SECRET RICHES

SECRET RICHES

Adventures of an Unreformed Oilman

John Masters

with Paul Grescoe

GONDOLIER

SECRET RICHES
© 2004 John Masters and Bayeux Arts, Inc.
Published by: Gondolier, an imprint of Bayeux Arts, Inc.,
119 Stratton Crescent SW, Calgary, Canada T3H 1T7 www.bayeux.com

Cover and book design by David Lane

Library and Archives Canada Cataloguing in Publication
Masters, John A. (John Alan), 1927-
    Secret riches : adventures of an unreformed oilman /
      John A. Masters ; with Paul Grescoe.
    ISBN 1-896209-97-1

    1. Masters, John A. (John Alan), 1927-. 2. Canadian Hunter Exploration. 3. Elmworth
    Gas Field (Alta.) 4. Gas industry–Alberta–Biography. 5. Petroleum industry and
    trade–Biography. I. Grescoe, Paul, 1939- II. Title.
HD9574.C22M38 2004   338.2'7285'092   C2004-905458-9

First Printing: September 2004
Printed in Canada

All rights reserved. No part of this publication may be reproduced, stored in a retrieval system, or transmitted, in any form or by any means, electronic, mechanical, recording, or otherwise, without the prior written permission of the publisher, except in the case of a reviewer, who may quote brief passages in a review to print in a magazine or newspaper, or broadcast on radio or television. In the case of photocopying or other reprographic copying, users must obtain a license from the Canadian Copyright Licensing Agency.

The Publisher gratefully acknowledges the financial support of the Canada Council for the Arts, the Alberta Foundation for the Arts, and the Government of Canada through The Book Publishing Industry Development Program.

This book is dedicated warmly to my beloved wife, Lenora, and my dear children, Chuck, Barbie, Robbie, Jim, our missing Alan, and his sweet wife, Alison.

CONTENTS

Mountains to Climb **1**

Roots **13**

My Right Brain **25**

The Navajo Years **39**

Learning from Mr. McGee **57**

Ambrosia Lake **69**

Chasing Oil **85**

An End and Beginnings **101**

Hunter **115**

Finding the Right One **129**

Deep Basin **149**

The Elmworth Miracle **163**

Families **177**

Checkered China **197**

Going South **209**

Endings **225**

Starting Over **245**

One More Mountain **261**

*And I will give you treasures hidden in
the darkness, secret riches . . .*

—*Isaiah 45:3*

CHAPTER ONE

MOUNTAINS TO CLIMB

I WAS SPRAWLED ON A SLIVER OF ROCK, slightly bruised and alone, trying not to glance down at the cliff wall disappearing below me. I'd just fallen 40 feet. One wrong move could finish me. I was only 25, fresh out of college. Ahead of me lay a life's work finding oil, natural gas, and uranium. Or falling over a thousand-foot cliff.

That summer of 1951, Leo Miller and I were deep in the Navajo country of northeastern Arizona, hiking the Lukachukai Mountains as geologists with the Atomic Energy Commission. Cold War fears had spurred the search for fuel to arm nuclear weapons and our task was to find uranium deposits. The Lukachukais stretch out from the main spine of the massive Chuska range, the upper slopes sprinkled with pinyon pine, and its peaks, 9,000 feet above sea level, white with the Chuska sandstone found nowhere else. We were mapping layers of grey sandstone exposed in the lower cliffs, and defining the channels of ancient streams where uranium ore might be buried.

For a couple of weeks Leo and I had jeeped down dirt roads, past silent Navajos in horse-drawn wagons. You don't just start up the hill. You have to get the whole picture. Neither of us could ever remember anyone teaching us that; it was in our bones. We drove where we could. Then we walked. Then we bushwacked through sagebrush and pine. *Then* we climbed. We had to orient ourselves first to the desert sand and the slopes and cliffs of the vast Lukachukai country.

My partner was a big-shouldered, athletic guy who could outclimb me and most anyone else up any cliff, even with a couple of quart water canteens on the belt of his green army fatigues and a pack on his back heavy with Geiger counter, hammer, and rock samples.

The day of the big fall, we'd started at the top of the Lukachukais, the end of the road up the north side of the mountain. We slid and scrabbled down the steep south side of for about fifteen hundred feet to reach the cliff-stepped layers of Jurassic sandstone that dinosaurs had footprinted 120 million years ago. (Do you know that in the northern hemisphere the south side of a mountain is always steeper and more rugged than the north because the sun always swings around that side? Result: fewer trees and brush, less soil, more exposed rock. Geologists learn that early.)

We walked the ledges, me up, Leo down, on high alert for the canary-yellow show of uranium. Spotting any, we would mark it on our map, measure thickness and width, and take several samples for later assays.

It was mid-morning. We worked our way along the Jurassic ledges until they began to merge into a continuous, vertical sandstone cliff. No sweat: we'd seen that before. Toes and fingers for a few yards and we'd find another ledge. Both of us had been on a lot of mountains. But this rock was crumbly sandstone. And now, suddenly, it gave way under one foot, and my hand-hold wasn't firm enough to take all my weight. It broke off. I slipped and fell, going faster, then cartwheeled down forty feet, the height of a four-storey building. Leo had frantically lunged for me, grabbing and tearing the front of my work-shirt as I fell past him. Clawing and clutching at anything that could break my fall, digging into the dirt with my boots, I crash-landed in a heap. It took a moment—or two—to calm down. I was

This big guy, Leo Miller, was my partner as we searched the cliffs and canyons of southeast Utah and northeast Arizona.

spreadeagled on a rock shelf about a yard wide. Below me, a thousand feet below, lay the bottom of the cliff.

"John, you okay?" Leo yelled down.

"I think so." Shook up, scared, but not badly hurt. "But I don't think I can get back up."

"I've got a rope." He pulled it from his pack, wrapped one end around his hips, tossed the other down to me.

I grabbed the rope, tied in with a climber's bowline, and rose gingerly to my feet, hugging the cliff face, careful not to step back into the void. "Okay, Leo. Here I come"

Slowly, deliberately, he belayed me up the cliff until I was safely beside him. "You know, you nearly went over the edge," he said needlessly. "We wouldn't have found you." Guys seem to say stuff like that.

The vertical red cliffs on Fall Down Mesa, where my story almost ended.

Suddenly the situation began to sink in. When he suggested I eat something and we unwrapped our sandwiches, I couldn't force mine down. I was on the verge of throwing up.

Leo, after patiently letting me talk out my fear for a while, said finally, "Let's get off this damn cliff."

Today's government topographic maps, if detailed enough, identify a little nick on the south side of the Lukachukais as Fall Down Mesa. I'm glad it isn't Dead Man Point.

If I'd had the gift of prophecy at the time, I might have foreseen that much of my career as an ore- and oil-finder would be balanced on a metaphorical cliff-edge, where a careless misstep could be fatal, both financially and emotionally. That certainly was the case when, after twenty years, I quit a good job with Kerr-McGee, a resource company based in my home state of Oklahoma. Leaving the comfortable employ of a man I revered, the remarkable Dean McGee, I co-founded my own venture, Canadian Hunter Exploration, on a geologist's hunch and an agnostic's prayer. Fortunately, I not only found the largest natural-gas field in the history of Canada but my partner and I also created a company that was memorialized in a book as one of the hundred best companies to work for in Canada, my beloved adopted country. We made many millions, sharing it with our employees, and then lost most of it in a new automobile-fuel idea that was two decades too early. Even today, my chronic risk-taking continues to endanger me. At an age when most men are unwinding on the golf course, I'm back in America trying to strike yet another motherlode of gas.

Along the way I've learned from and worked with some of the most renowned thinkers and doers in and outside my field. In my late teens, while an Oklahoma yokel at Yale, I was taught by legendary minds—including sociologist Raymond Kennedy and geologists William Twenhofel and Chester Longwell. Only a few years later, I was roaming the Arizona mountains with Leo Miller, who went on to fame finding giant ore deposits in Ontario, North Carolina, and Australia. In a colleague's words, "Leo spent much of his time in the air all over Australia, prospecting at speeds that caused birds to fly past him." Leo died when his plane crashed into a mountain in Colorado (five miles south of, and in view from, the front window of where I now live). On his way down, I'm sure he expected to overcome as he always had.

Perhaps if I'd been smart that day in the Lukachukais half a century ago, I might have tried to avoid real mountains from then on. But for one who has spent his time drilling beneath the surface of the earth, I've remained fascinated with its geological protrusions. While I eventually tired of roaming them personally to collect rock samples, I couldn't escape their allure. Throughout most of my life I have had a love affair with mountains—not just exploring them for the resources they hide but skiing their slopes for sport and climbing them for the mental and physical reward of attaining their summits.

What I didn't know then was that the mountains had the potential to murder me in another way. My family, I found later, has a genetic weakness that can lead to edemas—which can damage the lungs or the brain. It would kill one dearly beloved son and almost do away with me, though I was too mule-headed in the beginning to believe that I could be vulnerable.

What this says about me psychologically is something I'll leave to others to decipher. But clearly it is embedded in a credo I've followed in my life and career, summed up in the Eleventh Commandment that stays on the wall of my office: "Thou shalt not give up!"

Nowhere did my stubbornness express itself more sharply than in my role as an amateur climber. The poet William Blake put it well: "Great things are done when men and mountains meet; This is not done by jostling in the street." I got the mountain bug in my youth when I was working on my graduate thesis one summer in Wyoming. Nearby was the Grand Teton, the most famous mountain in mainland America, looming 13,700 feet over the valley of Jackson Hole in the national park named for it. A dozen other peaks form a garnet-studded granite range, 40 miles long by about 10 wide. It's the youngest in the Rockies—the mountains started to rise into place about eight million years ago—while featuring some of the oldest rocks on the continent. As well, it has the most comprehensive and complex geologic history. The only guide service permitted in the park then was co-founded by a school teacher named Glenn Exum, who in 1931 made the first ascent of the Grand Teton's difficult south ridge (in a pair of borrowed football shoes) and over the next few decades played an important role in popularizing the sport in the United States. "The Grand Teton is endlessly different, with its changing moods and attitudes, its eternal beauty," he once wrote. "It is a friend—and it is always a privilege to climb it." My first two-day climbs with Glenn were instructive and exhilarating and, in terms of any trouble, uneventful. It wasn't until much later that the Tetons truly humbled me.

Years farther on, I went back. My climbing partners were John Baker, a dear old friend from Yale, then a promising young State Department diplomat, and Breene Kerr, the son of Senator Bob Kerr, co-owner of the company employing me. Breene was a powerful six-foot-sixer who had rowed crew at MIT, the Massachussetts Institute of Technology. In this group I was the game little guy, eager for yet another encounter with the Grand Teton.

When I told my boss, Dean McGee, how I was going to spend my holiday, he said, "John, can't you figure out something better to do?"

"Well, you know, Mr. McGee"—it was always Mr. McGee—"I might be kind of dumb, but I can't think of anything better to do than that."

It proved to be pretty dumb. After we climbed some neighboring peaks over a few days, Glenn Exum arranged for a guide to meet us halfway up the mountain and take us to the top. We hiked to about 11,000 feet and slept in a hut till before dawn the next morning when we started up again to get the maximum daylight possible. The climbing was slow in that meager air as we stopped continually to catch our breath. During our time in the Tetons, we hadn't bothered to acclimatize ourselves by moving each night to higher elevations. Our lack of caution didn't bother my mates, but after we climbed the Grand and returned to the hut, my breathing began to signal pulmonary edema. Our guide left the hut at dawn to go all the way down to the valley for an emergency helicopter. No cell phones then. The wind howled around our hut all day. I lay semi-conscious. When the chopper finally arrived around 5 p.m., the wind died miraculously. This was 1965: choppers were pretty small. They strapped me into a stretcher on the struts and hoped like hell I wouldn't wake up and look out over the edge. I didn't awaken till I was wheeled into the Jackson Hole hospital, where they kept me for three days in an oxygen tent.

When I was in the hospital office, waiting to be released, the Kerr-McGee company pilot walked in. He said, "Mr. McGee sent me up here to get you. I've got a young geologist with me to drive your car back to Oklahoma City." That's what it was like for me to work for the great Dean McGee.

My doctor gave me a stern lecture about mountain sickness, which I heeded until the next time, in the mountains of Colorado. We were skiing at Aspen, and sleeping in a cabin at about 8,000 feet. After three days or so, I began breathing hard and now I understood what was happening to me. They got me off the mountain and drove me to the Glenwood hospital. Again, I had lost consciousness and had to recover in an oxygen tent for another three days.

By then you'd think I would have been wary. Approaching my fourth decade, while running Kerr-McGee of Canada in Calgary, I decided to climb in the Bugaboos. This series of spires reaches more than 11,000 feet amid glacier fields in the Purcell Mountains of south-central British Columbia. My guide was the storied Hans Gmoser, a great mountaineer from Austria who fell in love with the Rockies and introduced heli-skiing to the high glaciated slopes (which is a sport for 20-year-old bodies with 50-year-old incomes). I spent several straight days at altitude in the Bugaboos, climbing hard every day. One night as we camped out, I started drawing heavy breaths and by morning was falling unconscious. Hans recognized the problem instantly: acute mountain sickness. As it turned out, I was suffering from a more severe form, high-altitude pulmonary edema, a life-threatening condition in which fluid accumulates in the lungs after long periods in thin air. The most important treatment is to get down to a lower altitude fast.

Helicopters were either out of range or perhaps they couldn't land nearby. The only answer was to carry me down the mountain. Even Hans, rangy, muscular and so damn strong, had to enlist an assistant to share the descent, piggy-backing my unconscious form by turns in a rope sling. It took a few hours for them to climb down, often negotiating the sheer rockface one hand-hold at a time. Again, I spent some time in an oxygen tent but got a severe lecture from the doctor: "For Crissake, John, don't do high-altitude, high-powered exertion for more than two days at a time without coming down to sleep at five thousand feet. The next time may be your last!"

By not giving up until I was utterly forced to, I was being exposed to an important lesson that applied as truly in the office and home as it did on the mountain: the higher you go, the more precarious the path between triumph and failure. For decades I've recorded my thoughts and collected relevant quotations from others in a large leather-bound volume with a title stamped in gold: *The Unchanging Pattern of Human Behaviour*. One of my favorite quotes is from that much-maligned genius of Renaissance Italy, Niccolo Machiavelli: "It must be considered that there is nothing more difficult to carry out, nor more doubtful of success, nor more dangerous to handle, than to initiate a new order of things." That's it exactly, as I learned especially in bringing Canadian Hunter into successful being.

Drilling deep into my memory, I realize that my personal life, particularly my family, has also been marked indelibly by the triumphs and calamities that accompany a life lived large. I've fallen in love twice. My first wife died, broken-hearted, well before her time. My second wife and I have been married for more than a quarter-century. I helped raise two fine families—a creative daughter, physically and personally beautiful, and four stalwart, striving sons, only to lose one of them in the first flush of his daring, idealistic manhood. Alan was one of my two boys who were infected by my mountain fever. Singly and together, Alan and Chuck made some grand climbs in far corners of the earth. Tragically, Alan died of a rare form of high-altitude mountain sickness in the Andes, where he wasn't climbing for pleasure but selflessly volunteering his skills as a forester.

Ultimately, even veteran mountaineers know when to quit. John Roskelley, who has been on more successful climbing expeditions than any other American, admits: "You've got to know when to turn around." I haven't done any serious expedition climbing since my final ascent in Canada. In later years, I tried other adventures, from roller-blading and wind-surfing to hang-gliding and ultralight-flying—the last almost disastrously. Only skiing and sailing have survived the years.

But despite the thrill of mountaineering and other athletics, of all my adventures those of the mind have been the most exciting, the most fulfilling. I have long accepted the left brain/right brain theory of mental organization. According to this theory, the brain has two hemispheres that respond to outside stimuli in their own ways. Although one hemisphere may be more strongly developed in your brain, the two halves are not completely independent and the interaction between them keeps changing. The left hemisphere is the functional, rational, and analytical side that gives us the archetypical lawyer, accountant, or engineer. It's where the function of language resides. The right side is the hemisphere that appears to specialize in new ideas, creativity, conceptualization. It harbors the imagination and innovation that feed the artist and inventor. (Neither side has as yet accepted responsibility for politicians.)

Geologists can go either way. There is a role for left-brain, engineer-type geologists who process large sets of data. Right-brain exploration geologists are the ones who can create a conceptual model from scattered, sparse data. In what may be the most useful book I've ever read, *The Creative Brain*, Ned Herrman takes the theory even further. Herrman graduated from Cornell University with a double major in physics and music and went to work for General Electric, where he guided post-graduate education. While suffering a mysterious illness (which turned out to be heartblock), he took up painting and sculpting and crafted a second career as a professional artist. Researching at GE, surveying hundreds of thousands of people and analyzing the results by computer, he decided that the brain has four distinct specialized functions—harbored in the left front, left rear, right rear, and right front quadrants he labelled A, B, C, and D—"each with its own language, perception, values, gifts, and ways of knowing and being."

The dominant-A person likes to deal in facts and solve problems logically (mathematician). The B type is similar in some ways—distrusting emotions and intuition—but specializes in rules, methodology, and records (accountant). Cs are sensitive and receptive, more open to emotion than language (loving woman). Ds are visionaries who live for new ideas, hate structure and deadlines, and think in pictures rather than words (Walt Disney). Herrman concedes that "no quadrant exerts exclusive influence over any person" and "every quadrant brings critically important contributions to effective living and working." But in matters like problem-solving, we can broadly identify left-brain and right-brain approaches.

In *Drawing on the Right Side of the Brain*, Dr. Betty Edwards, a professor emeritus of art at California State University, Long Beach, neatly summarizes the strengths of the side which is dominant in me: "In the right-hemisphere mode of information processing, we use intuition and have leaps of insight—moments when 'everything seems to fall into place' without figuring things out in logical order. When this occurs, people often spontaneously exclaim, 'I've got it' or 'Ah, yes, now I see the picture.' The classic example of this kind of exclamation is the exultant cry, 'Eureka!' (*I have found it*)." Legend has it that Archimedes, the ancient Greek mathematician and physicist, shouted that as he ran home naked from the baths when he had the idea of using the quantity of displaced water to determine the buoyancy of similar-sized objects. Dr. Edwards describes the creative right hemisphere as "the intuitive, subjective, relational, holistic, time-free mode."

Eureka!

The theory has helped me to understand some of my own seeming contradictions and assess my place in the unusual universes I've created around me during my career in the resource industry. It has underscored the fact that, unlike most other scientists in my profession, I usually skip over the little details to emphasize the Big Picture. In other words, I ignore the trees to focus on the whole forest—or the individual gas wells to see a whole field or even the whole basin.

George Gilder has been a Fellow at Harvard's Kennedy Institute of Politics and the author of ground-breaking books on economics and technology. In *The Spirit of Enterprise*, Gilder argues that entrepreneurs pioneering in new industries are solving today's key problems. He devotes a chapter called "The Explorer" to my time at Canadian Hunter developing what became known as the Elmworth Deep Basin gas play. Immodest as it may seem to quote an approving passage from the book (and as myth-making as the selection may sound), I believe it captures the essence of what I was attempting and what I am all about:

"The importance of John Masters is measured not chiefly in the still-debated indices of [trillions of cubic] feet of natural gas at Elmworth but in his continuing command of the crucial underlying source of most business triumph: dedication to technological and scientific learning that does not eclipse an overarching knowledge of more profound truths." This was "the spirit of enterprise—the mysterious workings of creativity and faith" and the result of "a visionary idea that emerged in the mind of John Masters. . . ."

It took me a long time to realize that I am actually a renegade right-brain anomaly in a resolutely left-brain industry. If only I'd known that as a kid growing up Tulsa, Oklahoma, the center of the oil industry. Or when I tried to major in engineering at Yale and nearly failed freshman calculus and physics. My first experience with left- and right- brain theory was to demonstrate conclusively that I had little or no left hemisphere.

CHAPTER TWO

ROOTS

I WAS A FAT LITTLE KID who was raised during the Depression with a younger brother in a household full of women. That was enough to mark me as different from other boys, a very round peg in the neatly square holes occupied by my peers. Being ahead of most of them in reading and then skipping second grade were further impediments to winning their wholehearted approval. The role of the underdog has its advantages, however: many people tend to underestimate you, but a few root for you to succeed.

As a southerner—Oklahomans have always considered themselves more of the South than the Midwest—I grew up amid a society of underdogs. They were descended from the Confederates who lost the Civil War and who endured the worst poverty in the nation. One of my heroes has long been Robert E. Lee, the slavery-hating West Pointer who as a loyal Virginian felt obliged to abandon a shining future in the Union army to become the Confederate general-in-chief. Lee once said, "You can be anything you want to be, have anything you desire, accomplish anything you set out to accomplish—if you will hold to that desire with singleness of purpose." Ringing words to a kid from the South.

Oklahoma was suffering some of the first effects of the decade-long drought of the 1930s when I was born on September 20, 1927. But in the industry that was to become my career, that was a propitious time, around the globe and even in what I came to consider my home state. In the far-off lands of the Bible, prospectors continued to strike huge reservoirs of oil that promised a plentiful supply of petroleum in a world just beginning to hunger for fuel. Iraq was important to them, as it is now, for its reserves. In France that year, a company was born that would revolutionize the global industry: the two brothers who formed Schlumberger Ltd. (which has prospered for 70 years) recorded the first measurement of an oil well using an electrical-resistance log. Electric-log analysis—measuring the rock layers in a well to detect hydrocarbons—was a tool that would play an influential part in Canadian Hunter's success. And in Oklahoma, a state that once had to rely on cotton, a new resource was strenghtening the economy as wells gushed more than $400 million worth of oil that year. One wildcat a few years later in Oklahoma City launched a field that returned billions of dollars over the next four decades (one of those dollars would buy two dinners then). Five months after my birth, a foresightful lawyer named Robert Kerr and three partners incorporated an oil-drilling operation in Ada, Oklahoma. This was the forerunner of Kerr-McGee, the company that would one day employ me and teach me.

I was born, blond and ruddy-faced, in Iowa, a couple of states north of Oklahoma. My parents were Alan and Maxine Masters, who had family ties through my father to Shenandoah, a quiet, pretty, perfect little American farm town in the corn fields of southwestern Iowa. People would say "there's nothing much here, but it's the best town in the country." An old history of the county notes that "the early Mormons, who settled in the vicinity, were of the class whose love of morality and virtue prevented them from following the polygamists to Utah." (Decades later, as a neophyte geologist, I came to know and respect many of the descendants of those Utah Mormons.) Shenandoah's main claims to fame were being the self-described "seed and nursery capital of the world" and later the home of a woman's radio show called Kitchen-Klatter. Born the year before me, it aired in six midwestern states and became the longest-running homemaker program in the history of radio. My father had grown up in Shenandoah, his father was still an engineer for the town's electrical works, and his sister lived there. Dad was a roving publisher and editor for the small McGiffen chain of community newspapers. He went from town to town, working as a troubleshooter to whip a paper into financial shape and then moved on, dragging the family along. Perhaps I inherited my love of the language from him.

The year I was born, the pages of *The Shenandoah Evening Sentinel* advertised all-wool double blankets for $6.95, Lionel Barrymore was starring in *The Thirteenth Hour* at the Empress, and the editorial page was suggesting that "the ideal car would be one that could not be made to exceed the speed law on the country roads."

Shenandoah was a place of expansive shade trees and front porches with swings where neighbors came to sit and talk. Although we soon moved on, this classic small town remained an anchor for me as a boy when I came back to spend whole summers at my Aunt Mildred's home. She had twin daughters a couple of years older than me, the most beautiful girls I'd ever seen up to age six. Judy and Joanne were so identical that if I wanted Judy, I'd run around the corner of the house and yell her name and see who appeared. They had a big sandbox in the backyard under a shade tree; with the hose running it was probably the coolest place in Iowa.

The other cool spot in my young life was the family mansion on the south edge of Tulsa, the town where my mother's parents lived. Her father was Charles W. Day, the first dentist in Indian Territory (where the Five Civilized Tribes were forced to settle in what's now eastern Oklahoma).

My grandfather was a driving force in the community, the leader in getting a long-planned medical and dental arts center built in 1928. While remaining a dentist, he'd become rich by investing in lead and zinc mines during World War I and later in oil wells. The Day house was the largest in the city, built of stone and tended by black servants who would draw the shades early on steaming summer mornings. Daddy Day was an impressive man, always dining in a high starched collar and a tie, and Momma Day—my grandmother, Ermina—was a wealthy man's appropriately pretty wife. They had raised my mother and her younger siblings in luxury and sent them to the best schools. For our first few years, my brother Chuck and I had a taste of that high life, although no understanding of it.

Chuck—Charles Day—Masters was born in 1929. We were living in Oklahoma, at a spot on the map called Pawhuska, on the Osage Reservation. We moved two more times before Dad took us to Duncan, southwest of Tulsa. It was an agricultural and oil center that had grown up around an old trading post on the historic Chisholm Trail where Texas ranchers drove their cattle through Indian Territory to the railroad in Kansas. My Dad, tired of working for someone else, had finally bought his own paper, the *Duncan Eagle*. Dating back to 1894, it was founded by a Virginia printer named John G. Woods who became a prominent Confederate major, a Texas cowboy, and then publisher of several newspapers. The *Eagle* ran stories like this one:

PAT RICH KILLS
HIRAM THOMPSON

Wednesday afternoon about 1:30 Hiram Thompson came to Rich's barn where he had previously unloaded some hay without Rich's consent. It seems that Rich's mules had destroyed some of Thompson's hay and Thompson had accused Rich of stealing it . . .

Alan Masters didn't have many years to enjoy himself as an entrepreneur. He was a big, black-haired, confident guy, his six-foot-three towering over my mother, who was small, quiet, and beautiful. I still see him and his equally tall brother-in-law, Charlie, both handsome and athletic, talking and laughing together in a corner. Authoritative but kind with us kids, my father wasn't a particularly playful Dad. His newspaper work was so overwhelming that he came home tired, had dinner, and then retreated to his reading chair where our big police dog nuzzled up to him. He'd often tell my mother, "I'm having another of those damn headaches"—migraines. They became so bad that he had an operation to remove a piece of skull to relieve the pressure. Afterward he still felt some of the effects, including temporary blindness, but without the accompanying pain. Then one night in 1935, my father suffered an intracerebral hemorrhage as a hardened artery ruptured in his brain. He died in his sleep.

I was eight and his death changed my life immeasurably. I'd lost a Dad, the male in my life, the father figure, the teacher of masculine attributes. There's an old English proverb that says one father is worth more than a hundred schoolmasters. It took me a few years, and another man who became my mentor, to realize all that I was missing with his absence. Fortunately my mother was warm and giving—her arms were always around her sons—and she played both Dad and Mom to us, forever willing to listen to our problems. Yet she was firm in a gentle, feminine way. I am clearly her product and often felt like I had a slightly stronger connection with her than my brother did, something that Chuck himself mentioned as a grown-up with no apparent rancor.

My parents' relationship had not been untroubled, I found out years later. It seemed my father was something of a rake. My mother never gave me the details, nor did I ask her for them. But, selective in her counsel, she did feel compelled to tell me, "I was always concerned that your dad was interested in other women. And that made for a very difficult life because I'd been raised to think of a single, concentrated marriage—and your dad just didn't think that way. It made for a lot of sadness. I'm not telling you how to live your life, but the decisions you make in that regard are very serious." Her words would come back to me in decades to come.

Meanwhile, the fortunes of our extended, fatherless family had ebbed.

Daddy Day had died the year before—"of a broken heart," my mother said. The Depression was in full ugly flower and the aftermath of the Wall Street Crash of '29 had wiped him out financially. The Days had to move out of their mansion into lesser quarters.

Now, with her husband and father gone, my mother was forced to learn marketable skills. She studied dictation and typing at secretarial school but could only find jobs that paid less than $100 a month. We managed to move into the respectable southeast side of Tulsa, into a house rented by my mother's widowed sister. Ruth was artistic, amusing, and something of a party girl. She had a daughter, younger than me, and for a time Chuck and I had to deal with a girl cousin on the premises. My grandmother was also living with us, tying Aunt Ruth into Momma Day's new career as one of the city's rare female real-estate agents. Wealthy Tulsans trusted her because she'd once been a society matron herself in a city where pedigree counted (even today, they have a fancy ball to bring out the debutantes). The three women pooled their earnings to give us all a modest living.

In a decade when John Steinbeck was immortalizing desperate Okies in *The Grapes of Wrath*, Tulsa was one of the few profit centers in the state. The Indian Territory's first commercial oil well had been brought in at Bartlesville, to the north, in 1897. Four years later a couple of entrepreneurial doctors financed the first oil strike in the Tulsa area, triggering an initial boom. In 1905 a better well to the south opened up the spectacular Glenn Pool, one of the largest fields in the world at that time. Tulsa began to build its reputation as the Oil Capital of the World. Petroleum companies, suppliers, and workers flooded in, hotels went up, and banks were born to handle the fortunes being made. By the 1930s the population of Tulsa, a former Indian village and pony-express station, reached 140,000, swollen by the activities of 800 oil companies on the scene. By now my mother was working for one of them, Stanolind Oil and Gas (which later became Amoco). Looking back, it might seem inevitable that I would someday be in the business too.

Momma Day tried to capitalize on all that activity. She was a powerful, determined, high-powered woman who would just sail right over you if you got in her way. Our dinner hours were always a boring litany—"he said this," "she said that"—of the workday she and Ruth had as realtors. In reaction, I guess, Chuck and I tended to bond as brothers, especially when we had a mutual enemy, like the Church, Heaven forgive me.

My mother was a devout Methodist who taught Sunday school in Tulsa. She marched her boys there every week an hour or two ahead of time as she prepared her lessons and then insisted we stay on to attend the service. The church was the magnificent, skyscraping Boston Avenue Methodist, since designated a National Historic Landmark for its spectacular art-deco architecture. But for my brother and me, it was a prison. I came to dread Sundays, and the weekly force-feeding of Christianity might have helped turn me, if not Chuck, away from any form of organized religion.

I was always trying to look out for my baby brother, but as we grew he needed my protection less and less. We differed in a couple of distinctive ways. He was definitely a left-brain thinker who was never entranced as I was about taking risks and being creative and imaginative. But he was certainly a better athlete, whupping me in almost ever sport. Once, on a canoe trip as young guys, I challenged him to a race across a swift-flowing river. I'd been swimming steadily for exercise and thought I could take this kid two years younger than me. It turned out that in the water I was a turtle to his dolphin. As I dragged myself out of the river, Chuck stood commandingly on the shore and said, "Johnny, you've got lots of heart, but you just don't have any natural ability." It was one of the more memorable insults of my life. I wanted to bust him right there but realized he'd hit me back harder. An inch taller and at least ten pounds heavier than me even then, he went on to play college football as a rock-hard center and linebacker. He was a favorite of Yale's legendary coach, Herman Hickman, the All-American lineman who could quote Victorian poetry.

Chuck was right, of course. By the age of 12, I was a chubby little guy, five feet tall and 140 pounds. My mother and all the other women in the family, who kept filling me to the brim, just thought their fair-haired boy was cute and never encouraged me to do anything too vigorous. But I was fat and athletically challenged. At that point, providentially, a couple of men showed up in my life.

One was my Uncle John, married to another of my mother's sisters, who insisted, "These boys need some kind of outdoor activity." He was a superb sailor and his wife, Katherine, was an enthusiastic mate in their 14-foot, two-seater racing Snipe. He taught Chuck and me how to sail, let me handle the jib and absorb racing technique, and within a couple of years I was taking the boat out alone with my brother as crew. It was a wonderful gift. Ever since, I have found peace of mind and freedom in the liberating adventure of sailing. The right brain appreciates its beauty, art, and form—it smiles when you gaze up at the sails and laughs when the wind dances across the waves. And, perhaps best of all, sailing is not subject to the rules and regulations of a car on the highway.

But the most important male influence on my future was a high-school track coach named Bill Lantz. Compact and strong as a bull, he'd been an all-American halfback at Nebraska but an even better gymnast, lilting like a well-muscled ballet dancer on the parallel bars. His cross-country runners at Tulsa Central High always won the state championship. Always. More meaningful than the honors, Bill gave the kids true affection and leadership. And every summer, for a full eight weeks, he took only 50 youngsters to a boys' camp he directed in the Ozarks near Branson, Missouri. People described him as "a 24-hour-a-day, seven-day-a-week Christian," yet his brand of Christianity didn't turn me off the way my Methodist mother's did.

We lived a couple of blocks from his house in Tulsa and he'd seen my brother and me running loose around the neighborhood. One evening he knocked on our door and, when my mother answered, said, "I'd like to come in and talk to you."

"Well, if it's about your camp, Mr. Lantz, we just don't have the extra money to seriously consider it."

"Mrs. Masters, I want to talk to you about the *camp*—we'll talk about the money later."

He told her about a boys' camp called Kanakuk (named for an Indian chief) that through the medium of high-energy sports stressed teamwork, leadership training, and non-denominational Christian devotion for city boys aged 7 to 18. At some point I came in quietly to the living-room as he talked about how kids swam, canoed, climbed cliffs, ran on a quarter-mile track, high-jumped, pole-vaulted, did gymnastics and archery, played baseball and other games, and took long, long hikes on Saturdays.

"We try to make men out of boys. I can make a place for your boys. I can recognize good kids and John and Chuck are the kind of boys I like to have in my camp. I don't need money from everybody who goes to my camp. I'll figure out some kind of job for John by the end of the summer." He smiled and said, "We'll get some work out of him."

The great Bill Lantz, the Tulsa high-school track coach, owner of the Kanakuk Kamp for boys—and my surrogate father and mentor to all my sons.

In my first summer, I was given a silver cup as the honor camper and it was as if I'd been anointed on the greatest day of my 12-year-old life. Today, six decades later, I look back on that cup as the grandest honor in my whole life. Attending camp for the next five years, I worked at last as a junior counsellor, then a senior one, and the chief of the tribe. The world was at war, but we felt safe, protected in the camp. Uncle Bill made it all fun, even though we had to eat healthy. A brief history of Kanakuk described the food philosophy then: "Three terrific square meals a day with no Cokes, candy, or between-meal snacks was the norm." I began to lose girth—20 pounds of kid fat the first summer—even as I built muscle. Exercise has been part of my regimen ever after. I went back to high school each autumn all charged up, joining the football and wrestling teams and literally working my big fat butt off while acquiring self-respect.

I also gained a surrogate father. I tried to please him, to hear him say, "Hey, your shoulders are getting bigger, John!", as I digested the morals of his Sunday-morning sermon and watched him set an example by cleaning the lavatories and hoeing weeds off the track. He was mentor and hero to me.

Staying in touch with Bill over my years in Oklahoma, I visited him later in his home where, crippled in old age from previous athletic injuries, he held court every day with the dozens of ex-campers and students who wanted to keep in contact with him. Uncle Bill had turned over the camp in 1954 to colleagues who carried on his philosophy. Six decades after I left it, the operation has grown to eight athletic camps in Missouri and Colorado for 20,000 boys and girls each summer. This is not where Bill would have taken the camp, but it was deep in his nature to express pride and support for it.

My own children came to realize the importance of the camp in my life. My adult daughter, Barbara, told a friend not long ago, "To really understand my father, you have to understand his camp connection. I think he realized who he could be through that camp. He ran his family and his business in a very similar way, on the basis of friendly competition that brought out the best in you to create self-esteem, to foster excellence. If we did something altruistic, he'd say, 'That was a real Kanakuk thing to do.'"

I'm not a bit embarassed to admit that I still get teary-eyed (as I am now) talking about this glorious growing-up phase in my adolescence.

The next adult to set my course in the right direction was an oilman, George Jenkinson. He was head landman for Stanolind, acquiring and administering oil and gas leases from landowners. My mother was his secretary. I was among the top three students in my 1,300-student senior class in high school. But the Second World War was raging and if I'd thought of doing anything after graduation, it was to go off and join the Marines. George, a graduate of Yale University, asked my mom if she'd ever thought of sending her son to his alma mater. Well, of course not. But he told her that Yale was very generous with scholarships and with so many young men in the war, the competition was much less fierce. In fact, he was the scholarship representative for Oklahoma and offered to bring her the application forms.

When my mother asked me about taking college-board examinations to apply for a scholarship to an out-of-town university, I said I'd be lucky to get into Tulsa U. "Well, Mr. Jenkinson says you might be able to go to Yale on scholarship."

"Yale? I don't even know where Yale is."

I was a naive teenager, socially backward, a year or two younger than my schoolmates, not realizing that my age put me at a disadvantage, and consequently never thinking of myself as particularly smart. I was always trying to keep up.

None of that deterred her. She arranged for me to take the exams and I got the scholarship. In the summer of 1944, she put me on the train to someplace called New Haven, Connecticut, wherever the heck that was. It was wartime. We started classes July 1. I was still 16.

CHAPTER THREE

MY RIGHT BRAIN

KNOW WHAT YOU KNOW, and know what you don't know—you can fool yourself easier than anyone else. I knew so little about Yale that when I got off the train in New Haven, I actually expected to be met at the station and transported to the university in a horse and buggy. Somewhere I'd read this was the way they did things at colleges in New England. When I did disembark and looked around questioningly for a carriage, a policeman advised me to take the Millhouse Avenue bus.

I stepped off into a strange world of ivy-covered stone buildings and looming towers in Neo-Gothic style. Bizarre gargolyes grinned from the eaves, among them a carving of a student asleep at his desk and another with a cigarette and a mug of beer. Equally bizarre, in the courtyard of the Hall of Graduate Studies, there was a stone-carved quotation from Rafael Sabatini, the Italian author of swashbuckling novels: "He was born with a gift for laughter and a sense that the world was mad."

That was the beginning of the apprenticeship of John Masters, a thorn in the side of the Ivy League. Yale was the natural habitat of wealthy prep-school boys with gentlemanly graces who comprised up to two-thirds of the wartime classes, but I wasn't inclined then (or now) to adapt my personality to blend in with someone else's. My class included the wealthy likes of Herbie Dow II, the grandson of the founder of Dow Chemical, and George Bush Senior, a star baseball player who belonged to Skull and Bones, Yale's top secret society. I was only a member of Berzelius, a less-prestigious senior society. Most of my classmates wandered around in white bucks, grey flannel trousers, and J. Press jackets; I wore cowboy boots, Levi's, and a tee-shirt. When I'd enter the dining room, the manager would sometimes have to say gently, "John, there's a sport coat in the closet" (with a tie tucked in a pocket). I went to "the tables down at Mory's" a few times and, while enjoying myself, I really did feel like "a poor little lamb that had lost his way."

I was not so much a friend of, as friendly to, Jews, blacks, foreigners, and other students on the fringe like me. I openly acknowledged and accepted them, and this gave me a feeling for the psychology of the outsider. Some of the Jewish guys often gathered before dinner at one end of the common room to play classical music together and, even though it wasn't a popular thing to do, I sometimes sat and listened and said, "You're sure playing pretty tonight." There were only three African-Americans in an undergraduate body of 2,500. I admired Levi Jackson, the first black on the Yale football team and then the first to lead it as captain. So much did I value his dignity and grace that I later suggested to Bill Lantz that he hire Levi as a counselor at his camp. Patiently, painfully, Bill explained to me that the times had not yet changed enough for Oklahoma parents to accept a Negro counselor. I realized he was right, unfortunately.

Because of the war, Yale was on an accelerated schedule and my first term started at the beginning of July. At the first college party that summer, my counsellor offered me a choice of claret or Pepsi. "What's claret?" I asked. "You want the Pepsi," he quickly replied. Uncle Bill had so indoctrinated me about a healthy body equating to a healthy mind that I never even thought about smoking or taking a drink. I felt even younger than 16 when older soldiers returning from overseas entered or re-entered college. The only saving grace was their sartorial leaning to military fatigues and army boots.

My destiny at Yale, I hoped, was to be a jock. I went out for varsity football, wrestling, and lacrosse—in none of which, given my youth and immaturity, was I very accomplished. As a lightweight halfback, I broke three small vertebrae in my back in a pileup and then damaged my left knee in another game, the first of many insults that joint has endured. At no point did I consider getting involved in things intellectual, like writing for the *Yale Daily News*, where with my fondness for the language I might have shone.

I gave equal lack of thought to my courses in freshman year. Somehow I got it into my head that I should become an engineer while knowing little about what engineers do. Studying calculus, physics, and engineering convinced me I didn't want to know. The only first-year subjects that pleased me were history and Shakespeare. When I passed my calculus final after abysmal grades during term, my confused professor called me in and said, "You're not the kind of kid who would cheat, so what the hell did you do?" I explained that he just happened to ask the very test questions I'd chosen to memorize in the week of finals preparation.

Among my first real college friends was John Baker, my future climbing partner in the Tetons and one of the finest guys I ever knew. His father had been a successful mining engineer in Canada and his mother was a widely read, highly intelligent woman who became a brave pacifist during wartime. Because Tulsa was too far to travel during the Christmas holiday in my freshman year, John invited me home with him to Westport, Connecticut. The kid from Oklahoma meets the intelligentsia of New England—but they clasped me to the bosom of their family. The next summer, I proved to be a malign influence on John when we were hitchhiking to Tulsa to be camp counsellors and I said, "Why don't we go down and join the Marines?" Despite his pacifist past, he was as consumed by the progress of the war as I was and agreed we should try. It was 1945, we were only 17, and the recruiting officers had been advised the conflict was winding down. The sergeant knew we were lying about our ages and told us to come back with our birth certificates and a signed statement from our folks. Once outside, John assured me, "The jig's up. We're not going to get permission from our parents." It would be another six years before I considered volunteering again.

In my sophomore year I took my first aptitude tests. My counsellor looked over my results and advised me that the profession I should completely avoid—that I had no place nor promise in—was science. "Stay as far away from that as you can. You just don't have the aptitude." Certainly I couldn't do arithmetic, much less math, and was hopeless with any kind of formulae. "John, the thing you can do best is law and I seriously advise you to become a lawyer. You have the word skills and the mindset." In fact, I have never liked a thing about the law, its reliance on leverage and its failure to be balanced and fair. But he might have been right about science, so I decided to do a business major instead. That was another mistake: there wasn't a single economics course I gave a damn about. Although I couldn't put it into words at the time, all that quantitative content was much too left-brain for me.

With my oiltown background, my next summer's employment appeared to be a much safer choice. I got the job with some pull from my mother's new husband. He was an executive at her workplace, Stanolind, a brilliant geologist who had paid his dues in the field and become Manager of Exploration. John Bartram arranged for me to work for the first time in the Oil Patch. I was about to do a man's job and earn real money on a drilling rig in the hotbed of the petroleum industry, Texas.

Odessa, Texas, was a once-sleepy cowtown that had ballooned to 10,000 people as the center for drilling and operations in the mighty oil province of West Texas. The 19th-century railway workers had named the spot because it reminded them of their home in Russia. It reminded me of Hades, with not a drop of rain or a patch of green grass. A Union general, Philip Sheridan, once said, "If I owned Texas and Hell, I'd rent out Texas and live in Hell." That's what I thought of Odessa. About 300 miles west of Fort Worth, it's in the heart of the vast, productive Permian Basin, named for the geological time period 200 million years ago when the first great mass extinction of species happened. I thought I would be next. Someone defined the basin as "a geographic area covering portions of western Texas and eastern New Mexico, characterized by the presence of oil fields, mesquite bushes, and coyotes." The tumbleweed whipped across land as flat as a table composed of wind-blown, reddish sand. It was roughneck country where even the educated petroleum engineers dressed down in blue jeans and cowboy boots. And I was the brat from Yale parachuted in to help run pipe on a drill rig.

I was a floor man. A rig perches on stilts 10 to 20 feet high. On the floor beneath a large derrick is a big wheel called a rotary table. Cables from the derrick raise or lower heavy steel pipe through the table to the bottom of the drill hole. The table turns the pipe and rotates the bit, causing it to bore through the rock. Drilling mud—water mixed with bentonite clay—is circulated down through the pipe. It removes the cuttings from the hole, cools and lubricates the bit, and maintains the right pressure in the well. The driller runs the operation, standing beside a brake. If he releases the brake, the rotary table on the rig floor spins the pipe in the hole. My job was helping connect the 30-foot lengths of pipe. The driller simply said, "We're ready to run." I guided the big clamps, hung by a cable, which grabbed another section of pipe after it came up a ramp and hoisted it high into the derrick, suspended just over the rotary table. Then I put my shoulder to the pipe and horsed it to the connector pipe sticking out of the table. With six-foot-long steel tongs (giant wrenches), we clamped on to both joints of pipe and the other floor man and I screwed them together. The trick to was to keep your fingers out of the way. And don't slip in the mud. And hurry.

It wasn't real hard work except when we did it for eight hours straight.

Everything was heavy, everything seemed to weigh at least a hundred pounds—some a lot more. I was strong enough to do the job and learned it within a few days. What I never did learn was how all that damn equipment worked. There was always some kind of shouted command over the noise of the machinery: "Jawn, get up there and take that wrench and do this and do that!" The instructions were never clear to me; I never did understand anything I did outside of the floor operation or why I was doing it. The driller just didn't have time to explain it to me—dammit, I was a roughneck, I ought to know. The real roughnecks dismissed me as a dumb college kid who thought he was smart but didn't even know how to use a wrench. So I got the dirty jobs. The only pleasure was being by myself, making drilling mud. Each time, I toted about 100 sacks of mud, 100 pounds apiece, and mixed them in a hopper with a blast of water for two or three hours. Sometimes I escaped the searing sun by climbing under the rig floor, where water dripped down and there was a bit of shade. I never went home at night thinking I'd had a good day.

Home was a room in an old hotel. On my first day the desk clerk announced, "You have a roommate—a little guy named Shorty." There he was, propped up by pillows on his bed, reading a girlie magazine. I don't think he moved off the bed in the two and a half months I spent in Odessa. He was half-crippled from working on the rigs. We never exchanged more than a few words now and then. Out in the field seven days a week, I couldn't get to the bank so I stored all my cash in an envelope and hid it under my shirts in a drawer. One night, two weeks before work's end, I returned to my room—only to find Shorty gone, along with all my money except about $100, which he probably left out of some remnant of kindness of heart. Never saw him again. Aside from getting through *War and Peace* in the evenings, and one last pay check, I had to count the summer a dead loss.

College wasn't much fun without some spending money. Once in a moment of abandon, I went to New York for a couple of nights at the Waldorf-Astoria with a roommate, the likeable and lazy Dick Sandwick. I had my toilet kit, one shirt in a brown paper bag, and my ticket back to

New Haven. Somehow we managed to spend an evening on the town, taking a pair of girls to a nightclub. That left me with one dollar in my pocket. As we headed to the great hotel for the weekend, Dick's father had to meet us and, laughing at our penury, pay our subway fare. Although continually poverty-stricken and never much of a Lothario sexually, I did have a series of girlfriends, most of them at nearby Smith College. But the dearest one was Marian Roth, a high-school friend from Tulsa attending Wellesley. Because of her name and her appearance, she was rushed in her first week at college by a group of Jewish girls who were disappointed to find she was a WASP. While I was smitten by her dark good looks, she was a couple of years older and looking for a more mature man—a Bogart, not a Mickey Rooney. While Marian and I both went our separate ways, we've kept our friendship in the half-century since.

At the time, I was living in the Calhoun College residential dormitory in the same suite as William Clay Ford, the very likable younger brother of Henry Ford II, chairman of the automotive giant. Bill wasn't particularly interested in engineering either but decided to stick with it in hope the training would be relevant to his eventual work with the family firm ("It never occurred to me that I wouldn't work there," he once said). Bill had a wide smile for almost everyone, including me, although I learned later that he was tough-minded. At 21 the heir to the Ford empire inquired of the company about his financial affairs and was told that his father's and grandfather's estates would be kept in trust for him until he turned 35; "I want it now," he said, and received it. He was less forthright with his mother, keeping it a secret that he was dating a Vassar girl, Martha Firestone, the pretty blonde granddaughter of the tiremaker's founder.

Although shorter and slighter than me, too light for football, Bill Ford was captain of the tennis and soccer teams. We became pretty good friends. He had a convertible, the only new-model Ford on the road at the time, and on occasion let me borrow it. I was driving in town one day when another driver spotted this rarity and shouted, "Who the hell are you? Henry Ford?" I could have had my own car if only I'd accepted Bill's invitation to be an usher at his wedding when he married Martha. It was the highlight of the 1947 summer social season, but I wasn't there to claim one of the brand-new convertibles he gave every usher. Bill went on to help run Ford and later passed on the reins to his son, the current chairman. I have observed his career from afar and noted with pleasure that his marriage to Martha seems to be a very good one.

But the fact that I had only one good shirt wasn't the only reason I declined the invitation to their nuptials. I had to leave the East beforehand because I'd convinced another friend, Bill Swire, to join me for an unpaid yet highly rewarding summer job in Utah.

After my previous summer in Odessa, where I'd gained appreciation for the men who toiled on the oil rigs, the lesson for me was that I never wanted to do that again. Yet even in my third year of college I remained unclear what I *did* want. History was fascinating, as were two sociology courses under Raymond Kennedy, who a colleague called "a charismatic, square-jawed man with the short hair and intent eyes of a Marine colonel." Kennedy was an intelligence analyst in the OSS during the Second World War and an early critic of France's colonization of Indochina, a precursor to the Vietnam War. He was a marvelous lecturer on Southeast Asia who opened up part of the world to me by bringing alive the jungles and canyons he'd traversed and the headhunters and other natives he'd dined with. In 1949 he was on a research trip in western Java when an armed band killed him and a *Time-Life* reporter.

The most influential course I took, however, was an introduction to geology, given by one of the great minds in that science. William H. Twenhofel, a Kentucky farmer's son, had been a public-school teacher before he discovered geology and earned his Ph.D. at Yale, then went on to teach at the University of Wisconsin for three decades. Instead of retiring in 1945, he became a visiting professor at other major colleges, including his alma mater. In *Annals of the Former World*, a layman's primer on North American geology, John McPhee points out that "Yale had one of the better geology departments in the world, and its interests were commensurately global. It was syllogistic, encyclopedic, and stirred its students to extended effort. . . ." To me, Twen—as his students fondly nicknamed him—embodied all of those qualities. Bald like a monk and bespectacled, he had dancing eyes that lit up his long face as he described, with wit and vigor, all the things he loved about his subject. Every one of his lectures was a song to me.

He was an illustrious sedimentary geologist and paleontologist. I learned that sedimentary rocks (as opposed to igneous and metamorphic ones) are generally created from eroded grains of rock deposited in bodies of water that range in size from streams to seas. Occasionally, these sediments come to contain hydrocarbons, including petroleum. Dr. Twenhofel helped found the specialty that came to be called sedimentation. What I really learned from this engaging and enthusiastic seventy-year-old was that geology could reveal a fascinating hidden world I barely knew existed.

It was a young science: in 1793 an English surveyor named William Smith started following the course of rock layers in canals, noticing that certain fossils were found only in certain layers, and in 1815 unveiled the first real geological map of any spot on the globe. It was truly *The Map That Changed The World*, as Simon Winchester writes in a recent book with that title: "For the first time the earth had a provable history, a written record that paid no heed or obeisance to religious teaching and dogma, that declared its independence from the kind of faith that is no more than the blind acceptance of absurdity." While the science itself is a stripling, geologic time covers an enormous period, longer than six billion years and steadily being dated ever-older.

As a student, Twen himself had researched fossils from the Ordovician age, about 425 million years old, while hiking 700 miles around the wilds of Anticosti Island at the head of the Gulf of St. Lawrence off eastern Quebec. He later studied the processes of sedimentation on the islands of the Baltic Sea, where he was arrested briefly at the start of World War I. So he was speaking from solid, on-the-ground experience in teaching me that geology is not a static science. I learned too that it's highly interpretive and that in pursuing it "every faculty should be used—the *feet* to carry you across the strand, along the cliff, and over the rocky wastes; the *eyes* to search out the endless detail of the geological record; and the *mind* to analyze the significance of those details." Although I never suspected it at the time, the exercise of that last faculty was the one that would make my career in geology so captivating.

Near the end of that year, Twen let it be known that a Ph.D. candidate in paleontology named Reuben Ross was looking for two field assistants to help him complete the thesis for his doctorate. No money, but he'd give us transportation and food. I invited Bill Swire, from Albany, New York, to come along. He had no interest in geology, but said, "Sure! Where's Utah?" While the science intrigued me, the adventure of camping in the mountains of Utah was even more attractive to a boy from the flatlands of Oklahoma. I'd never seen mountains.

Bill and I saw plenty that summer. We were in a forestry camp outside Logan, north of Salt Lake City, in the Cache Valley area of northeastern Utah. It had been home to Shoshoni Indians, fur trappers, mountainmen, and eventually the Mormons led by Brigham Young. (I got to know many Mormons there and in the years since I've almost never met one I didn't like. I'm not so much a supporter of their faith as an admirer of the people themselves. At one point, years later, we had a dozen Mormons working for us at Canadian Hunter.) The camp was two or three large frame buildings which held about a hundred forestry students from Utah State College taking summer courses. Ross, Bill Swire, and I slept in tents nearby but had access to their showers and meals. We bushwacked all day through thick stands of scrub oak up the steep Wastach Mountains, devoured giant portions of food, and vented any remaining energy through volleyball with the forestry students in the evening.

Reub was documenting the paleontology and the stratigraphy of a thousand-foot-thick section of Ordovician rock. I had only recently learned that stratigraphy describes the arrangement of layers of rocks and their relationships in time as a means of interpreting both the rocks and their fossils in terms of Earth's history. Our leader was studying the cliff-forming Garden City rock formation of dark gray limestone with its black layers of flintlike chert. Studying always meant climbing a couple of thousand feet to reach the formation and then crawling up even further for close-ups. The formation was at the top of the peaks and we ascended them one by one, carefully measuring the entire section, describing each unit of rock. Our major objective was to collect telltale fossils of trilobites and brachiopods, ancient shelled marine invertebrates.

A couple of times, we had long, interesting hikes with Chester Longwell, the chairman of Yale's geology department, who had co-written *A Textbook of Geology*, the classic primer. He continued to do a lot of field work, especially in Nevada, where he made some key discoveries in the Great Basin, that desolate expanse of desert and high mountains between the Rockies and the Sierra Nevada. But Reub Ross, a quiet, serious guy, was our summer-long mentor. He went to work for the U.S. Geological Survey and, as Dr. Reuben J. Ross, became a ranking expert on the geology of the Ordovician.

I went back to Yale with an itch to learn more about this geology stuff. For my first three years in college, I had been making sloppy moves and backing off like a mismatched wrestler, never being any better than a B student. Only after I returned for my senior year did I get a clean hold on my future—although a boring course in mineralogy almost turned me off. However, the environment of that past summer had inspired me to consider geology seriously. Hiking, climbing, and sleeping out in the mountains seemed like a grand way to live. I had no idea that petroleum geology meant desert basins instead of mountain peaks and that, in fact, searching for oil and gas was no longer a physical pursuit but rather an intense intellectual exercise involving seven-day weeks, tons of geologic literature, and thousands of maps. But in my early 20s, I entered the profession joyfully, believing that it would be a splendid opportunity to live outdoors, enjoying the environment and the exercise. If I'd known the reality, I might not have stayed the course and found the love of my life.

The man who helped cement my resolve in 1948 was my mother's

Mother and her new husband, John Bartram—always steady, logical, and kind.

new husband, John Bartram. As a geologist, he knew the Rockies like the back of his weatherbeaten hand and was one of the real experts in surface mapping. He came into the business at the beginning of the new, heretical understanding that oil could be found in anticline structures, which are like underground inverted bowls: upfolds of rock that form arches. This insight was a turning point in petroleum exploration and John spent two decades field-testing it. He worked for the old Midwest Refining Company and then Stanolind, originally a pipeline company that was swallowed by Amoco. He was now Stanolind's exploration manager and his arrival in our family probably influenced my brother to follow me to Yale a couple of years later, on scholarship, to study geology. My stepfather certainly swayed me in my choice of graduate school and later linked me with a company that financed my master's thesis.

He was a practical man, who once told me that you should always pack your lunch before having your breakfast—because if your stomach is full, you probably won't prepare enough to eat at noon. Now, as I told him I was interested in becoming a geologist, he didn't paint the career in rosy colors but did point me in the right direction.

"John, geology's about rocks," he said in his quiet manner. "And going to a school like Yale or Harvard is not a very sensible way to study geology. I admire those universities, they have wonderful professors, but they don't have any rocks. If you've been at a rock school, you will know more than the fellows who come out of Yale. They will be more sophisticated than you, they will have read more thoroughly from the Great Masters. But you'll know more about rocks." He recommended that I take my master's degree at the University of Colorado, which had a respected graduate program and was set on the edge of a massive complex of mountains. So strongly did he suggest Colorado that he offered to support my studies there for the following three years.

It was good advice. I already knew what Yale had given me: a sense of social and intellectual confidence—a sense of possibility—that this kid from Oklahoma could not have acquired in any other way. But now it was time to use my left brain to learn about rocks. My right brain would be an interested observer.

CHAPTER FOUR

THE NAVAJO YEARS

THERE'S AN OLD NAVAJO SAYING that roughly translates from that impenetrable language as: "Tell me and I'll forget. Show me, and I may not remember. Involve me, and I'll understand." While I wouldn't meet my first Navajo Indian for another three years, I lived the truth of that homily during my heady time at Colorado University in Boulder. I started in September 1948. That's where I met rock and became truly involved in the long, slow, but engrossing adventure of geology. Not that I came to some sudden understanding; this isn't a science you can hurry along. While there are plenty of good young mathematicians, I maintain that you can't, by any means, be a good geologist in your twenties. Or your thirties. Or even your forties.

I was playing catch-up in a class of a couple of dozen graduate students in geology. Having taken only a few relevant courses at Yale, where my bachelor's degree was in economics, I spent my first year at Colorado doing undergraduate work. This year-long force-feeding, instead of the usual drip process over four years, proved to be a blessing. From seven in the morning till ten at night, I was immersed in nothing but geology. Among a variety of geologic subjects, I was soaking up a smattering of the oil industry's past along with the fundamentals of petroleum geology, which would shape most of my future.

Today, as the thoughtful American writer Jeremy Rifkin has noted, "Remove fossil fuels from the human equation and modern industrial civilization would cease to exist." Yet the fossil-fuel era had only begun in the late 1700s and for a long time the only thing people knew to do with the stuff was burn petrol in lamps and grease their carriage axles. In 1848 a Russian engineer drilled the first modern oil well, on the Aspheron Peninsula in Persia. The first well in North America was at Oil Springs, Ontario, where James Miller Williams went looking for water and found free oil at about 65 feet. That was a year before Edwin Drake—a railroad conductor whom his promoter backers elevated to "Colonel Drake"—brought in an oil well in 1859 at about the same depth in Titusville, Pennsylvania. By 1865 oil was America's sixth-largest export commodity. Five years later, John D. Rockefeller founded Standard Oil, Exxon's predecessor, and became the world's richest man.

I was more interested in how the petroleum came to be where it was. In his *Geology of Petroleum*, which became an essential text, Arville I. Levorsen, the Dean of Mineral Sciences at Stanford University, described the essence of a pool of crude oil or natural gas: "A porous and permeable body of rock, called the reservoir rock, which is overlain by an impervious rock, called the roof rock, contains oil or gas or both, and is deformed or obstructed in such a manner that the oil and gas are trapped." Petroleum, he pointed out, is always found in the water-coated pore spaces of sedimentary rocks. The hydrocarbons, lighter than water, rise to the top of the container—the trap—and the part of the trap that holds the petroleum is called the reservoir. I knew that Levorsen was an oil-finder as well as a priceless academic. His successful philosophy of exploration was down to earth in both senses of the phrase: "Find a trap—then drill it." He'd done just that during the 1930s in discovering the famous Fitts pool in the Wilcox sands of Oklahoma, which yielded 190 million barrels of crude oil (a barrel is 42 gallons).

By my second year, I was taking grad courses, mostly in structure and stratigraphy, while carefully avoiding the loathsome mineralogy, paleontology, and mining geology. My fellow students accused me of being poorly rounded because I knew nothing of the mining specialty. I consistently responded that I intended never to set foot in a mine. Ha! Never say never: The gods laugh at those who proclaim too confidently. (Iif that's not an ancient Navajo proverb, it should be).

In other areas, my peers were more respectful. My background at Yale impressed them and even my professors. The fact that I'd been taught by William Twenhofel and had rubbed shoulders with Chester Longwell, not to mention being friends with the likes of Bill Ford—all that, and my sense of self and purpose as a Yalie, combined to cut me out of the herd as slightly special. For the first time, my relative youthfulness was no longer much of a factor. In New Haven, I was just managing to keep up intellectually, worried that I'd lose my scholarship every year; in Boulder, I became one of the top students, which was a wonderfully validating feeling.

Equally empowering was the opportunity to step outside and be in the mountains I'd come to study. A thirty-minute walk from the geology building took me to my favorite lab. Rearing up behind the city are the reddish sandstone walls that form the sharp-peaked frontal range of the Flatirons, cloaked at the base in green pines. These steeply dipping rock plates are called hogbacks. They were an inspiration, an extension of the study hall, and an occasional escape hatch: I climbed the first three Flatirons twice apiece, mostly solo. But my real laboratory was next door in Wyoming.

One evening in early 1948, my stepfather took me along to a study-group meeting in Tulsa of a dozen selected senior geologists. Among them was Rodger Denison, vice-president of exploration at the great Amerada Petroleum company. Amerada's founder was a Renaissance man named Everette DeGolyer, known as the father of applied geophysics, the study of the earth's electrical, gravitational, and magnetic fields and the seismic waves within it. He was also publisher of the *Saturday Review of Literature* and a prominent collector of early Southwest Americana and literature. DeGolyer once said, "Prospecting for oil is a dynamic art.... The greatest single element in all prospecting, past, present and future, is the man willing to take a chance." Denison—whose quiet speech earned him the nickname Whispering Rodger—was the leader and final decision-maker of Amerada. I decided immediately that I wanted to work for him in my graduate-school summers.

Taking a chance on me, Denison became another of my mentors. Amerada gave me a salary and a Jeep and sent me out into the raw, windy plains of Wyoming. (My stepfather once told me, "The Laramie Basin is the only place I know where they use a logging chain for a wind indicator.") Those were sweaty, intensely physical days in the table-flat, dust-blown, sagebrush-dotted plains. Along with a few other young guys, I was learning to be a geologist. You have to see a lot of country, climb a lot of hills, have your vehicle break down a lot of times in the barrens, fix it, and then find your way home. In '48, I did recon geology—systematic reconnaissance mapping with aerial photos and a barometer to gauge altitude— in the southwest of the state. The next summer I was mapping on the Rock Springs Uplift, a huge anticlinal fold of late-Cretaceous sandstone (100 million years old). I learned to use the trusty old plane table, a field instrument John Bartram had used, which combined the telescope of the surveyor's transit with the draftsman's drafting board, all mounted on a tripod. And in my final college summer, I did field work for my M.S. in central Wyoming.

That last summer, I lived in a tiny, dilapidated schoolhouse and took my meals with a ranch family in their ramshackle house next door. To put food on the table, I learned to shoot antelope, deer, and sage chicken out of season. And by now I was absorbing geology through my pores, developing an affection for rocks and rock exposures to the point where the most satisfying thing in my life was to observe these natural structures rising from the ground and arcing off in the distance. I could put names and ages to them, estimate the angle of their dips, judge where they went underground—the whole physical world became more palpable to me. I finished researching and wrote a comprehensive thesis on the late-Cretaceous Frontier Formation. Covering the entire Rockies region from New Mexico to Montana, it was long enough to be a Ph.D. submission, thanks to my thesis supervisor, Warren Thompson.

I had a love/hate relationship with him. Originally my thesis was intended to focus on the Wind River Basin in Wyoming. When I brought it in for review, he said, "Jeez, John, you're covering such a little area."

"But that's the area you told me to do."

"Yes, but it sure looks puny, doesn't it? Why don't you add a couple of basins to it?"

So I expanded into the Bighorn and Green River Basins. When I showed him the revision, he asked me to describe how much territory the Frontier Formation covered. Between the Mexican and the Canadian borders, I said.

"Well, you'd better cover it all or it won't be much of a thesis."

Completing the rough draft of my partial thesis, I took it to Tulsa at Christmas to show Rodger Denison, who turned me over to two of his staff. I'd worked with academics but had never dealt with honest-to-God full-time, professional geologists up close. This pair spent a day analyzing my work, marking it up, and returned it to me with a dozen key suggestions. I was astounded at how informed these men were and how stupid I was. It was one of the seminal learning experiences of my career. I learned how far I had yet to go. As Picasso said, it takes a long time to be young.

When I finally finished the extended thesis over the whole U.S. Rocky Mountain region, I told Doc Thompson, "You sure put me through the wringer."

"John, you don't know enough yet to thank me. One of these days you'll be grateful to me for this because it's the best thing I could give you." It was—and I am.

In fact, for a master's grad, I emerged from college pretty knowledgeable about both the Rocky Mountains and the science I now intended to embrace for life. Under Professor Twenhofel at Yale, I had married geology. My time at Colorado consummated the relationship.

I would soon be married in the literal sense. In the last month of my thesis summer in Wyoming, I worked in the Amerada district office in Casper. Almost immediately, I met a slim, dark-haired, well-tanned girl named Helen—Susie—Mann. She was a year older and had graduated from Colorado in geology a year before me. Susie had been working a couple of years for Continental Oil Company in Casper, where she was the prettiest of all the women geologists. She was likely attracted by my new-found confidence. I was lured by her outgoing personality, her zest, and the Supergirl athletic skill she brought to any sport, from swimming and tennis to football and rock-climbing. On Christmas holidays, I used to play touch football with my uncles. Susie could outkick them—"Godalmighty, did you see that?" they'd say. And she could fire a pass like a bullet from a gun. But it was on the mountains that she showed how gutsy, beautifully coordinated, and light on her feet she could be. When I eventually took her to the Tetons, Glenn Exum remarked, "John, that girl climbs like a fly. She's just so damn good, she can climb anything. You can't shake her loose up there." The implication clearly was that I was pretty clumsy. Yet she was never overbearing about her talents, simply cute and desirable.

Susie came from a tony suburb of Chicago, where her father was a prominent attorney who had clawed his way out of a poverty-stricken background in Georgia. She was inordinately devoted to her parents and three brothers and they were over-protective of her. At the time, no warning bells rang. We fell in love and, as with most sweethearts, overlooked the personality traits that would someday pit us against one another.

Ours was a fairly whirlwind romance. We were married early in 1951, my last year at Colorado. She quit her job and moved to Boulder to be with me until I graduated. Again, the United States was at war, this time with North Korea; at 24, even as a newlywed with a college degree, I was prime draft material. Having missed out on the Marines in World War II, I decided to volunteer for officer training with the Navy. After doing well on the mental tests, I was sent to Dallas for a physical—which I failed because of the football injuries to my lumbar vertebrae and knee. My examiner warned me that while I couldn't qualify as a Naval officer, the Army would likely draft me to tote a rifle. The prospect didn't please me. At Colorado I'd heard that one way a geologist could avoid grunt service, while making a significant contribution, was to work for a critical federal agency like the Atomic Energy Commission.

The AEC was created in the wake of the atomic-bomb explosions that concluded the war with Japan and shocked the world into the Nuclear Age. The commission was charged with overseeing the nation's program of atomic energy, channeling it primarily to peaceful uses. J. Robert Oppenheimer, the brilliant physicist who directed the development of the A-bomb at Los Alamos, New Mexico, headed the committee of civilians who advised the commission on scientific and technical matters. Working for such a cutting-edge organization seemed like an intellectually stimulating launch to my career. It was looking for geologists. One of the AEC's mandates was production of new energy, which meant the mining of uranium. A light isotope of the radioactive metal, Uranium 235 is a highly unstable element, an ideal fuel for nuclear fission. But as the Cold War with Russia heated up, there was increasing talk of America's using uranium to build the biggest bombs in creation. And that's how I, who had vowed never to darken the door of any mine, found myself belowground in Utah.

Susie and I hadn't even taken the time to visit Tulsa before heading over the mountains to the Commission office in Grand Junction, Colorado, where I was inducted into the AEC at a dishwasher's salary of about $300 a month. The people there were managing the search for uranium deposits, focused mainly on the Colorado Plateau which ranges in elevation from 3,500 to 10,000 feet above sea level and contains the Four Corners Monument—the meeting place of Utah, Colorado, Arizona, and New Mexico. The AEC also bought uranium ore, operated a pilot uranium mill, and generally ran the nation's uranium raw-materials program.

They sent us down to White Canyon which, amid the red mesas and buttes of southeastern Utah, drains a vast area of virtually uninhabited rock and flows into the mighty Colorado River. Not that I saw much of the astonishing scenery, or even daylight, for the first several months. I was assigned to do underground mapping in the privately operated Happy Jack Mine on the canyon's southwest rim. This major producer of uranium ore through the 1950s and early '60s was located geologically on the Monument Upwarp, a monocline where uranium-bearing sedimentary rocks primarily of Triassic age lie exposed in the stream canyons.

My arrogant response to my school mates came back to haunt me: "Guys, I am never going to go underground. I have no interest at all in putting a light on my helmet and mapping muck and dirt in a mine." Which of course is exactly what I wound up doing, mapping channels of uranium in the dark bowels of the earth. There were many stories of how shabbily constructed these mines were. I witnessed miners tunneling through to rescue workers buried when a roof collapsed. While I don't recall being scared, I sure don't recall liking it. I was some concerned that the uranium itself could be lethal, as it proved to be for miners who worked with it for long years. Fortunately, ours was a reasonably low grade of ore, two-tenths of one per cent of uranium oxide.

And, luckily, after about four months, I was released from Underground into the Light and dispatched to northeastern Arizona. We went to Cove, a tiny cluster of Navajo hogans below the red-rock escarpments of the Lukachukai Mountains, while just to the north rose the southern slopes of the Carrizo Mountains. Susie and I were now delighted to be living in a trailer squarely amid the Navajo Nation, as the natives themselves called it. They gave us permission to park ourselves next to the tiny school at Cove, with its fresh water and shower facilities. The reservation territory stretched over 30,000 square miles, west from the Jemez Mountains of New Mexico to the Grand Canyon of Arizona and across the upper third of both states. Centered in this corner of Arizona, the

Navajos ranged the Colorado Plateau of sagebrush interrupted by pinyon and juniper evergreens and enlivened by the carmine hues of steep-walled mesas and canyons set against a vast electric-blue sky. The landscape runs from pine forests to bone-dry deserts which, in wetter years, erupt with red cactus blooms.

Then as now, the Navajos formed the largest tribe in America, about 55,000 of them in more than fifty distinct clans who were rapidly growing in population with a birthrate double the national average. The Dinè, The People, were then mostly shepherds, goatherds, and craftspeople becoming famous for their exquisite turquoise and silver jewelry and color-rich rugs woven on primitive looms. During the war years, the average annual income was about $80. Recently some of the men had begun working underground mining uranium and its associated vanadium.

The People intrigued me from first contact. The men were somewhat smaller than the white population but generally good-looking—handsome. Their skin runs from light to ruddy brown and all the shades between. The eyes of the women and children often have an oriental cast. While the men didn't look particularly well-muscled, just try outwalking them or outworking them with a pick and shovel in the mines. They chose to wear cowboy jeans, bright shirts and bandanas, and big felt hats. Women—in drabber Spanish-style calico skirts and velveteen blouses—were even more reclusive than the men.

The Navajos were caught somewhere between the 19th and 20th centuries. The majority of them still lived in hogans, typically six-sided, thick-walled log houses covered with mud and bark, topped by rounded roofs with stove pipes poking up from a central fire. Some of the men had cars and pickups, but most drove horse-drawn wagons, sometimes covered in canvas. Their farms might have metal ploughs and barbed-wire fencing or digging sticks and brush fences. Only after oil was found on their lands near Shiprock, Arizona, in 1923 did they form a Navajo Tribal Council to speak for the whole tribe, authorize expenditures of tribal funds, and deal with the oil and mineral rights that became more important in the years I was there. Their values were different than those of the white world. And they stuck to them. While they appreciated possessions, these often included intangibles like songs and stories. An old Navajo once told a researcher, "I have always been a poor man. I do not know a single song." Comfortable with them, I came to like and respect the Navajos, even though I couldn't claim to any deep understanding of their ways and their thinking.

Native Americans, including the Navajos, have been treated terribly in the U.S. and Canada. Resisting white men's culture, self-sufficient, they were an accepting people who mostly wanted to be left alone. The Navajos, despite their predatory past (they'd killed the first Indian agent ever sent them), had become a praiseworthy, peaceful people even while proving their bravery as soldiers during the Second World War. None of us working among them at the time knew one of the great stories out of that war: their proud record as Code Talkers. Three-quarters of the 540 Navajos who served in the Pacific theater with the U.S. Marines were trained to transmit details of tactics and troop movements over radios and telephones—in their native tongue, in code. Navajo, with no written alphabet or symbols, is such an unusually complex language that it was a perfect wartime code, one that the Japanese never broke. Navajo words were adapted to represent hundreds of common military terms: "besh-lo" (iron fish) was submarine and "dah-he-tih-hi" (hummingbird) was fighter plane. "Were it not for the Navajos," a Marine major said, "the Marines would never have taken Iwo Jima." Their story has only recently come to light, partly through a Hollywood movie, *Windtalkers*, starring Nicolas Cage as an officer overseeing these skilled and courageous soldiers.

From frustrating personal experience, I know just how difficult their language is. It's actually a southern branch of the Athabaskan spoken by natives in northwestern Canada, from where the Navajo migrated centuries ago (the Canadian tribes call themselves Dinè too). The language has 32 consonants and four vowels—but no r, v, f, q, or u. The sounds are strange to us and hard to imitate. Navajos might use just a catch of breath to make subtle distinctions between words: *tsin* can mean tree while *tsʻ in* (the ʻ denoting the breath intake) means bone. Aside from a relatively few common genderless nouns, the language depends on verbs. A single word might translate into an entire English sentence. And the tones of vowels are very important. In their 1946 book, *The Navaho*, cultural anthropologists Clyde Kluckhohn and Katherine Spencer note, "Sounds must be reproduced with pedantic neatness. Tones can be ignored in Chinese for the sake of stress. Not so in Navaho. The language of The People is the most delicate known for phonetic dynamics."

No wonder I felt tongue-tied attempting to communicate with them. While making real friends with a Navajo appeared impossible, I got friendly with a few men. I fell into conversation with one of them—squatting down on my haunches like a catcher, in the native way, which they could do for hours—and asked him to teach me the basics of his language. "Oh, very hard," he warned me but agreed to come to our trailer and try. Although he gave me a half-dozen or more lessons, it was a lost cause. He couldn't explain the convoluted grammar and I couldn't catch on to more than a handful of words; when I tried them on other Navajos, they never understood me.

Susie and I did come to appreciate what we observed of their spirituality. Their religion has long and involved ceremonies, rich with family and friends dancing and chanting, for every single major event in their lives, from birth through puberty to marriage and death. Occasionally we were invited to witness a lower-order event, such as a sandpainting ceremony to cure an ailing young woman by ridding her of evil spirits. We were in a mud hogan with a smokehole at the top, with the door opened to the rising sun in the east. A group of us, mostly natives, sat in a circle around the woman, who was naked near the fire in the center. A medicine man chanted while creating line figures on the ground of the malign spirit and then of a man, the hero, who would destroy the evil. The proper name for this technique is drypainting. While sand forms the backdrop of the image, the design is usually shaped by careful dribbling of charcoal and other pulverized materials (sometimes pollen and crushed flowers) in delicate lines. This medicine man was so skilfull that he could draw a straight line one grain wide. After a few hours, we noticed the weak-looking woman was beginning to revive and

Leo with our Navajo guides, Wallace Reed and Tom Joe.

at the end were convinced that this healing ceremony was doing its work.

Sometimes their beliefs in evil spirits became a problem in their encounters with the white working world. If there were rumors of a coyote man in the area, Navajos working in the local uranium mines would refuse to come in for a night shift unless the company sent a vehicle to pick them up and take them home. And in one mine operated by Kerr-McGee, a white supervisor had to be fired after he killed a snake—ignoring the Navajo belief that the dead return in the form of animals.

If one of many family ceremonies was scheduled, the Navajo miner would simply disappear for several days to a week—with no forewarning, no explanation. Dismissal was no solution: everyone would have wound up being fired. The Kerr-McGee foremen learned how to adjust. Navajos do not change; the family and the belief systems are like rock.

* * *

I was now part of a small team of geologists, engineers, and drillers exploring for uranium. For about a year, I partnered with Leo Miller, who was a couple of years older and had just graduated with a master's in geology from the University of Southern California. We were sent out into the Lukachukai Mountains to find mines. Our task was to map the distribution of the coarse fluvial Morrison sandstones, dating back about 120 million years, cemented together in layers ten to twenty feet thick. The sandstone was in irregular, interfingering stream channels. Uranium came in via fluids in the rock; the fluids followed the channels. The trick was to identify mineralization and then stay in that channel wherever it took you. In the Lukachukais, that involved a maze of vertical cliffs. Always we were seeking any mineralized portion of the Morrison that drillers could reach economically. We made our maps on aerial photos which we carried in our packs. It was on one of those expeditions that Leo rescued me after I'd tumbled 40 feet down Fall Down Mesa on the south side of the Lukachukais. As on every other day, we climbed steeply back to our vehicle, hot and exhausted, retrieved canvas water bags beneath the bumper, drank maybe half a gallon, slumped on the seats, and slept for half an hour before regaining the energy to drive an hour back down the mountain roads to home.

Driving every road, walking most of the major trails, we got to know the Lukachukais like amateur Navajos. Their name for the overall range of mountains was *choosh'gai*, meaning white-colored spruce trees, which became Chuska. They consider the Chuskas a sacred male deity whose forests provide them with timber and their grassy flanks with summer grazing land for livestock. Occasionally we would come across an Indian camp in the mountains where a woman might shyly offer us a meal. Sitting on our haunches, we'd devour hot bread with sauce and maybe some leftover lamb. The men would talk with us in pidgin English while the women retreated silently behind the fire and their kids ran into the hogan.

At the start, we hired two Navajo guides to lead us on horseback along trails through the dense woods of the upper Lukachukais. The first morning after camping out, we decided to make pancakes with a mix and water over a campfire. Our guides showed not a glimmer of emotion as they watched us create four bitty cakes in the fry pan. "Big fire," one of them finally noted. "Real little pancakes." Squatting down, he doused much of the flame with water to reduce it to hot coals, then asked for a second pan, into which he dumped the entire can of batter to make a single thick cake. Letting it cook for a while, he then flipped it over into the second pan, let it brown, sliced it into quarters like a pie and drizzled syrup on top. Navajo pancakes—oh man, were they good. (Lenora and I still fix them when we want to show off for guests.)

Baby Chuck at six months, in the trailer, preparing to be a field geologist.

As Leo and I bonded over those many months, Susie and his sweet wife, Julie, also became good friends. Most days the two women drove out in a big converted weapons-carrier to explore the deep canyons and the red-bed cliffs. Clad in bathing suits or shorts, they became as bronzed as the Navajos. They took a lunch, rode and walked for six or eight hours, and returned dirty, sweat-streaked, and keen to head out again the next morning. All that halted in the summer of 1950 when Susie had our firstborn, Charles—Chuck, named after my brother. She gave birth in Grand Junction and stayed there for about a month before we strapped him into a cradle tied on to the back seat of my Jeep and brought him home along bumpy roads to our trailer in the desert. He seemed a very soft, defenseless little creature. Later, I would record in my book of quotations the words of philosopher Joseph Campbell: "Human beings are born too soon; they are unfinished, unready as yet to meet the world. Consequently their whole defense from a universe of dangers is the mother."

While I was a typically inept young father, Susie was a suitably protective mother. If the heat in our trailer quit (and some Arizona nights hit twenty below zero), she aggressively shook me awake and pushed me out of bed to fix things before the little guy froze to death. The fact is, Chuck not only survived his infanthood, he flourished and grew up to be a wiry, well-conditioned young man, working for Leo Miller as a swamper when my former colleague was finding an enormous copper deposit in the western desert of Australia. By then Leo had his Ph.D. from Columbia University and was already building a reputation as one of the world's great exploration mineral geologists.

Although I had been a rank amateur on our geological team in the beginning, I was intent on becoming an expert on the Lukachukais. I read everything I could find on the subject and in a matter of months found myself being the answer man when other geologists wanted my opinion on this formation, that structure, the relationship certain trees might have to a particular igneous intrusion. I was intrigued enough to begin writing a government paper on this southernmost area of uranium on the Colorado Plateau, which pleased another guru who appeared in my life.

The AEC had cleverly designed a mentorship program that brought professors from various universities in the summer to do research projects with the assistance of AEC geologists. I was assigned to William Lee Stokes—recognized as the head man of Utah geology—a Princeton grad who'd worked for the U.S. Geological Survey, became the head of the University of Utah's geology department, and wrote several seminal textbooks, including *Introduction to Geology*. Lee Stokes, a damn fine geologist, embarked on a regional mapping project covering the Lukachukais and the Carrizos. Apparently impressed that the paper I was writing was equivalent to a doctoral thesis on the distribution of ore deposits in the region, he engaged me in long discussions. Soon, rather than lecturing me, he was picking my right and left brains about the local geology.

By this time, I had developed a hypothesis about how uranium had come to be only in the eastern half of the Lukachukais, avoiding the western part. Basically, my stratigraphic theory was built on the belief that uranium had been carried in solution through the whole Colorado Plateau wherever the geologic section contained ancient stream channels. In our region, the beds had developed in very large channels on the west side of the range, which created massive sandstone cliffs, while on the east they'd passed into a lateral environment with alternating layers, or benches, of shale and sandstone. The underground fluids would have moved more easily through the enormous sandstone section on the west than eastward through the interbedded sandstone and shale section. This latter environment, of course, is where the driftwood collected because stream velocity diminished. Wood is organic, it changes the pH (the acidity or alkilinty) of water, and that causes uranium to precipitate. This thesis contradicted the conventional wisdom, as expressed by most experts, that massive sandstones were most favorable for ore. These "experts" included the AEC's chief geologist, who developed a growing distate for me. I do not have a compromising personality. I didn't fashion it that way; it just grew.

Looking at my illustrated cross-sections of Morrison geology, which I'd color-coded, Lee Stokes said, "John, I've never seen such a picturesque—and accurate—description of a regional area in the uranium business." The U.S. Geological Survey guys had been working in southwestern Colorado for a decade, he remarked, and they didn't understand the distribution of uranium there nearly as well as I did here. With his encouragement, my research became the guiding criteria for the region, steering exploration crews away from uselessly drilling on those huge western cliffs where they hadn't been finding uranium. Publishing my first professional paper on the area—in the *Bulletin of the Society of Economic Geologists*—gave me the first burst of courage to dispute expert opinion; a long time later, General Colin Powell put it well when he said, "Don't be afraid to challenge the pros, even in their own backyard." At age 22, I was appointed district geologist in my own backyard, the Lukachukais, the commission's youngest in such a position.

It was while in that role that I met the man who had the most momentous impact on my career of anyone in my life.

CHAPTER FIVE

LEARNING FROM MR. McGEE

DEAN MCGEE, THE CO-FOUNDER of the Kerr-McGee Corporation of Oklahoma City, was a genius, the single grandest man I ever knew. But when some of his employees approached me in Arizona one day in early 1952, I had no idea of exactly how important an executive or how intelligent and far-sighted an exploration geologist he was. All a-flutter because McGee was about to visit the Lukachukais, they wanted me to give him and his people an hour's briefing on the geology of the region ("None of us wants to get up in front of him and make a fool of ourselves"). They asked me to describe the structure and the stratigraphy, the history, the larger context—the Big Picture. I knew I could do that. I could hardly wait.

Dean McGee wanted to go into the uranium business as a way of diversifying from the then-troubled oil industry. Several years before, a Navajo prospector had discovered a deposit of radioactive ore in a cliff

The legendary Dean McGee, head man of Kerr-McGee, obviously a genius—and my teacher and warm friend.

face on the north side of the Lukachukais. Two white owners had since mined uranium there and built a processing plant. Now, in early 1952, the Navajo Uranium Mine was for sale. As McGee assured his banker, "Drilling for uranium is no different than drilling for oil, for gas, or for any other minerals." The fact that no other oil company was considering such a possibility didn't dissuade him.

The Executive Vice-President of Kerr-McGee arrived on the Navajo Reservation with his entourage of VPs. I was immediately struck by the sheer presence of this handsome, vigorous-looking man with a square jaw and a shock of wavy black hair. He looked solid, barrel-chested, and walked with a kind of roll, like an old athlete or sailor, always appearing to be heading purposefully in a straight line toward something significant. Charming but controlling, he never raised his voice—never had to, as I learned. Wherever he sat was the head of the table. Although no taller than I, and unassuming in manner, McGee radiated power.

And so in our small plywood-sheathed cabin of an office, with a desk and a drafting table, I stood at a map and presented the geology of northeastern Arizona and the Masters theory of uranium-finding to this man for whom I had instant respect.

After the presentation, Dean McGee took me by the elbow, led me outside, and said, "That was a darn good talk, John. You were putting the uranium into a geological context. . . .What are you going to do when you leave the AEC?"

"Well, Mr. McGee, I want to work for an oil company." I had concluded that three-fourths of mining geology was a waste of time. I was getting tired of climbing two thousand feet to reach an outcrop, and driving a Jeep on dirt trails too many miles from home, changing flats and then thumbing a ride when a spark plug failed. In the oil business, I suspected, you'd have file cases full of maps and data in your own office and have the time and encouragement to work your mind instead of your body.

Undeterred, he replied, "What would you think about coming to work for me and running our uranium program?"

"I don't want to offend you, but I'm really not interested in staying in uranium. I think I can learn to be a lot better geologist if I get into the oil business and start working with people who are really well trained in geology. Is there any chance of doing that?"

Yes, McGee said measuredly, he thought he could entertain that notion. Why didn't I fly in to Oklahoma City at their expense and we'd decide what I could do for them?

A week later, I flew in the company DC-3 and met him at the Kerr-McGee Building, an eight-storey concrete structure, as substantial-looking as McGee himself.

Kerr-McGee had grown out of the little oil-drilling operation Robert Kerr and his partners incorporated in his hometown of Ada, Oklahoma, in 1928. That venture developed into A&K Petroleum Company, which Dean McGee joined in 1937 as a Production Vice-President. Kerr, a lawyer, became the state's first native-born governor in 1942 and a Democratic senator six years later. In 1953 the medium-sized company—

now Kerr-McGee Oil Industries—had grown to 800 employees and thirty operating oil rigs in the western U.S. and the Gulf of Mexico.

Kerr—six-foot-four and an unathletic 250 pounds—was an orator, a bibliophile, and a skillful poker player who once won enough cash to buy an oil lease with his brother. He was also a hard-driving businessman whose main goal in making money was to support his other interests, primarily politics. Fifteen years before, he'd needed a competent 2-I-C who could gradually assume the presidency of his petroleum company—and in Dean McGee he found him, in spades.

Dean Anderson McGee was the son of a wildcatter who finally drilled one too many dry holes and went broke. The youngest of four children, Dean was born in 1904 in the shacktown village of Humboldt amid the rolling grass hills and blackjack oaks of southeastern Kansas. The local high-school library had a single book on geology, which inspired him to pursue the science. Working his way through Kansas University, doing four jobs at a time, he earned a degree in mining engineering, the closest he could come to geology, and spent a further year in graduate studies. He went to work for Phillips Petroleum Company in Peru, returning in time for the finale of the oil boom that had begun in southeastern Oklahoma with the Seminole field.

But his first major play was the Oklahoma City discovery, which McGee made two years later, in 1928. He had come to the conclusion that the real oil would be in the Wilcox sand on the west flank of the structure below the crest where the first, short-lived wells had come in. He persuaded Phillips to take leases there. Later that year, another company's "wild Mary" blew in from the Wilcox and for eleven days coated much of the city in oil. (In the Great Depression, that was considered a major achievement, not an environmental disaster.) Phillips acquired a dominant position in the new field and became one of the top producers in the state as the field ultimately flowed 800 million barrels. Dean McGee was

26. Five years later, he became Phillips' chief geologist. To everyone, he was a hero. To founder Waite Phillips, he was a genius.

Not that he confined his successes to Oklahoma. Explaining his early philosophy of oil-finding, he said, "You can figure out where to explore by where the most millionaires live. Houston has a lot more millionaires than Wichita. I just decided to put the money where the rewards would be the greatest."

At 33 he joined Bob Kerr's company, lured by the promise of share participation. Phillips was so loath to let him go that it promised to underwrite 75 per cent of the company's exploration expenses for a 50-per-cent share of the profits. In those days—still the Depression—that was what we call a helluva deal. His initial big find was a field at Magnolia in southern Arkansas, which had to be sold when there wasn't enough cash to exploit it. However, the exploration decision that ranks McGee among the giants was tackling the seemingly insurmountable problems of exploring, drilling, and producing oil on the shallow offshore waters of the Gulf of Mexico. The major companies simply could not figure out how to do that. "It looked better to us than staying on land, where the first-class spots were already leased and drilled," McGee explained. "Some said it took courage. Others just said we were foolish." But as one colleague put it, "McGee just knew there was oil out there and as good drilling contractors we believed we could solve the producing problems." That's an after-the-fact quote. At first, it was McGee alone who was sure it could be done.

Geologically, Louisiana is a prime breeding ground for hydrocarbons (maybe hydrocarbons have some relation to mosquitoes). The sedimentary section beneath its coast and offshore forms a significant portion of the richly productive Gulf Coast Continental Margin Basin stretching from Mexico across Texas and Louisiana to the Florida Panhandle. The most favorable traps in the state at that time were salt domes, masses of salt forced up into sedimentary rocks. While the ones on land were taken, those in shallow water were virgin territory. In what became the Ship Shoal fields, the company did marine seismic work, inducing shock-wave reflections from underground layers of rock to build detailed models of the underlying geological structure. In 1947, McGee did the unthinkable: he directed construction of the world's first stationary oil platform at sea, out of sight of land. He was in eighteen feet of water a dozen miles from shore. No one in the global oil industry had conceived of doing that. The equipment cost a mere $250,000, one-quarter of what the majors eventually spent for floating platforms including crew quarters and storage space for supplies. The first prospect in Ship Shoal at Block 32 found oil at only 1,500 feet on the top of a shallow salt dome. Some months later, a second well found a major gas field at 13,000 feet on Block 28. Within 12 months McGee had made back-to-back discoveries with the first two wells ever drilled in the open ocean and set the prevailing course of the oil industry around the world for the next century. That was McGee: a genius—with guts. A tiny company showed the whole industry its future.

Over the years, he successfully integrated his company into pipelines, gasoline plants, refining, wholesale distribution, and retail marketing through a chain of 800 Deep Rock service stations in 23 states. But even in the early 1950s, he was starting to define the oil company more broadly as an energy company. His company was the first to begin acquiring coal properties, one of several primary energy sources he knew would eventually be needed to meet America's insatiable demand. He bought the nation's second-biggest reserve of sodium borate salts—an essential ingredient in glass, agricultural chemicals, and pharmaceuticals—at Searles Lake, California, and developed an industrial-chemical arm. The company later operated the only private helium plant in the U.S., became a large harvester of forest products, and produced uranium, copper, zinc, silver, lithium, titanium, potash, and phosphate from many, many mines.

For the time, moving into coal, chemicals, and uranium was a conceptual leap. But while Dean McGee was a great conceptualizer, his execution was not always on a grand scale. In part, this was because he liked to keep the decision-making authority in his own hands and never allowed the organization to function independently. (An embarrassing *Time* magazine story in 1954 told how he'd taken charge of bids for oil leases off Lousiana and mistakenly wrote down map numbers instead of sale numbers of the tracts he wanted. Kerr-McGee was the highest, and only, bidder on several tracts it didn't want. Senator Kerr finally got the $3-million down payment back, but the Interior Department wouldn't let the company apply that bid to the blocks it did want; it was too late.) The more McGee set up management committees and vice-presidents and decentralized operations, the more he retained ultimate and final authority over almost everything. McGee simply was never comfortable with building a large, autonomous company staffed with experts strong enough to proceed on their own. He never knew anyone smart enough to do things better than he could do.

Nervy enough to discuss this with him one day, long after joining the company, I said, "Mr. McGee, you don't seem to spend as much effort choosing your people as you do about a lot of your other ideas."

"Well, John, that's true. I have a bad habit of picking people that just do the janitor jobs around here. As a rule, I don't need anybody supplying me with ideas."

As a result, he failed for many years to build Kerr-McGee's oil exploration organization to a size and quality that could compete effectively with large companies in offshore, domestic, and foreign ventures. He never developed a state-of-the-art organization in geophysics (the interpretation of subsurface structure from underground seismic energy waves). His geological organization never had a special competence in any one particular field of technology that would give it a significant competitive advantage. Nor did he develop groups of different specialists to work tightly together to solve mutual problems. By observation — observing what *not* to do as well as the many things to do — I came to realize the importance of building teams, strong teams, in the oil business, a concept I took with me to Canadian Hunter. I had to do that: I wasn't as smart as Dean McGee.

In smaller-scale operations, such as exploration for uranium and other minerals, the competitive field was neither as wide nor as intense as petroleum exploration. In those areas, the company, working with relatively small units in close touch with McGee, could be very effective. There were periods when Kerr-McGee was the pre-eminent player in the American uranium field.

Before seeing Dean McGee in Oklahoma City about a new job, I went to Tulsa to visit my mentor at Amerada Petroleum, Rodger Denison, to discuss my overall problem of finding the right place in the oil business. He was in a bind because his Wyoming district manager, whom I'd known in my student days, disliked me—perhaps because I wouldn't go drinking with him or because he didn't share my youthfully immodest opinion of my intelligence. Denison counselled me to consider Kerr-McGee. It was good advice.

When I met McGee in his office, he asked the usual questions—especially, how did I learn to find uranium? After all, I was only 23. He listened carefully, letting me ramble on, and then, with his incredible skill at summation, succinctly fed back the essence of what I'd said. He realized that even though he had a more immediate need for someone in his uranium group, I was serious about becoming an oil geologist. He hired me and for the next two years that's what I tried to be.

The petroleum geologist is the key link between an oil or gas pool and more than twenty different interpretive disciplines, ranging from geophysics and engineering, through stratigraphy and surface mapping, chemistry and mathematics, to sedimentation and petrography—which is describing and systematically classifying rock with the aid of a microscope (a specialty that would loom large in my later career). As A.I. Levorsen has pointed out, a potential oil or gas field is only a concept in the geologist's mind: "Imagination, then, is an indispensable quality of the petroleum geologist. The world's future supply of petroleum is as dependent upon the imaginative powers of the petroleum geologist as on the presence of favorable rocks—of which there appears to be an abundant volume."

In 1953, I began learning some of this at Kerr-McGee's Oklahoma

City headquarters. For about a year, I did some well-sitting—being the on-site geologist at an oil rig—and found the mechanical nature of the job uninspiring. The fact is, though, this field preparation is an important first step before you graduate to the more interesting job of mapping prospects. It's not an area in which I'm strong today because Mr. McGee was impatient for me to begin exploring.

Our family had moved into a rented bungalow only a few blocks from McGee's house, where he lived with his wife, Dorothea, and their two daughters. Occasionally he dropped me off in his car after work, giving us a chance to talk. One day he said, "John, there's no place like West Texas to learn about the oil business." There was an opening in their office in Midland, the operational heart of the district's oil industry. Because I had no idea how important the geology of that region would be to my future, he allowed me the time to visit my knowledgeable stepfather in Tulsa. "Oh, it's really simple," John Bartram told me. "You're not an oil geologist until you've worked in West Texas. You'll learn more oil geology and see more complex stratigraphic and structural problems out there in a state that has more oil than any other place in the entire country."

So we moved again, the three of us, and in the beginning Susie was a good oilman's wife, viewing it as an adventure. She soon came to hate the barren flatlands surrounding the town of 21,000. So much grit came through the taped windows and doors of our jerkwater little house that it would take her a couple of days to clean up after a dust storm. It was too hot and windy to play tennis, there was too little grass to play golf, and not enough water to swim in. Instead, the young oil families like us actively socialized, making the rounds of each others' backyards for barbecues.

The first big oil well in West Texas had blown in near here in 1923 and Midland almost doubled in growth with every decade. Although a challenging place to raise a family, it was better for me because of what I was learning—in spite of my boss there, who wasn't a particularly astute geologist. I was helping develop prospects in shallow beds to avoid digging deep, expensive wells. The company's geologists hadn't investigated the shallow section closely enough to detect any pattern to the fields.

Bypassing them, I asked who the best geologists in town were and became friends with two of them: an independent developing his own prospects, Bill Humbard, and a respected senior geologist working for Phillips, Addison Young. Having coffee with them twice a day and filling my notebook with observations, I got another college education as they taught me practical oil geology. One day a light went on and I announced to them, "You can't explore the Permian unless you know the reef distribution!" Broadly translated, that meant you can't be an effective explorationist if you simply try to understand a prospect in a localized area without comprehending the distribution of the whole rock section over the whole region. They looked at each other, laughed, and agreed that I was catching on. It's humbling how long it takes to grasp the Big Picture. Addison and Bill were miles ahead of me.

I developed my first regional map, displaying the entire Grayburg reef trend in the Permian which looped around the basin for 600 miles. I showed Mr. McGee. He told his Vice-President of Exploration, Gene Finley, that they needed this kind of comprehensive mapping in all their offices. Gratifying as that recognition was, I realized that to succeed in the company as an oil geologist, I'd have to work my way through several layers of managers I didn't respect, including Finley. So I was primed for an approach from another company that invited me to be, of all things, a uranium geologist again.

J. Paul Getty, the oilman's son from Tulsa who became one of the world's richest men, had acquired Tidewater Oil in 1953 and now intended to diversify into uranium on the Colorado Plateau. The Vice-President of Mineral Exploration came to Midland and invited me to manage the operation at a salary triple what I was earning. The offer turned my head. Many of my colleagues at AEC had leaped to private uranium ventures at inflated salaries. However, I felt it only fair to meet Dean McGee face to face to announce my decision to leave.

He had recently become Kerr-McGee's President and Chief Executive Officer and, if anything, exuded more power than ever. However quietly expressed, his enormous presence humbled everyone around him, inhibiting all but the most confident. "John," he said, "you made a deal with me. You told me you wanted to work in the oil business when I wanted you to work in the uranium business. I changed my plans to accommodate you. And now you come in and tell me you're leaving because you want to go back into the uranium business. If you'd told me that then, I would have given you the same job Tidewater is offering you. And I still will. I'll set you up in a Denver office and you can run our uranium operation and be a Rocky Mountain district oil geologist on the side. I think your future is here with me."

He had dealt a royal flush to my pair of aces. "Mr. McGee, if you let me take on a job where I can have some authority, that's all I want," I replied. "I didn't think I was going to be able to do that here."

In early 1955, we moved to Denver, the four of us—our daughter, a beauty we named Barabara, had just been born in Midland. Almost from the start, Barbie reminded me of my mother in her strength and determination: nobody tells her what she can do, and yet she combines that steel spine with a marvelous sense of warmth and support for other people. Like me, she was right-brained and an avid bookworm, encouraged by my reading of *Winnie the Pooh* and *Charlotte's Web*; on family holidays I'd recite *The Cremation of Sam McGee*. Unlike me, who had a boyhood ambition to become a cartoonist, she became a gifted artist ("I was an artist since the day I was born," she says). At age three, she used to play Cinderella, in a scarf and little high heels, while I was the Prince in a Tyrolean mountain hat who would do anything she asked. Or it might be the game of Bus where we lined up the chairs after dinner; I was the driver and took Barbie and Chuck anywhere they wanted to go. Ours was a child-centered household, where the kids would make tents under the table and the place would look like a bomb hit it until ten minutes before I arrived home, when Susie would quickly clean up.

Growing up, Barbie visited her grandmother in Tulsa and, while

Chuck considered Maxine Masters a bit demanding and controlling (the Methodist Sunday-school teacher), his sister loved being with this cultivated, motivated woman of similar temperament. Susie was a bit of a tomboy, so it was left to grandmother to teach Barbie how to sew, take her shopping, and do all that girl stuff together. Back home, their mother took Barbie and Chuck to museums and zoos and taught them how to play baseball.

Denver was in the midst of its first big oil boom, spawning instant millionaires as petroleum companies from around the world set up shop. The city had begun as a boomtown when prospectors found gold nearby in 1858. Two decades later, it became the capital of Colorado and transformed itself into an agriculture-fueled cow town. Now it was an oil town, an attractive place to raise a family with its abundant parks and tree-lined boulevards and easy access to hiking and skiing in the surrounding Rocky Mountains.

Life in Denver was sweet, and it was about to get sweeter—as sweet as ambrosia.

CHAPTER SIX

AMBROSIA LAKE

"I NEVER KNEW WHERE ALL THE CROOKS from East Texas went until I got into the uranium business and they all turned up again," Dean McGee said more than once. Let me describe the background for that comment.

Beaumont, Texas, on the coastline of the Gulf of Mexico, near Houston, was the real birthplace of the American oil industry. On January 10, 1901, the Lucas gusher roared in at Spindletop from a depth of 1,020 feet. At 100,000 barrels of oil per day that one well exceeded the total production from all the wells in the world. Forget gold, silver, even diamonds — their total dollar value was inconsequential compared to the gigantic wealth of hydrocarbons in the machine age.

More fields were quickly found in Texas as well as in California, Oklahoma, Kansas, New Mexico, Louisiana, and other states. The biggest of them all, the grandest field in the whole U.S., was found in East Texas in

1930. Like Spindletop and many of the great new fields that broke open whole new provinces, it was discovered in an area already discounted by the recognized experts of the day. This situation opens the door briefly to the fleet of foot—not only the scientists who can create a new image out of scattered data that are widely perceived to have already settled into a logical picture, but also crooks who are quick enough to recognize from the new wells a new opportunity for profit. It's interesting to reflect how similar must be the brain types of these two human groups generally considered to be at opposite ends of the human spectrum.

In East Texas, 200 miles north of Spindletop, in an area thought by most oilmen to have scant promise, an ignorant little man named Dad Joiner had some kind of hunch that oil could be found there. He teamed up with a really phony old "geologist" and together they conned elderly investors into giving them their life savings. Remember, this was 1930, in the Great Depression. America was in a deep hole. Joiner oversold the whole venture by 300 per cent. Everyone bought in at a cheap price, but they got only one-third of what they paid for. Joiner leased a large block of land with some money and a lot of promises.

The first well to 1,098 feet was a dry hole. The second well was a dry hole. The third well at 3,592 feet blew in at 300 barrels of oil per day and unleashed the largest oil field ever found in the U.S. Every oilman in the region knew a discovery had been made, but they all had the normal human reaction to a new idea: there must be something wrong with it. All of them except H.L.. Hunt, a gambler, and Wallace Pratt, exploration manager of Humble Oil Company, later Exxon. Pratt was the greatest oil geologist ever.

Hunt went after Dad Joiner. With booze and promises and threats, he convinced Joiner to take $1.3 million for his acreage. That laid the foundation of the oil empire that ultimately made H.L. Hunt the richest man in America. Pratt went after huge blocks of land north and south of the well. He realized that the Woodbine pay sand, because it was not present updip (at a higher elevation) to the east, must be caught in a gigantic pinchout trap (one that tapers out of a reservoir into non-porous rock, sealing it in). Hunt knew there was an important new field. Pratt knew how important and its approximate shape. And he had unlimited money.

East Texas was such a large field, it stretched much farther than even Wallace Pratt's projections. Many other operators, large and small, got pieces of this bonanza. Land prices, total land costs, numbers of wells, total production, total investment, numbers of deals made from the original deals, trespasses, theft, lies—all of these factors, in quantities never before experienced, at the bottom of the greatest Depression in history, created a vast outpouring of wealth and a cesspool of corruption.

The uranium business had to go a long way to match that sordid history. It made a good try. Many of the characters were certainly as venal as the worst in East Texas. There just weren't as many of them. Fortunately, some of the first ones had died.

This time, some of the characters doing the conning were a sweet-talking old woman named Stella Dysart, a jewelry salesman and self-styled geologist I called Loathsome Lothmann, and a double-dealing oil-company employee nicknamed Bufalo Kennedy, who buffaloed some naive landowners out of their valuable uranium holdings. And I was there to witness much of it—while helping to identify the largest uranium deposit in the world.

Uranium was the gold of the 1950s. It brought out all the greed, duplicity, and crazy dreams of overnight fortunes that fueled the Gold Rushes in the late 1800s. Prospectors had discovered radioactive metals in the western U.S. in the early days of mining. An initial boom in Colorado erupted in 1912 with the development of radium, found in uranium oxide ore, for medical uses and luminous paints. Before the Second World War, the ore was mined on the Colorado Plateau as a co-product of the vanadium used to strengthen steel. But it took the Manhattan Project's creation of the first atomic bomb to spur a landrush demand for uranium. While most of it came from the old vanadium mines in southwest

Colorado, some was from new mines in Arizona, Utah, New Mexico, and Wyoming.

Only after the war, amid the danger of an arms race with the Soviet Union, did the Atomic Energy Commission launch a serious search for a domestic supply of uranium. Government and privately employed geologists found significant deposits in Colorado and surrounding states. The reports of fresh finds touched off a hunt by amateur prospectors. By 1955 the commission estimated that more time had been spent searching for uranium than for all other metals in history. As the search reached a crescendo of activity that year, *Life Magazine* offered a basic pictorial guide for the civilian uranium-seeker—while reporting "some 10,000 people spend weekends tramping the hills for uranium" and "colleges are giving classes in uranium prospecting for amateurs."

One of the most colorful of many uranium characters was the heroine of a nonsensical book, *Stella Dysart of Ambrosia Lake*, which veers igorantly between non-fiction and fiction in recounting her story. Written in 1959 by a graphic designer named Merle Armitage (with a foreword by a New Mexico senator), it's an astonishing whitewash of a woman who drilled dry holes, peddled worthless parcels of land to thousands of dirt-poor investors, and went to jail for one of her crooked deals. As the editor of *Uranium Magazine* writes in an introduction, "this woman being Woman is in part inscrutable. There must be a little more of her story, but as someone said of Truth—'it lies hidden in a crooked well.'" He sensed a little of Stella, but he wasn't even close to the full story.

When I encountered her, she was deep into her seventies, although still a commanding woman. Another *Life* article at the time showed her looking elegant in a fur stole and a rose-garnished hat; the caption read: "Wealthy landowner, Mrs. Stella Dysart stands before abandoned oil rig which she set up on her property in a long, vain search for oil. Now uranium is being mined there and Mrs. Dysart, swathed in mink, gets a plump royalty." I met her once in her home in Albuquerque, which looked modest from the outside but had a heated and air-conditioned indoor swimming pool. She sat there with a servile female companion

("You're exactly right, Stella") and spun stories about her oil and uranium plays and how she was pursuing all her projects for the benefit of the poor investors in California.

This ambitious daughter of a Missouri sheepherder and a school teacher attended a minor college to take theology and public speaking, skills she didn't need to be taught. After owning dress shops in St. Louis and Los Angeles, she got a real-estate licence and began hawking "potential oil property" in California during the 1920s. Under the mentorship of an L.A. lawyer, she bought pasture land in northwestern New Mexico—desolate, arid land in an area unaccountably called Ambrosia Lake, which *Time* would later describe as "a misnamed patch of sunbaked, bone-dry limestone." (It's not limestone, but that's how *Time* tells its stories.) She then flipped it for more than triple the price she'd paid for it.

Someone explained to Stella that Ambrosia Lake was on a small anticline and that anticlines hold oil. A light went on, and she decided (1) to lease more land and (2) to drill for oil, and (3) to make money along the way. She turned loose as many as 150 salesmen at a time in Los Angeles. Even her admiring biographer admits some of the salesmen were, in his term, "opportunists . . . it was something Stella Dysart could not completely control." She was, of course, hardly the person you would select to control such a situation. During the Depression her sales force peddled lots a sixteenth of an acre in size for $18 apiece (or $288 per acre) which was at least 576 times the market value to sophisticated oil people. The owners were impoverished, trusting, evangelical church-goers whom she impressed with her constant quoting of Scripture and her assurance that this was God's way to wealth. At one point, legal records showed that a single 640-acre section had 2,596 lease-owners. While she was touting Ambrosia Lake as being rich in oil, her own attempts at drilling came up dry. "With her failures came controversies galore," the editor of *Uranium Magazine* concedes in the Armitage book, "notably a tangle with California authorities wherein she admitted a technical violation of the securities act as a result of what she regards today as mistaken legal advice." She also tried drilling in Utah, but as her biographer ambiguously explains, "through unbelievable technicalities was obliged to abandon her operations, and the courts forced her out of the state."

Stella was, as they say, a piece of work.

What saved her was the discovery of uranium nearby and the eventual surfacing of Louis B. Lothmann. In 1950, a local sheepherder found an odd yellow rock on railroad land around Haystack Butte, near Grants, New Mexico. It was uranium ore and two companies quickly opened mines in the area, luring a passel of prospectors who hit minor paydirt. Among them was Loathsome Lothmann, as I thought of him. This young, actually rather good-looking Texan—once described as "a very friendly great Dane"—was a slick traveling salesman of cheap jewelry who on his rounds of New Mexico had the wild idea he might find a mine. He always carried a high priced scintillometer in his car—more sensitive than a plain old Geiger counter.

Lothman's biggest coup was courting Stella Dysart and getting a lease on Section 11 of her Ambrosia Lake land to scout for uranium. He turned to another con artist, more devious even than himself, who had a Jeep station wagon outfitted with, believe this or not, an old nickelodeon—today's jukebox. It had a switch that could be turned to gold, silver, or uranium. When the time was right for the kill, the driver would press a button under the dashboard. The old music machine would flash lights and ring bells. Each mineral had a different group of such signals.

(Looking for oil has become pretty sophisticated; the screwballs have pretty much lost their footing there. But the mining business still has a lot of them. I'm not going to try to explain that. It is just a fact of life you'd better be prepared for if you're going to look for mines.)

Lothman got the station-wagon guy to drive over Stella's Section 11 at Ambrosia Lake. They drove over a piece of it here, another piece there, and the guy says, "It don't look any good." Lothman starts to slump, and then his colleague presses the button. Lights and bells! The guy is yelling, Lothman is yelling. But the strangest part of this story is that they were actually ringing that stupid nickelodeon over the biggest, richest uranium deposit ever found in the whole world. Unbelievable, but you're in the mining business now and it can get pretty crazy. Loathsome Lothman had stumbled blindly onto the giant Ambrosia Lake uranium deposit. Ultimately, it would make America the nuclear power of the world. It became one of the key factors in ending the Cold War because the Russians finally realized they couldn't keep up.

At the time, Lothman didn't have any money to explore his big nickelodeon find. It had to be drilled. I don't know how the next step happened, but Lothman found Ellis Dunn, owner of a trucking company in Dallas. Dunn thought it would be a good idea to spend the summer at Grants. He'd get his swamper, Red, to look after the drills. Dunn would entertain Red's wife. The drilling proceeded, cuttings were collected, and they were trucked to Kerr-McGee's uranium mill at Shiprock for assaying. Which is where Kerr-McGee, Bufalo Kennedy, and I came in.

It had taken Kerr-McGee two decades to generate resource revenues of $15 million a year. Now it was in the middle of a five-year surge that would see it tripling in size. An admiring *Time* reporter (who described Dean McGee as "a tall, rawhide-tough wildcatter and geologist"—about the most inaccurate description of him ever penned) quoted McGee as saying, "When you pull yourself up by your bootstraps, it's like a flower opening up—slowly at first, and then it finally spreads out." In 1952 the company was the first of the oil producers to decide that uranium was a complement, not a competitor, to its main product. They paid $50,000 cash and future considerations for the small Navajo Uranium Mine in New Mexico and then built a mill at Shiprock, one of the Navajo Nation's largest population centers. Three years later, at Ambrosia Lake, Kerr-McGee was on the road to becoming the nation's number-one uranium producer and was spending $100,000 a month in exploration.

For me, the story started in early 1955 with a phone call to my office in Denver from Marion Bolton, the manager of the Shiprock mill, who was a good mining engineer. "John, you know we run an assay service, mostly for the Navajos who find a curious-looking rock and bring it in and ask us to assay it."

I knew that most of the rocks didn't show any uranium, but the service was a clever way of exposing the company to potential discoveries.

"Well," he continued, "we've been doing these free assays for years and I've never seen a sample come in that looked very good. Now I've got a set of samples, two or three hundred, and I never saw so much uranium. Every single one of them assays uranium. Let me read them to you."

Minimum ore-grade uranium measured one-tenth of one per cent U308. Anything above a half-per cent was pretty rich. And many of the figures he read were showing one per cent—which I'd never seen before. Bolton read assay after assay result until he said, "Have you had enough?"

"Jesus, Marion, I'll never get enough of this. . . .I can't get down this afternoon; I'll get a plane and be there first thing in the morning."

We arranged to meet in Grants, northwestern New Mexico. I flew into Albuquerque, rented a car, and drove west for an hour through the crisp air of mile-high country. Grants was a small highway town on Route 66. When Marion Bolton and I met at a café there, we were just a couple more guys passing through. Showing me the assays, he said the fellow who'd brought the samples in had first shown them to geologists around Grants, who assured him that uranium deposits just weren't possible that far north of town. The samples came from a section of land held by Ellis Dunn—a trucker from Dallas.

I phoned Dunn and, casual as hell, told him I was with Kerr-McGee, had been passing through Grants, and heard he might have some uranium on his property. We met that afternoon at his trailer near the Ambrosia Lake acreage, about a ninety-minute drive through mesa and desert, past a few sheep. Dunn was a prosperous-looking businessman with the air of an Italian mobster. "I suppose you'll want to see the drill holes," he said.

"Are the samples out there?"

"Oh yeah, they're stacked up alongside the holes." He turned me over to his swamper, who wasn't much of a help. Neither of them really believed there was anything promising to see and probably figured I was wasting their time. They hadn't even tested the radioactivity of the samples with a Geiger counter. His land was the Section 11 he'd received from Lothman. I walked to the drill area alone and saw that they'd drilled about forty holes, up to 300 feet deep, at hundred-foot spaced intervals instead of the usual distance of 25 feet. Mounds of fine-grained sandstone were arranged in neat piles representing ten feet of drill hole. But these samples were dark grey, almost black. All my experience with uranium was in light-grey sandstone with yellow uranium mineralization. I looked through the piles with decreasing enthusiasm. Finally, I decided to fetch my Geiger counter from the car.

I ran it over one mound and *pow!* — the needle hit the end of the scale and had to be turned back to read at second and third levels. Almost every mound knocked the needle off the first stage.

My God, this must be pitchblende, or uraninite — unoxidized uranium. The high-grade mineralization retained its dark original colors. I had never seen this stuff before. The kind of material that Marie and Pierre Curie worked with in the early 1900s and got radioactive poisoning from because it was so rich.

And there was so much of it! I'd never seen a uranium deposit thicker than two and a half feet and this sonuvabitch was 150 feet.

By the time I finished mapping those drill holes on an envelope I found in my pocket, I had recorded the largest deposit of uranium in the United States. In my head I kept the size and shape of every major mine in western North America and the number of pounds of uranium it held. This was at least five to ten times bigger than anything I knew — ultimately, we learned the deposit had a much larger area and had a hundred times more uranium ore than the nearest competition. It turned out to be the largest uranium deposit in the world. By late afternoon I strolled back to the trailer and Dunn asked, "How'd you do, John?"

"I put my counter on every one of those piles and got some flicker occasionally, so you've got some show. But I didn't really see a hot one. It's interesting to us because we don't see uranium show very often, but I don't know whether we can find a commercial deposit out of this or not." It's called dissembling. But it's really lying on a massive scale. I should have been struck down by lightning.

I drove back to Grants at 80 miles an hour, fast for me, and stepped into the glass cage of a telephone booth that was broiling in the heat. Although I'd been Dean McGee's uranium specialist for only a few months, I had no hesitation in calling him with this news at his Oklahoma City home in the evening—even when his stern-sounding wife said he was at dinner.

Introducing myself, I said, "I'm his uranium manager and I'm sitting here in the hot sun and I just have to talk to him. I promise you this is so important that he'll be glad to hear from me."

Reluctantly, she called her husband to the phone. After I reminded him who I was, he was cordial and listened silently as I rattled on: "Mr. McGee, this afternoon I've seen the most exciting thing I've ever seen in my whole life! I think I have identified the largest uranium deposit in America!"

He made me repeat myself and then asked what I wanted him to do. "Could you have a landman out here tomorrow to see if we can buy this? You'll become, overnight, the largest holder of uranium ore in the United States!"

He said they'd have someone fly out the next morning—their head landman and manager of uranium exploration, Bufalo Kennedy.

Bufalo—he spelled it with one "f"—was an anomaly in the Kerr-McGee organization. A hulking braggart of a man with a bison's belly, Gilbert Kennedy had been a major stockholder in the Navajo Uranium mine, which Kerr-McGee had bought three years earlier in the Lukachukais. As Marion Bolton said later, "The gentleman who was handling the negotiations—I said gentleman; I'm not sure—was Bufalo Kennedy." In doing the deal, Kennedy wangled himself a position with Kerr-McGee. A company history quotes McGee's secretary, Elizabeth Zoernig, as saying, "Many of our men felt that it was highly out of line for

Mr. McGee to keep a man around like Bufalo Kennedy.... He had many faults, but we learned a lot from Bufalo Kennedy in the uranium field."

Among other things, they learned how someone could hornswoggle both Kerr and McGee. When Bufalo arrived in Grants, I briefed him about Dunn and Lothmann. At that point, he took over from me, in his inimitable way. What nobody in the company knew until later was that he called Ellis Dunn, introduced himself as an oilman from Oklahoma City, and invited him to a meeting there to discuss the Ambrosia Lake property. They met downtown in the historic Skirvin Hotel, built by an oil magnate in 1910. Kennedy falsely presented himself as an independent, with no links to any other company, and convinced Dunn to sell him the land. When Kerr-McGee discovered his double-dealing, they launched a lawsuit against him. But, as I've heard from many people since, Kennedy had the nerve to confront the senator and McGee and threaten them that he would bring up, in court, every even slightly offside maneuver the two partners might have made in the years he'd worked for them. The suit was dropped.

That left us looking for other choice parcels of Ambrosia Lake. The so-called lake was now a large patch of sand that looked vaguely out of place in the sagebrush. By this time, I had combed the geologic studies of the area and knew there was a small anticlinal dome at Ambrosia Lake. Oil had collected in the anticline trap when water levels were fairly high in the San Juan Basin, which covers about 7,500 square miles of northwestern New Mexico and southwestern Colorado. In the Tertiary period (about 50 million years ago) the water table and the oil dropped; the air left at the top oxidized the oil, turning it into a ring of asphalt around the dome. The oil was in the same Morrison formation beds that I had worked in the Lukachukais. Eventually, uranium fluids encountered Ambrosia's asphalt and formed deposits there, which are still the largest known in the world. The asphalt of the old oil field provided a prodigiously larger quantity of organic material than sticks and logs in old streambeds. As a result, the giant uranium deposit was precipitated by the change of pH created by reducing action of the asphalt.

Discovery at Section 22, the first Kerr-McGee uranium drill hole at Ambrosia Lake, the largest deposit in the world.

Putting together a comprehensive geologic story of conditions millions of years ago from scattered clues is what I do best. It's actually as much art as science. It comes out of the right brain.

I told Dean McGee that we might have lost one section to Bufalo, but the best section in the whole play would be next to Section 11: "The best piece of land in North America is Section 10." We bought it from some ranchers and, sure enough, the uranium ore deposit continued right across Section 11—but stopped dead at the barbed-wire fence which marked the east edge of Section 10. Kerr-McGee ended up acquiring nearly 80 per cent of Ambrosia Lake. We had lots of sections full of ore, but Section 10 was a disaster. The main ore trend was on the other side of the dome. There, even though we were drilling at hundred-foot spacing, we kept hitting big. The deposit was about a mile wide and ten miles long. It reached 200 feet of thickness. The major deposits in Colorado that the industry was built on were only 100 feet wide, 500 feet long, and a few feet thick.

The official history of Kerr-McGee sums up the insanity that ensued as competitors tried to sew up the uranium leases in the area. In *Innovations in Energy: The Story of Kerr-McGee*, John Samuel Ezell, a University of Oklahoma history professor, writes:

> A mad scramble followed to stake claims, with Kerr-McGee representatives in the middle of it. The dreams of possible fortunes made tempers run high, and claim jumping became a way of life. Massive legal problems ensued because the then current mineral law was based upon surface visibility whereas this uranium was hundreds of feet deep in the ground. Kerr-McGee officials theorized that such superficial actions as scooping a few surface ditches did not establish proof of subsurface mineralization, or proof of discovery. So to substantiate their claims, they relied on core drilling, retrieving cylindrical samples of rock. In some instances Kerr-McGee core drillers were actually shot at by other claimants. After long litigation the courts finally upheld the company, and a group of the hardest-fought-over claims [in Section 22] became one of its best mines.

Although never shot at, I did indulge in some guerilla warfare. It ended up in a messy lawsuit over claims to Section 22. General Patrick J. Hurley had founded United Western Minerals Corporation of Santa Fe, NM. He was a tough old bird who'd served during the Truman presidency as the U.S. Ambassador to Chiang Kai-shek's China. Hearing that Hurley's people had jumped our claims, I drove out to the section that night with our landman, Buddy Tinkle. Buddy used to be a bodyguard to a legendary West Texas oilman who liked to drink. We found Hurley's rig on our land. A fairly excitable 28-year-old, I told Buddy to help me trash the truck's engine and then we dropped a heavy link chain down their well. They wouldn't soon be drilling again. The next morning, I cussed out the driller while saving my most colorful profanity for their landman. We were pretty brave because Buddy had a rifle in the car.

Afteward, I drove fast to Santa Fe and called on General Hurley. We had a lot of hard words and he said he didn't appreciate a kid swearing at him. "General, when you were my age, this is just what you would have done."

He began to smile. "Boy, I think I'm gonna like you."

But not enough to avoid seeing me in court.

Kerr-McGee's lawyer in New Mexico was wise old Henry Glascock, who'd founded the first law firm in Gallup in 1927, the year I was born. Henry had told me that under no circumstances should I repeat in court the swear words I'd wielded: "We want to paint the other people as the bad guys."

When I took the stand, Hurley's lawyer said, "Mr. Masters, you used very threatening language to our men at the well. Would you tell the court what you said?"

I was Henry's attentive pupil. "I'm sorry, I can't do that. The language was just right around a drill rig. But this room is full of ladies. I don't swear in front of ladies."

In two or three different attempts, he tried to have me repeat all the dirty names I'd called the men. "I have a full vocabulary of four-letter words," I admitted. "I probably know just as many as you do. But I was taught not to use them in front of ladies. Maybe you weren't brought up that way. If you want to know what bad words I used, if that's important to you, why don't you just say the words you're interested in knowing about and I'll tell you Yes or No."

The courtroom, even the judge, erupted in peals of laughter. The lawyer leaned over to his partner, exchanged whispers, and then turned to the judge: "Those are all my questions, your honor."

Henry Glascock told that story to so many people that even I got tired of hearing it. Kerr-McGee won the lawsuit and months later we sank our first shaft on the section we'd defended in court. In 1957 the company began building a $30-million uranium mill, based on the reassuring knowledge that it controlled roughly a quarter of all known uranium reserves in the nation. That year, *Petroleum Week* credited us with several firsts in developing the ore—among them the fact that using petroleum geology and methods, we'd introduced regional stratigraphic and structural mapping (of the kind I'd done with the AEC) to integrate all the geological data at Ambrosia Lake.

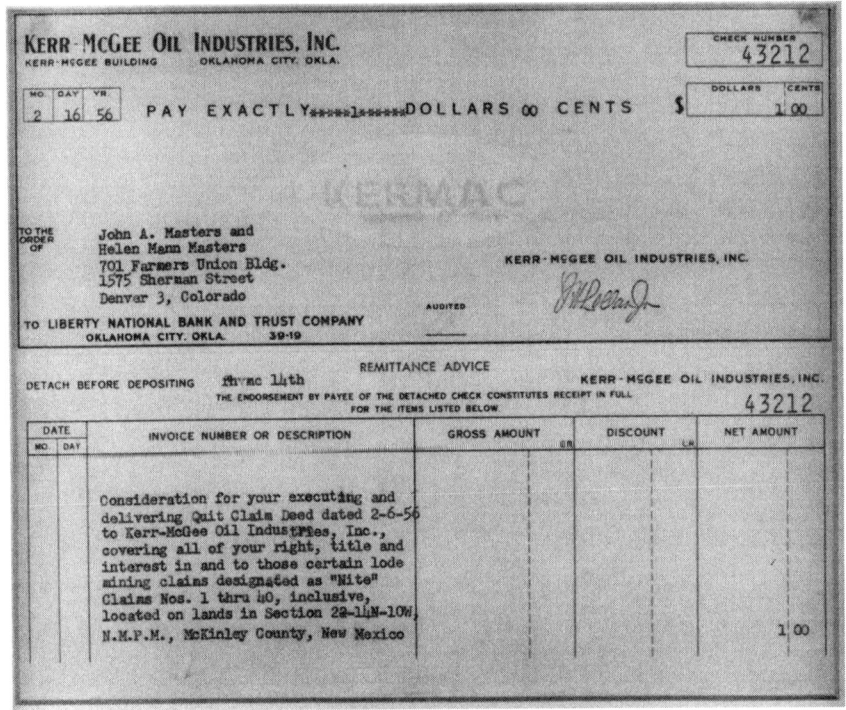

$1 check from Kerr-McGee in payment for the Nite Claims (stacked at midnight) to hold the key land at Ambrosia Lake.

Framed in my office today, I have a copy of a check from Kerr-McGee Oil Industries, paid to the order of John A. Masters and Helen Mann Masters, in consideration of our delivering a quit-claim deed to the company for our rights to claims we staked to override the claims staked by Hurley's company. We called them the Nite Claims. The check is for $1. That same night, we moved in six drilling rigs collected from all around the state. The next morning, Hurley's man knew how the Japanese felt at Iwo Jima.

Later, the company gave me about $100,000 in stock options, which over the years grew into several hundred thousand. But I knew what I'd discovered was worth far more than that and was kind of resentful—until years later when Dean McGee recalled the amount of the bonus and said, "John, I just don't think it's good to put a lot of money into a young person's hands. I remember when I was young, and it probably would have harmed my career." I had so much confidence in the man that when he explained his rationale in that soothing, reasonable way of his, I walked away thinking, *Oh, that's why he did it. Well, that's okay with me.*

CHAPTER SEVEN

CHASING OIL

A PHOTO GALLERY OF PERSONAL HEROES hangs in the hallway of my present office in Denver. Next to the picture of Dean McGee is one of Wallace Pratt. Along with H.L. Hunt, Pratt was the only other man who was ready and willing to act in 1930 when Dad Joiner's first well flowed at East Texas—America's greatest oil field. Rumors of an oil show in the barren region of East Texas had brought a huge collection of oilmen to the well when Joiner first tested oil. Several hundred people measured and recorded and dutifully reported the promising data but then did nothing with it. In the next few months, two big wells came in a good many miles from the Joiner play to demonstrate conclusively that East Texas was a giant field. At that point, everyone leaped in. But it was too late because Hunt and Pratt had already moved on the basis of the first well's evidence. Pratt went on to build Humble Oil into the largest producing company in the U.S., later absorbed into Standard of New Jersey

85

Wallace Pratt, the greatest oil finder in history, seen here in 1964 speaking to members of a geological society visiting McKittrick Canyon in Texas, where he donated some of his land for a federal park.

and then Exxon. Only Pratt and Hunt had the judgement and decisiveness to act on the initial information in a timely fashion. Only they were oil-finders. My friend Elliott Riggs, a very successful explorationist, calls those types "first movers."

An oil-finder will usually see a mere flicker, a momentary opening, yet he must blast through it like a Panzer general, committing men and material and assets to pry and hold it open. If he flinches, he is lost. If he is wrong, he is lost. If all goes well, he has the luck of the gods.

Following my lucky foray into uranium, I spent the next decade and a half with Kerr-McGee looking for oil and gas in the U.S. and Canada. Finding oil is like making love: it's wonderful, but you can't do it all the time. While I succeeded just often enough during many of those years, there were bitter dry spells when I wondered whether I was in the right profession. If you make oil your mistress, they say, you have to put up with her moods. But you must always have an optimist's faith in the mere *possibility* of having a relationship with the fickle lady. In 1952, Wallace

Pratt wrote a paper titled "Toward a Philosophy of Oil-Finding" which contained these cautionary words: "This conviction of our best minds that little or no oil remained to be found has continuously handicapped the search for oil. Unless men can believe that there is more oil to be discovered, they will not drill for oil."

Like Pratt, Dean McGee believed that oil is found in the minds of men, and he wasn't handicapped by any lack of faith in its existence. In 1957, *Forbes* profiled McGee, noting his "reputation of being one of the best prospectors in the business...known in the oil country as a man who can smell oil in the ground." That's why, the same year, he sent the thirty-year-old me to Calgary, Alberta, to become the district geologist for Canada, a long way from our uranium mines. "John," he was saying in effect, "we don't need you here anymore." He wanted me to gain some breadth of experience, some seasoning, by exploring in a new frontier and seeing if I could find a place for Kerr-McGee there.

A quarter-century earlier, my stepfather, John Bartram, had reported on Canadian petroleum potential for the old Midwest Refining Company. In 1914, Alberta's first major find, the Dingman Discovery Well, had blown in with abundant natural gas in the Turner Valley field south of Calgary. A dozen years later, the Royalite No. 4 wildcat well came blasting in at 21 million cubic feet of wet gas per day. John made a prescient recommendation for a careful study of the province's promise. Before Midwest could implement it, oil prices started declining as discoveries in the U.S. Mid-continent came on stream. Production rose until it peaked in 1942 and then declined because of the immense war effort that stripped the industry of steel.

After the Second World War, Alberta's prospects seemed gloomy. Imperial Oil had drilled 133 dry holes in a row across the prairie provinces and was planning to depend in future on offshore petroleum supplies. In 1947, a geologist convinced the reluctant and disbelieving company to try last-ditch exploration in a belt of the central Alberta plains south of Edmonton. Imperial gave him one more well. Leduc #1 astounded Imperial and the whole industry by ushering in a boom that made Canada self-sufficient in oil for years to come. Now, only a decade later, I was heading to Canada. The idea was for me to absorb a solid background and understanding of the Canadian petroleum scene, rather than worry about identifying prospects immediately. Dean McGee was preparing me for the future he could see.

This was my introduction to a land and a people that I came to love almost from the first day Susie and I and our two kids landed there. I have found Canadians to be a gentler, softer, and more accepting people in personality and relationships than Americans, who are more combative. I've never heard anyone who knows both cultures well question that distinction. We left Calgary after a year, but went back ten years later to live there for 27 years. We came to know the people of the prairies and the mountains of western Canada as cordial, courteous, and gentle with one another. My personal theory—which I don't pretend has much intellectual background—is that this might reflect the division of people that took place in the Revolutionary War. The United Empire Loyalists who wanted to remain British citizens were made unwelcome in the northeastern states where the rebellion began. They left of their own accord for Canada. The collective personality that represents those people in my mind seems less rebellious and aggressive than the American psyche. I've found ordinary Canadians are more given to consensus, to allowing their neighbors room, to not insisting that by God, things better be done my way. I felt very much at home with those qualities and, when returning to the U.S. on business, found the Americans I'd grown up with measurably different. I grew much more comfortable with the Canadians' way and thought it superior to the pugnaciousness of their southern neighbors. While not fully approving of that American attitude, I realize its value: taming the frontier, winning wars, making the United States the preeminent power in the world. You have to accept that such bellicosity made the Romans dominant and gave Britain its supremacy for a couple of centuries, but it comes at a high price. Canada can afford its people's more kindly attitude because they live in the protective shadow of a generous neighbor. Rome and Britain didn't have that comfort.

The Calgary of the late 1950s was still a small town, known if at all for its legendary annual Stampede. Although it had doubled in size during the past decade to 30 square miles, there were still fewer than 250,000 Calgarians. The major oil companies were there—Imperial, Chevron, Texaco, Shell—but little supporting infrastructure of small oil companies and independent consulting services. Kerr-McGee was kind of a curiosity in town and nobody in the business paid much mind to us. That allowed me to make mistakes without attracting too much attention. For the first time, I was in charge of my own operation and could choose most of my own people. I hired three geologists, but head office in Oklahoma City foisted a petroleum engineer on me who proved to be a bad apple in our bunch and was finally dropped from the branch. One of the geologists who proved out well was a University of Colorado classmate, Gerry Loucks, who eventually returned to Denver and became one of the important finders in the Rocky Mountains. While never impressing you as being particularly intellectual, he could find oil—again and again. Gerry was the first of the stars I emplaced in the Calgary firmament over the years.

Because we didn't have the finances to compete in the same areas as an Imperial Oil, I quickly identified our best bet as being in the shallow Cretaceous sands of Alberta. In recounting my modest results during the year I was there, the authorized company history reports that in early 1958, "Tennessee Gas Transmission signed a farmout agreement whereby it assigned Kerr-McGee part of its leases in the Sylvan Lake area in the Province of Alberta, Canada, in return for Kerr-McGee's agreement to drill no less than two test wells there at its own expense. The first well, completed in March at a cost of $113,525, found gas, but had to be shut down for lack of a market. The second well was dry. Kerr-McGee had, nevertheless, earned an interest in twenty sections. A similar arrangement was made with Canadian Superior Oil of California, Ltd., and three holes were sunk. But in this case again only one of them produced gas and oil." Wells at Sylvan Lake did eventually go to market and became a property of some repute within Kerr-McGee.

Looking back on that time—without benefit of full medical or psychological evaluation because I was never willing to discuss my weakness—I believe I was physically and mentally exhausted from a year of continuous 12-hour days in New Mexico. An emergency would follow immediately after a disaster, be replaced by a triumph, then instantly came another emergency. I finally left the uranium Crisis Center but went directly to a new life and fresh problems in Canada. While the new job didn't have all the combat urgency of New Mexico, I think the reptile remnant in the subconscious part of my brain signaled that we'd had enough. I suffered long, sleepless nights, took pills, avoided long discussions, was uneasy with new people, had difficulty concentrating, and would suddenly lose a train of thought. For a rest, I went alone to Lake O'Hara in eastern British Columbia that fall and camped in the snow for a week. There was not another soul up there; it was too cold. I hiked and climbed every day. My apprehension was transferred to the rugged, sometimes dangerous

Hiking and camping alone for a week at Lake O'Hara.

routes I was taking. The trip, intended to be rest and "getting away" from a long period of over-concentration, turned into the usual challenge and defiance. Well, whatever was wrong with me wasn't resolved by risky climbing and freezing nights in my tent. Returning to Oklahoma City a few months later, I was still under some kind of a spell, which took several more months to gradually disappear. Its most disconcerting aspect was during normal conversation when I suddenly couldn't find the words to express myself.

All in all, I was somewhat incapacitated for part of my Canadian stint, which lasted less than a year. Putting my successor in place, I returned to head office.

But I'd got my feet wet as a manager and when Dean McGee brought me back, they became even wetter—at least figuratively. Now, with promotion to Chief Geologist for oil and gas in Oklahoma City when I was 33, I turned my mind to the exploration program in the Gulf of Mexico off the coast of Louisiana. The company had leaped a long way since pioneering offshore drilling just a decade earlier. As McGee said, "In a small way, ours was kind of like a step on the moon. We were exploring a new, hostile environment."

The Ship Shoal waters I was searching (from the comfort of my office) were well named: drilling in the shallows there was always an adventure. Some of the rigs weighed in at about 6,500 tons and loomed twenty-five storeys tall. They were sitting ducks for tempests like one on my watch in 1961: Hurricane Carla was the largest and strongest Gulf Coast hurricane in decades. Fortunately, we escaped with only about $50,000 in capital losses.

The company paid a little more than $6 million to acquire a part interest in leases totalling 20,000 acres of Ship Shoal. They included one salt dome and a large "roll-over" structure. It was there, in 1960, that I took part in the major development at Block 28 which became an important gas field at 13,000 feet.

I had a more important role in Block 214, Ship Shoal. I'd identified this area, in some of my earlier mapping, as having a particularly favorable ratio of sand to shale. I was one of a small group of Gulf Coast geologists just beginning to understand that the different percentages of sandstone in the offshore sediments was highly significant in recognizing the richest producing trends. Too much sand—not good for source. Too much shale—not good for reservoir. In applying those rules over a wide area of the Gulf, I introduced Kerr-McGee to stratigraphic mapping in the area. Exploration was being run at the time by the Vice-President of Production, an engineer who thought the less money you spent, the better your department was performing. When Block 214 came up for sale, we argued vigorously over the price. He finally decided on a really dumb, low bid. In total exasperation, I went to Dean McGee two days before the sale, apologized profusely, but said I couldn't bear to see us make a horrible mistake. The block covered a big salt dome right in the middle of a fat sand-shale trend with just the right ratio. You never argued with McGee. He would either see the point immediately and decide yes—or disagree and say no. In this case, he doubled the bid, we won the tract, and made a big oil discovery. Mr. McGee called it John's Dome. How could you have a better reward than that? The only unhappy guy was my boss.

You had many more potential petroleum targets on a dome where the ratio of sand to shale was 60 to 70 per cent compared to one of 30. After my maps indicated which structures were initially attractive, we did seismic work to select the best ones. Sometimes, though, a good seismic structure wasn't in a good sand belt and I might advise bidding lower on that acreage.

Divining the favorable trends for offshore oil was another early example of my gift for regional geologic thinking. While not much good with numbers, my right brain can make an overall picture of seemingly unrelated data. In a new area, I want to know the conventional wisdom—which I usually avoid. I don't attempt to become better than everyone else at dealing with old ideas.

Now, it's true that my mode of thinking, my visualization of the Big

Picture, sometimes doesn't stand up to intense probing. In that case, I try again. If you want to build a bridge, don't let me near it because I'll screw things up. But if you want to pinpoint some productive oil wells in an enormous sea or a wide plain, come to me — I'll think of something.

In 1977 the company celebrated the thirtieth anniversary of bringing in the world's first well in the open ocean. Around the world, offshore rigs were then producing more than 20 million barrels of oil and 29 billion cubic feet of gas a day — roughly 20 per cent, respectively, of the global supplies. My part in all this was infinitesimal yet personally rewarding. In my journal, I quote the great Canadian novelist Robertson Davies about the aftermath of discovery: "It asserts itself in sudden unaccountable bursts of well-being."

In my role as chief geologist, I'd hunted oil in Oklahoma and north and west Texas as well as along the Gulf Coast. But apart from the finds at sea, my other discovery wells were, as the saying goes, better than a kick in the pants, but none of them were earth-shattering in size or scope. As I once tried to explain to a journalist, "The reason is that too many people were jiggling my aim, or telling me not to shoot just yet."

I needed another Ambrosia Lake.

I remember reading what A.I. Levorsen, the professor and oil-finder, had once written: "An opportunity must be provided for those men with the capacity and with the ability for doing creative geology to actually do geology, and in addition, to be able to spend a part of their time with their feet on a desk looking out of the window where they can generate ideas and where they can reconstruct in their mind the conditions and the environments of past geologic ages." One Sunday afternoon in 1964 — four slow years since Ship Shoal — I was sitting in my Oklahoma City office staring at the wall. Then I had one of those lightning flashes where the right brain has been subconsciously rearranging data in the memory bank and finally presents it to you whole cloth. The subject was an old one: the Chuska

Mountains around my former stomping grounds at Cove, Arizona, and a strange anomaly that had obviously been haunting my silent mind for the past ten years. Why this insight emerged at this point still baffles me. But I suddenly realized, in a thought quite unbidden, that the Chinle redbeds at the north end of the Defiance Uplift could not dip under the overlying Chuska formation, continue dipping northeastward for ten miles and then suddenly re-appear on the eastern side of those mountains, *still dipping eastward but at the same elevation* as they were on the west side.

Translation: the Chinle redbeds are sedimentary strata, mostly red in color, named for a community in Arizona (pronounced *chin-LEE*). Back in my Atomic Energy days, I'd observed them on both sides of the Chuska Mountains but didn't have maps to tell me their elevations on either side of the mountains. Who cared? Now I realized that somewhere under the Chuskas they had to reverse the direction of their dip—by arching back into an upfold of rock, an anticline—and only then return to their eastward dip. There was no other way to put everything in place on both sides of the mountain. A look at a regional geological map confirmed that thirty-five miles farther south along the Chuskas, the southeast-trending outcrop of Chinle redbeds swung sharply westward. There was the southern end, the critical southern closure of the structure. Translation: closure is continuous dip around an upfold creating a dome or canoe-shaped anticline.

It took only a few moments to conceptualize an anticline thirty-five miles long with perhaps a thousand feet of closure. Toadlena, as it came to be called, was one of the largest anticlines still undrilled in the whole United States. Mr. McGee liked anticlines even more than I did. Once, after locating a large anticline in Colorado, I told him my paleogeographic maps indicated there might not be any favorable reservoir beds to contain petroleum there. "John," he replied, "you just find the anticlines; we'll let God put the reservoirs there."

Nobody else had recognized the Lukachukai anticline over the half-century that prospectors and geologists had been in the area, mostly in the great gas fields of the San Juan Basin only a few miles to the east.

But then, no one had studied my particular locality two whole years as I had, on foot, climbing, falling, soaking up the data. You couldn't absorb it in one fell swoop because there was just too much country to comprehend and the mapping wasn't sufficiently detailed. Why it took me eleven years to reach a conclusion is another matter. Maybe I'm just a real slow learner.

Now that I had it, how could I prove my thesis? Dean McGee wasn't about to spend cash way out in Arizona, where everybody knew there was no oil, unless I could convince him about that anticline. Gathering up my maps and my guts, I went to Mr. McGee's office and briefly explained my idea to him.

He speculated that the dip problem I'd identified could be explained by a fault—an up-down displacement of the rocks—which would destroy my anticlinal theory.

I responded that this country didn't have faults; I *knew* that.

But how could we check this out without spending much money while preventing any competitor from discovering what we were doing?

Here's where my uranium experience in the Lukachukais came into play. Recalling that the Navajo Tribal Council granted uranium drilling permits at no charge if you committed to drill a certain number of test holes, I phoned their offices at Window Rock. Were there any permits outstanding on the Chuska Mountains? None? Well then, please reserve some for Kerr-McGee.

No one had to know we were really mapping for oil. We could bring in a small uranium rig, I told McGee, then drill through the Chuska sands and plot the elevation of the Chinle marker beds. With enough drill points, we could map the structure and perhaps prove my concept.

In typical fashion, he made the decision promptly and gave me the go-ahead. I called on Mach Vaughan, my good friend, a tough operations geologist from our Amarillo office, to do the field work. Mach was conscientious and knowledgeable about all phases of the business: samples, wells, drill rigs. A good country boy who grew up around the drilling rigs in Oklahoma, he was also half-Indian and liked the Navajos, particularly the girls. Mach went to Shiprock, where Kerr-McGee had its uranium mine and mill, to become familiar with the nearby Chinle redbeds and their three fairly distinct subdivisions. All by himself, he handled our core rigs, chose our locations, surveyed them, found drilling water, logged the cores, and mapped the structure. To do the same work, a major company would have needed two engineers, a surveyor, and a truck driver. Our challenge was to figure out which part of the Chinle formation we'd encountered in each hole as we drilled through the overlying Chuska rock. Taking core samples, Mach should know if he was in zone A, B, or C, and by drilling into the next zone could determine by the thickness exactly how far he was from the top of the formation. With enough drill holes, he could map the structure. Piece of cake.

When he was ready to show me what he'd been doing, we jeeped out to Cove, my old home on the reservation, and were soon hiking up a familiar trail. Mach, out in front, remarked, "The only thing that worries me is snakes. This looks like snake country to me."

"Oh, Mach, don't be a wimp; there aren't any snakes out here. I worked this country for two years and never saw a single snake."

It couldn't have been more than a couple of minutes later: Mach just about stepped on a small rattlesnake coiled in the middle of the trail, almost invisible in the dust. The damn thing buzzed and Mach never even put his foot down. He ejected into the air, did a figure-skater's 180-degree turn, and passed me at roughly a hundred miles an hour.

After he settled down, I offered to walk ahead of him. A few minutes later, I apparently stepped over another rattler, stirring it up. When Mach came upon it, the snake was coiled and shaking its threatening rattle. He about died—from fright, not a bite. I kept swearing to my disbelieving trailmate that these were the only two rattlesnakes I had ever seen legging it through the Lukachukais for two years.

We survived our outing and eventually moved in a rig to start drilling—supposedly for uranium. None of our rivals in the industry suspected our real mission was to map the structure for potential oil plays. And lo!, just as I'd thought, there was a huge closed anticline, the biggest untapped anticline in the U.S. Was there any reservoir rock accompanying it? After worrying about that for a while, I accepted my employer's advice and let God fret about it instead.

Choosing several four-section blocks of land at the top of the structure, we asked the Navajos to advertise a lease sale and I talked Mr. McGee into bidding $104 an acre on the best block. It cost us $263,000—and, as it turned out, there were no other bidders. We could have had it for a pittance of that price. My popularity quotient dipped that week, but I consoled myself knowing that McGee had gone through the same experience at much pricier Gulf of Mexico sales (although I didn't point that out to him).

Months later, in 1965, we moved a sizable oil rig into the Chuskas and began drilling. We hit very low-porosity sandstone—what we call tight sands—along with tight dark-grey limestone and shale, all of it relatively impermeable, unpromising for oil production. Tight, tight, tight. No reservoir beds; the God of Oil wasn't helping us.

Then, at 2,875 feet, the wellsite geologist found white crystals in the shale stained with oil. Were they sand? Didn't seem to be. He couldn't see any meaningful porosity, the characteristic holes in rocks that allow fluid to flow in a reservoir and contain it like a sponge holds water. (In the 1860s a young American civil engineer, John F. Carll, interviewed oilmen in Pennsylvania and New York about both their successful and non-producing wells and was the first to record in a published report that oil was found in porous rock formations and was composed of the billions of tiny droplets held in that rock.) After drilling another 800 feet, with no recognizable reservoir, we plugged the damn well. In examining those crystals, lab technicians identified the rock as a volcanic sill of Oligocene age (about 30 million years old), which had intruded the limestones and shales of Pennsylvanian age (about 170 million years), when marine life was abundant. I'd seen a lot of such syenite in the area in the form of volcanic intrusions of magma. But I'd never seen any porosity or signs of oil. We were sunk.

Well into the next year, after moving to Canada, I was still pondering that oil stain in those white crystals. One day a drilling engineer sat down with McGee and described to him the showings of oil in the drilling mud and in the mud pits. McGee was perplexed that no one had ever described that to him. He said, "I want to test that well. I don't care if its volcanic rock or cement if it's got oil in it!" The engineers were instructed to re-enter the well and test. They did. Nothing. McGee said to acidize it. They did. Nothing. Then McGee said to frac it—which is to pump a liquid mixed with sand into a well under pressure to create a fracture in the rock and then prop it open with the sand, allowing hydrocarbons to flow into the well. I remember the Production guys saying how dumb that was. All we could do in those days was a little 20,000 pound frac. *Boom!* The well came in flowing oil at 648 barrels per day!

Eventually we drilled fourteen wells into the igneous sill, which was unnaturally porous and which just happened to extend, like a thin blanket, over most of the area that we'd bought for a quarter of a million dollars. That, however, was the extent of it; the rest of that enormous anticline appears to be dry.

In fact, despite all my calculations, the anticline had nothing to do with the presence of the oil. The sill we drilled was igneous rock, crystallized from hot volcanic magma injected into a section of grey shale. The shale had never been buried deep enough, to get hot enough, to generate oil. It was immature. But because of the volcanic sill, the shale had heated up enough to generate oil and squeeze it into the sill. That particular sill, responding obediently to the God of Oil, had crystallized with a significant amount of porosity. We were just lucky that the sill happened to be exactly where we decided to drill at the top of the anticline for carefully mapped structural reasons—all of which, in this case, had nothing to do with the accumulation.

Over the years, a story grew among the usual group of conspiracy theorists that we had delayed bringing in the well in order to buy land at a cheaper price. Baloney: the land was already bought. The only mistake we made was falling in love with our prospect and paying too much for it. We delayed simply because we were confused.

The play marked an important turning point for Kerr-McGee. The last I heard, the wells had yielded net income of about $60 million by producing 20 million barrels of oil. Not a great field, but the largest ever found in Arizona. The wells produced wide open because they weren't restricted by allowables (the rate of production that a state or other governing body permits from a well or group of wells). The field provided unexpected cash flow at a critical time for the company. Once again, McGee had pulled a rabbit out of his hat. The Navajos christened the field Dineh-bi-Keyah, Field of the People. If it had produced at today's price, we would have netted $20 a barrel—or $400 million. Drat: I would have been famous.

Dean McGee later congratulated me for making the discovery, remarking that my selection of the land had been "prescient". I had to look the word up: the ability to see into the future. Who said the man who lives by the crystal ball learns to eat broken glass?

The improbable success of Dineh-bi-Keyah—the field that should never have been—suggests another Masters rule: You don't have to be entirely right. Just right enough. This isn't a chemistry lab. We're drilling tiny holes into the crust of a planet.

Those years working in Oklahoma City may have been a mixed blessing for me, but for our children they were wonderful. Alan MacGregor Masters (named for my father and Susie's family) was born to us in 1960, a lovable blond brother to Chuck and Barbie. From the start, Alan was a gem as a personality, as a person, and though never an all-around athlete like the other two, he later took up skiing and moved with such fluidity that it was like letting a stream loose down the mountain. I was always encouraging the kids to exercise, to excel in sports as a way of developing self-esteem. Actually, only Barbie had any desire to compete. Chuck confesses now to hating Kamp Kanakuk, where I'd grown up, because he found it too sports-oriented and competitive. But he grew up to be a Himlayan mountaineer. Barbie, a natural athlete like her mother, loved the fun and discipline of the camp for girls—especially the day that both camps went to the Silver Dollar Amusement Park, the boys walking several miles in the heat while the girls rode in a cattle truck. Sometimes our holidays were in places like Colorado where there were lots of rocks and I tried to teach her to toss them in the overhand style of a big-league pitcher. She still throws like a girl ("I *am* a girl," she reasons). But Barbie enjoyed birdwatching with her Mom, learning the names of many species by age five. By the time she was nine, I took her weekend sailing with me in a Lightning racing boat on the city reservoir. She still remembers lying on the deck, watching the stars, and then going for a root beer afterward. By her teens, Barbie excelled in every sport she tackled.

All of our vacations had an element of adventure. On a five-day canoeing trip through the Ozarks, we braved rapids and I challenged the kids to a camp-like contest every day, often to their collective groans. There's a family story that gets told time and again: on one expedition, I took nine-year-old Chuck up a limestone cliff. As the ledge got increasingly narrow, he became frightened. Finally Chuck looked at me through tears and said, "It always turns out like this." And it always did, the children still insist.

Barbie, in particular, has fond recollections of Oklahoma in the 1960s as a stable time for an oil family that had moved around like a traveling carnival. We lived in a pleasant neighborhood in Oklahoma City, which was finally becoming somewhat like Tulsa. On Saturdays, I took the older kids to the Kerr-McGee office with me and on Sundays, they went with Susie to the Unitarian Church. We each had our own religion.

It all seemed as picture-perfect as a Norman Rockwell cover on the *Saturday Evening Post*. But fissures were beginning to appear in our marriage—problems of communications and divided loyalties—and the breach between Susie and me would widen with the years.

CHAPTER EIGHT

AN END AND BEGINNINGS

THE CANADA OF 1967 seemed like a nation that had finally found its soul. Canadians were celebrating both the centennial of their country and a magnificent world's fair, Montreal's Expo 67, that focused global attention on their creativity and vitality. Calgarians, meanwhile, were revelling in their new-found energy, in both meanings of the word. In the decade since we'd last lived there, Calgary's population had exploded by nearly sixty per cent, to 335,000, driven by recent discoveries of new petroleum reserves in Alberta. With the province still supplying most of Canada's crude oil and natural gas, Calgary was Action Central of the boom. Office towers, hotels, and shopping centers erupted on the skyline so quickly that, in Mordecai Richler's famous remark, the city looked as if it had just been uncrated. In 1967, as Marathon Realty and Husky Oil were establishing head offices in town, they began building what I thought was the perfect visual symbol of the optimism, confidence, and

101

machismo of the locals: the Calgary Tower. It rose like an exclamation mark 625 feet above the heart of downtown.

Susie and I, and our three children, arrived that year with our own burst of enthusiasm about new beginnings. We probably both hoped the fresh start would at least paper over the problems she and I were having in our relationship. This time, Dean McGee had given me the mandate to truly run my own show in Calgary and actively hunt for petroleum as President of Kerr-McGee Canada.

The move was spurred by George Hardin, a geologist who'd found a string of Gulf Coast fields before joining the company in Oklahoma City as Vice-President, Exploration, for oil, gas, uranium, coal, and other minerals. He was a squat, sarcastic, cigar-smoking, smart sunuvabitch who was always one jump ahead of you. Beneath his toupee was one of the better brains in the industry. After I worked under him for a couple of years, he told McGee that I needed to mature more and learn to take charge of my own operation. Not only was I glad to get away from Hardin's ill temper, I also had good memories of Calgary, not least its nearness to great skiing on the mountains at Banff, Lake Louise, and eastern British Columbia.

Returning to take over the Canadian operation, I made two significant moves early on. They were both decisions that would have profound effects on my career and my life. The first was to hire Jim Gray. In my hunt for an exploration geologist to backstop me, I interviewed several candidates, but the one who stood out was this energetic, enthusiastic guy who laughed a lot and seemed to brim with gusto. Jim was born and bred in the gold-mining town of Kirkland Lake in northern Ontario, where his father was a mine manager for Noranda. The son studied at the University of British Columbia and in 1957 became a geologist with Great Plains, a subsidiary of the British-owned Burmah Oil. He cut his teeth in the mud and cold of central Alberta, sitting on wells drilled into the 400-million-year-old reefs of the Devonian. Leduc #1, which launched the Alberta boom, had found oil in those mounds of corals built up in the waters of primeval seas that have long since vanished. In our first year, Jim was responsible for the discovery of South Clive, an important Devonian reef

Jim Gray, Hunter's vice-president and my partner, on the left.
We looked alike and understood one another.

field. Six years later, he recognized a potential gas reserve on the Suffield Block, a huge military reserve in southeastern Alberta. Acting as a concerned citizen, he convinced Premier Peter Lougheed to drill 100 wells on the site, which confirmed the presence of two trillion cubic feet of gas and kick-started the creation of the provincially owned Alberta Energy Company.

We were well-suited then. Both of us were athletic, skiing and playing handball together, and we socialized as couples, my wife enjoying the company of his wonderful Josie. Six years younger than I, Jim has a voluble, outgoing personality compared to my quieter, more intellectual nature. In *The Blue-Eyed Shieks: The Canadian Oil Establishment*, Peter Foster noted that physically we might have been brothers: "Squat and muscular, both with short-cropped sandy hair, they look like the sort of men it would be wiser not to get involved with in a bar-room brawl." He went on to list the real distinctions between us, a perceptive third-party description worth quoting:

> Although so similar in appearance, their characters are totally different. Gray is perhaps the most gregarious man in Calgary. His energy, and enthusiasm, are seemingly boundless. His barrel chest seems to contain some great and unstoppable motive force that demands that he keep constantly in motion.
>
> Masters, however, is more reclusive by nature, an intellectual who avoids, indeed looks with distaste on, the Petroleum Club cocktail party circuit of the Calgary corporate establishment.
>
> One thing they do have in common, however, is their selling ability. Again, their styles are different. Gray sweeps you along with a tidal wave of enthusiasm; Masters bears you along more gently, but just as firmly, with a seemingly impregnable, almost hypnotic logic.

The other life-shaking decision I made as president of Kerr-McGee Canada was the seemingly prosaic one of hiring a new receptionist in 1970. One of our secretaries called a friend to suggest she apply for the position. In came this tall, elegant-looking twenty-two-year-old named Lenora Johnson. Interviewing her for the job, I was impressed by her gentle manner as well as her physical beauty. Lenora had been Sweetheart Queen at her high school in Medicine Hat, Alberta, and I could see why. Standing five-foot-nine (too tall for the stewardess she'd wanted to be in those days of low-ceilinged DC-3s), she had big brown eyes and long, lovely legs that were strikingly visible in the mini-skirts of that era. There was a grace about her, with her high forehead, aquiline nose, and tapered fingers, and a quietude in her soft voice that made me listen all the more intently to everything she said. She told me about her secretarial work over the past three years for a geophysical-services company in the Calgary oil community. We wound up talking about her off-hours devotions, including travel and skiing, and the fact that she was engaged and was about to be married in three weeks' time. But she'd be available to join us after the wedding and when I asked her about salary, she hesitantly suggested a modest $300 a month—$60 more than she was earning.

A couple of days later, I called her to say, "We'd like you to come to work for us; what would you think about $400 a month?" Although Lenora shone as a receptionist, it wasn't long before I switched her to my personal secretary and she took a shorthand course at night to bring her dictation skills up to speed. She was left-brain clever and highly organized. I soon fell under the spell of this congenial yet private, young yet wise woman.

These were the years I truly began to learn the geology of Alberta. It was soon evident that, as in 1957-58, Kerr-McGee's Canadian operation was neither large nor technically advanced enough to compete with the major companies. They were mainly involved in the exploration of Devonian reefs of the kind Jim knew. I decided we would stay in the shallow, much younger Cretaceous sands where rivals were fewer and the costs of acquiring and drilling land much lower.

In 1968, Kerr-McGee had 19 producing wells in Canada, and of the 162 new wells drilled by the parent company that year, our Canadian operation was the second-most active, after offshore Louisiana. For the next few years we were involved in completing a couple of dozen wells a year. But none of this was too impressive. Perhaps surprisingly, I wasn't worried about my reputation in the company or in the industry. No one else in Calgary had found the biggest uranium deposit in the world and the only real oil field in Arizona. I would continue inquiring, interpreting, and exploring, and eventually the hard thinking and hard work should combine to generate a good discovery.

You find petroleum by analyzing and reconstructing geologic history to determine the most probable hiding places of oil and gas accumulations, which are buoyant, mobile, and constantly seeking upward escape.

The process has elements of detective story, spy thriller, and gigantic jigsaw puzzle. Even then, although I was finding nothing of note to report back to head office, pieces of the puzzle were beginning to form in my right brain.

I was investigating the basins of Alberta and neighboring Saskatchewan. Basins are depressions in the earth's crust where sediments accumulate. If rocks rich in organic material are buried to the right depth and for the right length of time, a hydrocarbon system can develop in the basin. Based on my studies, I had an intuition that western Canada probably had large, unexploited reserves of natural gas in sandstone of low porosity—tight sands. Because porosity measures the capacity of rock to hold gas, oil, or water, the higher the percentage, the better: low porosity means less volume and less-profitable wells. Yet from my U.S. experience, I recalled that much petroleum development was happening there in second-class gas reservoirs with porosities less than 15 per cent. In Canada most of the reservoirs found to this point were above that level. Amazingly, most Canadian geologists insisted then—although they'd probably deny it now—that there were no sandstones in the country with less than that lowball figure. Either that or, if there *were* lower porosities, the reservoirs would never produce economically.

It would be intriguing to chronicle all the misconceptions in the industry by prominent experts who were later proved wrong (such as the Standard Oil executive who said, "I'll drink all the oil west of the Mississippi"). Over the past 150 years, the oil business has been littered by hundreds of false pronouncements that seemed entirely wise and informed but turned out to be disastrously wrong. The human mind receives with comfortable conviction what it wants to hear.

Another reason for my optimism was that new hydraulic-fracture methods in use down south could make low-porosity sands produce. When I came to Canada in 1967, Kerr-McGee was fracturing wells in the U.S. with 20,000 pounds of sand, the equivalent of putting no more than a firecracker down the hole. Scientists at Amoco had now come up with frac techniques that utilized everything from chemical foams to nuclear explosions. And Steve Holditch, a professor at Texas A&M, had invented the "massive frac" in which fluids could be introduced to an underground formation at a pressure high enough to crack the rock into fracture patterns up to 2,000 feet long. Steve has been an advisor and warm friend to me for 35 years.

Finally, I felt sure that Canadian oil and gas prices would rise and justify any additional costs in developing tight sands, which was not a theory that had much currency with the majors during the early 1970s. By then the western Canadian petroleum industry was going through another down cycle. The Organization of Petroleum Exporting Countries (OPEC), whose five founding nations produced eighty per cent of the world's oil, would introduce an embargo and quadruple the global price to record levels in 1973. But our domestic industry—historically plagued by fluctuating markets and low prices—was suffering from serious government intervention. As federal and provincial royalties and taxes increased, and the feds and Alberta became locked in a bitter dispute over petroleum profits, the industry lost momentum. Producers, caught in the middle, cut back exploration programs. They began to shift their activities to the nation's far frontiers and to foreign countries. Another reason for all this negativity was the conviction that the southern Canadian basins really did not have much oil and gas left to discover. This was wrong, but it was widely believed.

At that point in my thinking, six years after my return to Canada, I had a summons from head office. George Gilder, in *The Spirit of Enterprise*, suggests that in 1973 "Dean McGee's patience with his protégé was running low." More likely is that his optimism for Western Canada was ebbing. Given the downturn, and my own mixed record in making discoveries, he wanted me back in the Gulf of Mexico where, he often said, "you can find more in the Gulf by mistake than you can anywhere else by design."

But Calgary, Canada, and the hidden potential of western resources had claimed my heart. I didn't want to leave now, not when my mind percolated with all the possibilities. I told Jim Gray I would try to talk McGee into letting me stay put, but if necessary I'd resign. "You'll never quit," he replied. "He won't let you."

I flew to Oklahoma City to tell McGee: "I'm on to something so important up in Canada that I want to stay with it, but I don't know where it's going."

"Well, tell me where the idea is."

"It's in the foothills of western Alberta, it's a big thick sand section, it has gas shows, and it's caught in the frontal structures of the mountains. There ought to be a whole lot of gas in it. I don't know where it is for sure, but I'm just positive that there's a big gas field out there somewhere and I want to find it."

He allowed that it was the kind of idea he expected from me—"but our business is in the Gulf of Mexico and I need you there."

"Mr. McGee," I said measuredly, "I just don't want to do that."

He tilted back in his chair, crossed his arms over his wide chest, smiled, and said, "I know, John, you just can't keep a stallion in the corral forever. You're ready to run."

This was not what I'd expected; I simply didn't believe he would decide to cut me loose. Still startled, I was caught off-guard when he asked me what Jim was going to do.

The question came like a thunderbolt. Although I seldom if ever stammer, I did then: "Well, Mr. McGee, I don't really know—I suppose—well, I'm pretty sure—he'll probably go with me."

"That's kind of what I thought would happen," he said. "I wish you guys lots of luck and be sure to let me know if you need any help."

After edging out of his office, shaken, I went to the nearest telephone and called Jim. He and I had never discussed the possibility of his resigning.

"I've got some good news and bad news for you, Jim."

"What's the good news?

"I quit."

"Oh, fantastic. I didn't think you'd have the guts." A pause. "But what's the bad news?"

"You quit too!"

For a man with a wife and three kids and no real savings, just like me, Jim took it quite gracefully.

But what was I doing, taking leave of Kerr-McGee, Dean McGee—and probably my senses? There's no question I hero-worshipped McGee, as did most of the business press. That year *Forbes* said "the company's biggest asset is above ground, not under it. That asset is the company's chairman, geologist Dean A. McGee." I had learned more, been more inspired, by watching him operate than by any other man I ever knew. Most of the company's discoveries after 1950 occurred when he was chief executive officer. While he wasn't the originating geologist, nothing was ever done in that organization to which he did not contribute concurrence, guidance, and overarching judgement. He was a visionary geologist businessman who took the company in many different directions, building it both financially and technically, from a tiny drilling contractor to one of the nation's most important independent oil companies. An industrial genius.

Later in his career, Dean McGee's attention was diverted to overall corporate activities and, although remaining effectively in control of exploration, he couldn't give it the undivided focus required. Strangely, he had almost a perverse resistance to advanced exploration technology, was slow to adopt new seismic techniques, and didn't foster or encourage such specialties as electric-log analysis and petrography. McGee did his early exploration when intuitive geology was more important, and I think he persisted in the belief that if you were good enough, you could keep doing it that way without all the complications and expense of advanced technology. *He* probably could have. During the 1970s, the company began restructuring and reduced investment in research and development. His failure to give R&D scientists better salaries reduced his competitive strength.

One thing I did learn from him—but wouldn't always apply—was not to persist over the long haul to complete an oil play at all costs. "It's important to know when to quit. The hardest thing to do is quit," he said. "Someone has to learn to say No. You never have enough money to keep on saying Yes."

I couldn't forget the aura McGee had about him, almost a visible mist that dominated a room or meeting when he was present. Once, several of us were having lunch at the Petroleum Club in Oklahoma City when there was a bit of a stir at the entrance and in walked Senator Bob Kerr, company President Frank Love, Operations VP Tom Seale, and Dean McGee. Love and Seale were men of dignified bearing, Kerr was a towering figure, and behind him came McGee with his sailor's gait, square face and build, and overwhelming presence. A younger geologist at our table whispered, "Uh-oh, Murderers' Row." But of them all, McGee was the softest—an agreeable and generous person who rarely expressed a superior attitude and always remained appreciative of the work you did.

After my leave-taking, he faced times of terrible trouble. A year later, a Kerr-McGee plutonium plant in Oklahoma City was charged with creating faulty products and poor worker-safety conditions as well as falsifying records. Karen Silkwood, a young lab technician and union activist, suffered radiation exposure in a series of unexplained incidents, and was killed in a car crash en route to meeting an Atomic Energy Commission official and a *New York Times* reporter. Her ambiguous death was well publicized, inspiring a Hollywood movie, and sparked a federal investigation into the plant, which was shut down. In 1986 the company settled an $11.5-million lawsuit with Silkwood's family although admitting no liability. The mystery has never been solved. However, I know with absolute clarity that Dean McGee had no connection whatsoever with it.

McGee was a man of integrity, who was deeply involved in charitable causes. He endowed an eye institute in Oklahoma City; named for him, it became one of the ten largest in the U.S. Knowing this about him, and knowing him so well, I realized the personal pain the charges against the company caused him. His peers valued his decency too: in 1975, a year after the Silkwood charges, the American Association of Petroleum Geologists awarded him its highest honor, the Sidney Powers Award, "for being an eminent petroleum geologist, energy developer and industrialist—but above all, for being a gracious man, willing to contribute his time and talents for the benefits of his fellow citizens."

He stepped down as Chairman in 1983, yet came to work every day in the next few years, even when he was diagnosed with cancer. Shortly before his death, I came to see him at his office. Although a shell of the dynamo I knew and loved, he still had the McGee skill of summarizing what I told him in his succinct, accurate style. Leaving, I said, "Please don't get up" and he said, "I'm getting up," hoisting himself slowly from his chair and graciously seeing me out. When he died a couple of months later, in 1989, I recalled that last moment when he told me, "You are doing the most important thing a serious man can do. You are creating wealth and thereby providing hundreds of people with the opportunity to live meaningful lives." That was a description of the life he lived, yet he was too modest to claim it for himself or to mention that he had done it so generously and kindly. He pronounced his own requiem.

That was the giant who first recognized me, then befriended me, later guided and counselled me. I never had a hard word from Dean McGee. From him, I received only direction and judgement, kindness and encouragement. For him, I will always feel the deepest love, respect, and appreciation.

And here I was, in 1973, leaving him to start my own company. Leaving the security of a salary, modest as it was, the reputation of a respected corporation, and the infrastructure of support it had provided for twenty invigorating years. Most people prepare for their exodus with the liberal use of a copying machine to send out resumés, then job interviews, and the strong possibility of a new position—all designed to make the big leap as safe and painless as changing apartments. Employed continuously by the Atomic Energy Commission and Kerr-McGee, I had never been out there on my own since graduation. My brother, Chuck, was making a similar decision that same year. But after working as a geologist for Stanolind, Pan American Petroleum, and Amoco, he was leaving private industry for the safety net of government as chief of the Office of Energy Resources at the U.S. Geological Survey. I was about to willingly walk a slender financial tightrope without any net.

Meanwhile, I was still supporting our two youngest, Barbie and Alan. Our daughter had long since come out of a tempestuous period in her early teens when she rebelled against everything we represented. My theory is that she believed girls had forcibly to take anything they wanted because a male-oriented society wasn't going to share equally with them. Whatever the reason, she drove Susie and me wild. She began running with a motorcycle crowd when I'd told all the kids that we would buy them any piece of non-motorized equipment, from skis to canoes, that didn't require a button to operate. Luckily, Barbie heard about a student-exchange program and elected to live on a farm in southern France for the summer. It was a working farm and did they ever make her work, milking cows and pitching hay. Their daughter, who had the heft of a wrestler, made it clear that if this Canadian kid didn't follow orders, she'd beat the hell out of her. Well, Barbie came back from France transformed, appreciative of her parents and her life at home. At 18, she was an achieving senior at high school, a year away from attending the University of Alberta in Edmonton.

Younger son Alan was in his early teens, a sweet, big boy, gentle and genial. A good student, he was a tinkerer who liked to mess around with electronics and came to love outdoor adventure, especially deep-powder downhill skiing. On the ski hill, he was a hurricane, blowing past every other skier. He didn't talk about it, but his presence on a mountain exuded supreme confidence. Yet Alan could be obstinate in his dislike of organized sports: taken to the pool at my urging to join the swim team, he refused to leave the locker room. He and his sister were developing strong bonds that deepened after she left home for college.

Our oldest was far away that year. Partly, at least, from my forceful encouragement that he become a doctor, Chuck had gone to Queen's University in Kingston, Ontario, for pre-med studies. After just squeezing through his second year, he decided to take time off to get some perspective on his life and went to Western Australia for eight months to work with my old friend

My first progeny: Chuck, 19, at Queen's University, Barbie, 16, in high school, and Alan, 12, in grade school.

and AEC colleague, Leo Miller. In a mineral-exploration crew, Chuck surveyed and sampled rocks while hiking through the Outback, sleeping in tents and trailers. With $5,000 in his jeans he flew to Thailand. There, he had the brainstorm that would transform his life.

I had sent 14-year-old Chuck to mountaineering school at Banff and over the following summers this youngster, who five years before was frightened stiff on a limestone ledge, became entranced with climbing the Rockies. Five years later, traveling through Burma and India, he reached Katmandu in Nepal, where he launched his incredible adventure: a solo tramp to the edge of Everest and the ascent of a 19,000-foot flanking peak.

Many westerners had gone there, and climbed much higher, but typically in large, organized mountaineering expeditions with scores of porters. Chuck went with two Sherpa hillboys, carrying his own pack, planning his trip day by day, making his own judgements about whether he could enter a village, dare sleep there or drink the water, and make his food last till the next stop. In a month, he learned to speak basic Nepalese ("Dad, they weren't talking anything else!"). Over some of the most rugged, steep, exhausting country in the world, he booted for almost a month and more than 200 miles, then climbed with one of the Sherpas to the summit of Pokalde—at 19,050 feet, higher than most mountains in North America. There, he recorded in his diary, "we sat in silence marveling at what was around us. I took a Canadian flag out of my pack and with mittened hands painstakingly wired it to my axe. Then, in exhaustion and ecstasy, I took the one final step to the top, lifting at the same time my Maple Leaf high into the icy thin air."

When he came home, Chuck wasn't a boy anymore. Back at Queen's, he was the first of his class to be accepted to medical school and graduated in 1979 to become a GP and eventually a pathologist. He has a favorite quotation from Goethe which could have served as a motto for what I was about to attempt when I returned after resigning from Kerr-McGee:

> *Whatever you can do, or dream you can, begin it.*
> *Boldness has genius, power and magic in it.*

CHAPTER NINE

HUNTER

IT WAS EITHER A CRAZY TIME or the perfect time to be launching a company in the North American petroluem industry. A global recession was growing, the worst since the Depression. The OPEC oil shock was crippling economies around the world. Most Canadian companies had abandoned southern Canada as the major companies and the National Energy Board pronounced solemnly and pompously that there were no more large fields left there. They all went to the Arctic. In the U.S., as the Vietnam war ended and the Watergate scandal boiled up, the Nixon administration was trying to encourage exploration for natural gas by ending federal regulation of the fuel. Meanwhile, Canada and Venezuela supplied most of America's much-needed imported oil.

Jim and I started our new company in March 1973 with a borrowed office, a telephone, two chairs facing one another across a desk, a pair of yellow Ford Pintos as company cars—and maybe a few hundred dollars between us. The idea was to find petroleum in second-class reservoirs, but first we had to find money. Neither of us had enjoyed large salaries with Kerr-McGee, had no savings to speak of, and I damn well needed some income within the next month or two. Working out of the small space that a couple of consulting engineers generously lent us, we started casting about for corporate angels who would bless us with operating capital. We figured the still-unnamed company could be launched with at most three or four geologists, one landman, clerical help to handle our files of logs and scout cards, and some outside land-map services—requiring no more than a modest $250,000 to launch us that first year.

Creating charts to show our price projections, we had the gall to predict that someday the price of gas to producers would quadruple to 60 cents per thousand cubic feet and oil might eventually climb to $6 from $2.50 a barrel. (Read on: these numbers don't quite qualify me as an investment counselor but I do okay as a gambler.) We compiled a list of up to twenty probable investors—oil, industrial, and financial companies, almost all of them in Toronto—and sent them letters describing our proposed approach while trying to convince them that the current downcycle was temporary:

"No matter what various politicians do to impede these changes, supply and demand, with a big assist from OPEC with regard to oil, will force these prices to levels that are difficult for us to conceive of today. These price factors make it possible to review old well information and re-interpret fields that were discovered and discarded years ago as uneconomic. For a few years, some of the most economic hunting grounds in the world will be the partially drilled areas of North America. Not the frontiers, but the areas of well control, moderate drilling costs, and pipelines. Opportunities exist in the U.S. to be sure, but nowhere are those opportunities so great as in western Canada."

Foresightful, as it turned out, but when Jim followed up the letter with phone calls, nobody seemed to be buying our arguments. As he recalled later, "The response was always the same. The President would be all enthused with our pitch. Then later he'd arrange dinner with some so-called expert. The guy would tell him we were wingy and anyway gas was something everyone was piling out of. We always had several CEOs on our list, adding more while the earlier ones dropped away."

If we got to meet the top people in a company with no connection to the resource industry, the discussion first dealt with our financial needs. And then, with the inevitability of sunset, the prospect of a decent return on their investment. And there would always be an accountant or a Vice-President, Finance, who said, "Now, John, you've spoken about dry holes. If I understand correctly, a dry hole is a well that's unsuccessful, is that correct?"

(The textbooks describe a dry hole as "a wellbore that has not encountered hydrocarbons in economically producible quantities." Probably the only dry hole this financial guy had ever encountered was a cocktail of that name made with rum and apricot brandy.)

"And how much does a dry hole cost?" he persisted.

"It's quite a range, but at medium depths, it would probably be a million dollars."

"And how many dry holes might there be?" By now he was leaning forward, on the hunt, and there was a tension in the room as his colleagues paid close attention.

"You might have to drill five or six before you found a productive well." Only one exploratory well in 1,000 finds a major field in North America, I could have told him.

"Five or six million dollars in dry holes?"

He caught the eyes of the others, who I now realized were already saying to themselves, "We're not going to touch this crazy project."

Among the companies we tried were the B.C. forest-products behemoth MacMillan Bloedel; the chemical conglomerate CIL; Canadian Pacific's international mining subsidiary, Cominco; and two eastern steel companies that ranked among the top two dozen Canadian corporations in terms of sales: Dofasco and Stelco. Along with all the others, Dofasco quickly said No, but then—to our delight and increasing excitement—the Steel Company of Canada began to seem interested.

But our best bet was still a family connection Jim had with the Toronto-based multinational, Noranda Mines. The giant natural-resource company had annual revenues of well over $1 billion and assets approaching $2 billion. Jim's father had run the Noranda gold mine at Kirkland Lake in the 1930s when Bill Row was a mining engineer there. The Grays and the Rows became good friends—and Bill was now the blunt but kindly executive Vice-President of Noranda. He was an old-time miner, who had built the Kerr Addison mine in Ontario into a huge gold producer. Row was obviously well connected and listened to Jim's pitch intently. He understood the nuts and bolts of resource industries like ours.

Alf Powis was President of Noranda, a quiet, courteous, unusually young financial wizard who got the job Row might have had. Powis was clever and engaging, as we discovered that spring when Row convinced him to stop over in Calgary briefly when the company jet was flying to Vancouver. As the four of us dined at the Petroleum Club, Jim and I presented our case: untapped, overlooked gas, new technology to make wells productive, and the promise of rising prices. All this against a background of common agreement in the industry that Alberta was finished and the future would be in the Northwest Territories. The drum-beater for this concept was the National Energy Board.

Bill and Alf were predisposed to be sympathetic. Noranda was heavily into copper and they knew that, after the nationalization of mines in Chile had raised that mineral's world price, even second-class deposits in Canada became profitable. Powis had a lightning ability to grasp new and unfamiliar opportunities. "When everyone else is leaving somewhere and you can see a reason to stay—that's opportunity," he said as we drove him back to the airport. And: "When all the wise men are saying something, then it's very often wrong." Sweet music to my contrarian ears.

How much did we need? The way of the world, I now know, is a very carefully constructed economic projection. But I thought about it for ten seconds and said, "Alf, I don't see how we could spend more than $5 million a year." Noranda was willing to put up half that amount if we could find a partner.

Wonderful: we could go back to Stelco and sell the steel company's executives on partnering with a very credible mining company. It took much to-ing and fro-ing, but Stelco Chairman and CEO Peter Gordon and President John Allan finally agreed to have us pitch the project to their board of directors in December. Two weeks before that date, the company learned that the cost estimates of their major new steel plant being built on Lake Erie had unexpectedly soared. The management decided, in crisis mode, there was no excess cash to gamble on a startup in an industry foreign to them. Jim and I flew back to Calgary with our tails dragging out of the plane behind us.

Noranda was looking, too. At one time, it had the executives of a manufacturing company on the line as a possible partner. But when asked about the potential rate of return on a proposed five-year, $12.5-million investment, Row admitted that they could lose every cent. There was no bail-out, no way to sell and cut the loss. "They ran like rabbits," he said later.

We had further meetings with Noranda. They involved more damned accountants who displayed the same excess of caution as all the others had shown. This time the question was about the limits of our signing authority on expenditures. Bill Row was there, but we hadn't discussed any fixed numbers with him. "Jim and I could operate quite effectively if we had an expenditure limit of a million dollars," I said, throwing a number on the table.

The inquisitive head accountant blanched. "We have Vice-Presidents running great big mines in Ontario and Quebec who have limits of a hundred thousand."

At that point, Row, who understood the nature of our industry, saved us. "We're not talking about the mining business," he told his people. "In the oil business you've got to be ready to spend big bucks competing against some of the biggest companies in the world." He knew that in buying or leasing land for exploration, the trick is not to nibble at it a bit at a time, over several sales. You have to hit hard the first time. It's what we came to call the "stun 'em" policy: take all you can at a solid price and don't worry about leaving money on the table—because the next time the price will be considerably higher and your first bids will look beautiful.

Looking around at his colleagues, he said, "You're not getting this, are you? Being in the oil business is like shooting ducks." He swung in a shooting position. "You've only got from here to here."

We got our million-dollar signing authority. Now all we needed was the rest of the cash. Noranda was having a good year and did want to be in the oil business. So they decided to take all of us. Alf Powis agreed to a $5-million annual commitment for the next five years (at least that's what he thought he was doing). Jim and I negotiated a 12.5-per-cent net-profit interest between us for our sweat equity. I became President and CEO, Jim Executive Vice-President. All of this had to be approved by the Board. We went back to Calgary. Three days later the phone by my bed rang early one morning. Powis's assistant, Ozzie Hinds, said, "It'll take a while to write up the agreements. You can wait for the whole nine yards or I can park a hundred thousand in your account and we can start with a handshake." It took me eleven seconds to decide. "Ozzie," I said, "we'll take the handshake." *Lift-off!*

By then we had a name for our venture. We'd tossed several possibilities on to the table—and tossed all of them out. A couple of favorites, Everest (for obvious reasons) and Chimo (a friendly Inuktitut greeting) had already been claimed by other oil companies. Bill Row re-ignited our thinking by recommending we have "Canadian" in the name. Somewhere along the way, Jim and I came up with hunting as a good metaphor for what we intended to do. As Dickens said, there's a passion for hunting deeply implanted in the human breast (and Bill Row obviously liked duck-hunting). So Canadian Hunter Exploration—less formally Canadian Hunter and just Hunter—it was. The name was one of the most enlightened ideas we ever had. We never could decide which of us thought it up.

We put a sign on the door of a group of offices we rented on Eighth Avenue downtown, about two blocks from the heart of Calgary's oil business. Then we set about hiring men and women who were expert in areas we weren't. Half of being smart is knowing what you're dumb at. One of the smart choices was Lenora Johnson, my efficient, sharp (and, yes, attractive) secretary. We didn't want or need public-relations people, personnel managers, corporate development staff. We were looking for professional hunters.

Among our first employees was a bright young landman from Mobil Oil, Jim Chaput. One formal definition of the job is "an employee whose primary duties are managing an oil company's relations with its landowners and partners, including securing and administering oil and gas leases and other agreements." Petroleum landmen have been called many things, some of them only marginally flattering: leasehounds, horsetraders, amateur psychiatrists, poor man's diplomats. A typical story tells of the landman in mid-1970s Alabama who had to convince a reluctant elderly widow to lease her thirty acres in the middle of a key play. Unfortunately she was in the hospital and, her memory fading, told him she'd have to consult Henry—her long-deceased husband. The enterprising landman stepped out into the hall and returned a few minutes later to tell her he'd talked to Henry who thought it was a good lease and she should sign it. She did.

Landmen's work goes back to the 19th century with the need to check landowners' titles in courthouses, and then developed during the growing days of the North American oil industry to negotiate leases and acquire partners before setting up rigs on a site. They had an unprofessional image—"about the same category as a used-car salesman," one of them recalls—until the late 1950s when the University of Oklahoma designed a course to train landmen. College grad or not, a good professional landman is part scout and spy, part salesman and negotiator. He—and, more recently, she—needs the right kind of personality to talk and listen to everybody from small farmers and wealthy landholders to engineers and executives. Jim Chaput, a gregarious guy comfortable communicating with geologists and average working joes, had those skills. He nimbly orchestrated leases for the site of our first well, in the Barons area of south-central Alberta, and for hundreds of subsequent wells.

The other pivotal position in a budding exploration company is chief geologist. We hired straight-thinking, left-brained Dave Smith as our scientist of rocks, our field-finder, to study the buried strata, map the structure of formations, and anticipate the presence of hydrocarbon fluids. Smith, a good techical geologist rather than an explorationist, was less interested in the Big Picture that consumed me than the small but important details. At first, he and I concentrated on low-grade conventional reservoirs like the thin oil-bearing sandstone of the Barons field in southern Alberta. With only a little money, you stay close to home. It was there, on October 1, 1973, that Canadian Hunter spudded its first well—began the drilling process. A pretty sure bet, we thought, just the thing for a new company to cut its teeth on.

Now we had to see if there was any appreciable amount of what the petroleum poets like to call black gold. We snuggled up close to the old wells on the north side—and drilled a dry hole. Damn! But every oil field ever found was between dry holes. So we tried again on the east side—and hit. Our first oil discovery, at 3,000 feet! We and Noranda knew it wasn't much, but at least our baby had taken its first step.

To exploit this zone, by year's end Hunter had drilled seven wells—four finding oil and three abandoned. A modest beginning, yet our people were no longer so-called company geologists; we were oilmen. There's a vital difference, which colors how you conduct yourself, examine a prospect, and probably even the way you walk into a room. We had our diplomas.

The first exploratory well of 1974 took us out of the familiar, shallow oil region of the south into the far northwestern part of Alberta. The farming community of Keg River is as far north as the northern tip of Labrador on Canada's east coast. In early February a Hunter rig hit bottom at 2,000 feet—and all of a sudden we were in the gas business. It was Dave Smith's prospect. We'd tapped into the Cretaceous-age Gething Formation, a gas-saturated sand covering a sizable area. Our competitors, seeking oil, had drilled right through the shallow sands to a reef formation four or five thousand feet below. Jim Chaput eventually accumulated 380,000 acres for us in this area, which delivered our first significant gas reserves. A fine, large field. *But you ain't seen nothing yet.*

(Let me say, parenthetically, that 380,000 acres in any lease play is a lot of land. But Canada is very big and many companies had gone into the far north. We leased extremely large blocks of land again and again in these early days of the growing gas business.)

For a company on the make like ours—and, hell, for the planet—natural gas had a lot going for it. It's mostly methane—the simplest form of petroleum gas—with lesser amounts of ethane, propane, butane, and pentane. Long a poor cousin of crude oil, it was increasingly playing a major part in the petroleum universe and soon would account for almost a quarter of total energy consumption in the hungry U.S. market. Its share would keep expanding because of its low cost compared to other fuels and its relative harmlessness at a time of tightening environmental standards. It's a clean-burning fuel and while an oil spill anywhere is a disaster, a gas spill is no big deal. In the petroleum world, gas was the less-competitive way to go for Canadian Hunter—if we could find enough to make it worth our while. Today, that sounds like a pretty obvious solution. Thirty years ago, that was by no means cut-and-dried. I think it was just luck—not sophisticated analysis—that took us in the right direction.

Natural gas did have a downside: locating it could be like looking for a pearl in an oyster bed—you knew it might be there, but you had to shuck a lot of shells to find it. I like what one of our young geologists, Nick Wemyss, once said about it: "Gas is *subtle* because it weighs so much less than water or mud does, and in drilling for it, gas is more easily pushed back into the rock than oil is. And the rock isn't stained by gas as it is by oil. You don't see it in the rock the way you do oil. The whole basis of Hunter's edge has been developing a mastery of that subtlety." Nick was so quiet, he surprised us when he got so articulate.

Keg River was our baptism in using one of the weapons we'd wield to become leaders in the detection of gas: the analysis of electric logs to evaluate dry holes. In this process, each vertical drill hole (or wellbore) is recorded electrically on a striplog from bottom to top. Like an electrocardiogram, this electric log measures the electrical properties of the rock layers, including electrical resistivity. Because hydrocarbons don't conduct electricity (high resistivity) while most formation waters do (low resistivity), careful analysis of this data can detect gas and oil in the rock pores. This exploration technology, based on skilful interpretation of old electric logs, was not new. Such well logs had become an invaluable source of information since shortly after I was born; geologists could now map the subsurface using well-log control, no longer having to rely entirely on surface geology. And, half a century after the technology was developed, the logs from about 125,000 wells drilled in western Canada to that time were in public files. Within the year, by sweat and determination, we would take a giant step forward in the use of electric-log analysis.

Dave Smith had recognized tell-tale electrical resistivity in the Gething sand and mapped a sizable area which he interpreted as nearly proven gas. All we had to do was pop a hole down the middle of it. Within two years Keg River would be an Alberta hotspot, but now, in 1974, we leaped ahead of the pack by turning Chaput loose to start acquiring acreage.

In the same month, we found a gas well at our Barons oil field in thin Viking sand a hundred feet below the Barons oil. Pure luck: we had no idea it was there until doing a drillstem test. That's when you isolate the zone of interest in a well and open valves to release reservoir fluids through the drillpipe (or drillstem) and let the well flow for a time. This measures a reservoir's pressure, permeability, and productive capacity. It was a nice test, recovering a million cubic feet of gas per day. Yet our first reaction was to forget it; who wanted to milk a skinny streak of gas-bearing sand? But then someone pointed out that we were only a mile from the main TransCanada Pipelines system which transports gas from Alberta to eastern Canada and the U.S. You might deem this a rather serious oversight. It was. We were a small group, just learning to address the full scope of problems associated with finding and producing oil and gas. We got a lot better.

Dave Smith, studying old well logs around Barons, in the Kipp-Coaldale area, realized that earlier wells had not tested those Viking sands adequately. There was a substantial gas field here that other companies had overlooked. We hit the ground running and tied up 250,000 acres. This became a Hunter characteristic: to take large land positions on our prospects. The big mistake in exploration is not when a good idea fails but when a hit is not fully exploited.

At the same time, we were investigating a very different type of fuel: heavy oil, which is thick, sticky, and costly to upgrade into something usable. Crude oil can be measured in kilograms per cubic metre (kg/m3). (It can be measured a lot more sensibly in pounds per cubic foot, but the Quebec politicians—who controlled the government then—insisted characteristically on distinguishing themselves from the English.) In Western Canada, oil up to 900 kg/m3 is considered light to medium crude – above that it's heavy oil or bitumen (which contains hydrocarbons such as asphalt and mineral wax). It can range in heaviness from the tar-like oil near the surface at Fort McMurray and Cold Lake, Alberta—which is very expensive to mine or dig up by draglines—to the thinner variety that can be pumped up more cheaply from deeper deposits in the province. It's a serious matter because Canada's heavy oils represent one of the world's largest supplies of petroleum.

I had no experience with the stuff. But we did understand that the heavy-oil prospects around Lloydminster, on the Alberta-Saskatchewan border, were light enough to pump and could represent an opportunity for us. This was the lowest-priced oil in the free world and at the time only one company, Husky Oil, was even interested in getting it out. Perhaps Hunter could make a modest investment, take a modest risk, and have a modest return—but, with luck, enough to generate a steady cash flow. We were just starting, and any income looked good.

In our profession, gambling is a way of life and the element of doubt can seldom be eliminated. To roll the dice for us in heavy oil, Hunter needed an expert. We found one of the rare ones, both in background and talents. Jay Christensen was a gentleman, a petroleum engineer, four years older than I, but always looked fifteen years younger than his age. He was a friendly, stocky Dane with a farmer's crinkles around his eyes. Raised on an Alberta farm ("We were so poor we had to ride pigs"), during the Second World War he became a Canadian radar specialist. Based in places like the Bahamas and Egypt, he guided aircraft that were shuttling across the Atlantic to Europe. Afterward, an uncle in Texas suggested he become a petroleum engineer. Jay studied engineering at college in the U.S. and went to work for Magnolia Oil (which became Mobil Oil) in Louisiana, Texas, and New Mexico. Later he joined Husky to learn the heavy-oil business in Alberta. As production manager, he became a leader in the tricky technology of actually producing the heavy, viscous oil, a task that was complicated by frequent equipment failures, wellbore problems, and the challenge of disposing the saltwater and sand that inevitably surfaced with the heavy oil.

Hunter had been scratching around the Lloydminster area to no good effect, belatedly realizing we didn't know what we were doing there. When we approached Jay, he had left Husky to go on his own as a consultant. He was available to assist us in acquiring and developing a group of wells. While I've not been comfortable with most engineers, he was an exception, an all-around oilman. Jay helped locate the land, drilled the wells, produced the heavy oil, and sold it on our behalf. He drilled about fifty wells in new fields or field extensions on the Alberta side of the border. We had properties in Saskatchewan too, but when the government in that province abruptly increased royalty charges, they went on indefinite hold. Governments can do with impunity what would be criminal actions by companies or individuals.

From the first, Jim Gray and I fell into our distinctive operating styles which we would enlarge throughout our relationship. He never had my passion to draw and pore over maps, think long hours about what I saw in them, and then try to compose the puzzle pieces into a recognizable pattern. He saw his role as the bush-beater in the on-going hunt for investors, the gladhander who made the social connections at the Petroleum Club and industry functions, and often the corporate spokesman (although I sounded off in public when issues aroused me). Our confluence of personalities set the overall tone in the company—his outward-looking and political, mine more introspective and analytical.

Again, it's instructive to quote from Peter Foster, a shrewd observer of the Oil Patch, in *The Blue-Eyed Shieks*:

> Many people are unaware of Masters' existence, since Gray has served as 'the front man' for the company since it started. But Masters is really the intellectual driving force behind Canadian Hunter. Gray may go around spreading the word, but if he is the prophet, Masters is Allah. . . .His approach to both geology and Canadian Hunter is a supremely intellectual one, and his conversation abounds with images and analogies. . . . Some of his memos are almost philosophical in style, containing phrases like "we all see the world through the lenses of our self image." He is one of the very few oilmen likely to bring Samuel Johnson into the conversation.

You can see why I like Peter (even though I don't think I've ever referred to Samuel Johnson).

Collaborating during those early days, Jim and I developed various technical teams. We started by choosing our one log analyst to work hand-in-glove with us in our role as geologists. The concept worked well for us and soon we realized it made sense for others in the company. Individuals operating separately generate a one-plus-one sum of effectiveness. Two complementary specialists operating as a team spark a two-times-two product. The real value of the system lies in always having someone equal in stature and equally familiar with the total problem to bounce an idea off—and have it bounce back, bigger. It's not like trying a concept on a subordinate, whose response is apt to be a little mushy. A peer can generally bounce it back to you sharply, at a different angle, and with a different spin on it. While the volleys of ideas between us dwindled later, Jim and I launched our relationship at Hunter with all the fervor and effectiveness, I believe, of Lewis and Clark setting out to explore a new world.

Gradually, we broadened our team concept, designing a specific team, made up of certain specialists, to solve a particular problem. When the problem disappeared, so did the team, to be reconstituted and re-assigned to new problems. Ultimately, we had many teams, some of our specialists serving on two or three at the same time. A cardinal rule was not to let a team persist if its problem had been solved. The team organization at Hunter was extraordinarily effective. It was adopted by many companies in Canada, is now common organizational practice throughout much of the oil industry, and has even stretched out into other industries. It has become so widespread that its origins have largely been forgotten.

By the spring of 1974, our company had grown to eleven imaginative, innovative technical and business specialists. That summer we were all as hyper-active as rabbits in planning and drilling nearly two dozen exploratory and follow-up development wells. There's a truism that is so simple, it sounds stupid: you find oil and gas only when you drill wells. It's amazing how few people in the business truly understand this. While they may think they're finding petroleum by drawing maps and studying logs, they have to drill the damn things. Then they have a chance not only to discover what they were seeking, but sometimes the extra pay zones they didn't even know were there.

In our second year of existence, we were hoping to find both the originals and the extras. I want all that science can do for me but, please, give me luck too.

CHAPTER TEN

FINDING THE RIGHT ONE

WHILE CANADIAN HUNTER WAS COMING TOGETHER, my marriage was falling apart. The tensions between my wife and me had mushroomed during our years in Calgary. Part of the problem sprang from her family's continuing influence on Susie and her emotional dependence on them. Her father, who'd earned his law degree taking night courses, was resentful of people educated at Yale and Harvard and often spoke of his superiority to them. L.B. tried to establish the same superior position in our relationship and made it clear to me that his beloved daughter had only to call him if she had any complaints about me. He couldn't bear the thought of losing his little girl. And if I took a stance that contradicted what Susie had learned growing up in her family, she let me know I was on the wrong track. She knew. I did not. Minor irritations grew into full-bore verbal battles. It didn't matter how much familiarity, how much logic, I brought to an argument—if it disagreed with the family thinking, I couldn't sway her. Her parents and brothers could do no wrong and increasingly I could do no right; they loomed like phantoms in the background of almost every major disagreement we had. Father was "B" to close friends and family. I never got past calling him Mr. Mann. I didn't know his name for me because he never addressed me.

The differences between Susie and me had deepened with the years: she couldn't understand why I wasn't interested in her interests, such as birds and flowers, and I couldn't comprehend her determined anti-intellectual approach to the things that mattered to me. While Susie was educated as a geologist and worked several years for an oil company, she—like many wives of her time—didn't pursue her professional career after marriage. But she was a wonderful mother to our children. By then, however, I felt as if I had wed the wrong woman.

As our marriage continued to deteriorate, so had Lenora Johnson's with her insurance-salesman husband. She'd leapt into it naively—all her girlfriends were getting married—and after less than three years had left him. At that point, I started considering our relationship as more than boss and secretary. We started having an occasional lunch together. Very soon, I was positively enamored of her. One day I asked her to send a large check to my brother, Chuck, part of the proceeds of a sale of Kerr-McGee stock I wanted to share with him, and she remembers being impressed I would want to do that. While knowing that Lenora liked and respected me, I had no idea if she could ever fall in love with a man twenty-one years older. Much later, she said the age difference just melted away. "You seemed ever-young—you always could out-climb and out-ski me." Eventually I let her know my deep feelings for her. To my delight, she encouraged my advances and, guilty though she felt, we grew closer and closer. In one of the best novels I've ever read, *Fugitive Pieces* by the Canadian writer Ann Michaels, there's a line I copied in my journal and marked with a star: "We're never ourselves until we contain two souls." That's how I was thinking of Lenora.

But she felt torn between her growing affection for me and her self-reproach at being involved with a married man. In 1974 she quit

Canadian Hunter and fled to Australia with some skiing friends, to get as far away as possible, and end our affair once and for all. I was devastated at losing this woman who had brought me youth and wisdom combined. She was gone for months without letting me know where she was, how she was. I learned finally that she'd made her way to the Great Barrier Reef in northern Australia, become a barmaid at a place of palm trees and sandy beaches called Daydream Island, and then moved to Darwin where she was working as a switchboard operator in a hotel. Her postcard to a friend back home finally tipped me off to her whereabouts. Lenora picked up the hotel phone one day and was surprised to hear my voice, telling her how much I loved and missed her. How I drove by her apartment every day, how I couldn't live without her in my heart, in my arms. Would she join me in Europe, where I'd be meeting some potential investors? I'd send her the ticket immediately. We could decide our future there. Would she come?

She would. I reserved a sumptuous room in the Haus Munchstein, a castle overlooking Salzburg, Austria, Mozart's birthplace, one of the most beautiful cities either of us had ever seen. It was a perfect place to fall in love, strolling along wooded trails, attending concerts, and wandering the beautiful castle. She explained her confusion after coming out of a broken marriage, wanting a new relationship, but unsure whether I'd ever leave Susie. We talked long and hard the rest of our stay in Salzburg and finally broke through the wall between us.

Coming home, I was determined we would have a life together.

While my personal drama was playing out through 1974, Canadian Hunter was well into the first phase of its own saga. In Alberta I was initially drawn to the thick sand section on the western edge of the basin. But it took more study to get it clearly in my sights. At the same time, we were seeing conventional, individual prospects in the south of the province. These are for the unsure. The most significant step in 1974 was making a string of small discoveries—drawing blood, in effect, gaining confidence. Ultimately these were important only as starters, but it's hard to be very realistic about your first babies.

The *Daily Oil Bulletin*, the industry Bible, tallying the statistics for that year listed the leading operators in terms of drilling completions:

"Perhaps the most surprising firm to be shown in the Top Ten (seventh position) is the small independent Canadian Hunter Exploration Ltd. This Calgary-based company was only formed in September of 1973 [but] during 1974 chalked up 84 drilling completions, including 62 wells that indicated hydrocarbon potential."

Note that they described us as a "small independent." No one knew we were backed by Noranda. Not telling everything is not lying.

We were pleased with the recognition, of course, and glad to make a little income for Noranda, but that was way short of my dream. I wasn't interested in rabbits; I wanted a grizzly bear.

Our geology was still fairly basic. We hadn't stretched out yet. But our tactical thinking was already maturing, starting to separate us from the pack. I knew, by absorption from Dean McGee, that an oil company gets rich only by good timing in acquiring real estate. You can always get a good prospect drilled, but you can only buy it once. And there's no substitute for having the guts to act fast—on good technical information.

I couldn't stop thinking about the enormous thickness of Cretaceous sands and shales in the foothills of the Rockies in the westernmost part of the Alberta Basin. From there the section wedged rapidly eastward to perhaps a tenth of its maximum thickness. We found several formations in northeast B.C. with small accumulations of gas and water in the updip area and a widespread area apparently of continuous gas saturation with no water in the downdip part. It reminded me of the productive San Juan Basin with its updip water.

Our target was the Halfway formation, Triassic sand, and we were defining favorable areas by drillstem-test information. Did the test get gas or water? Eventually we were a lot more sophisticated but at first that's all we knew how to do.

In the first four months of 1975, we leased 400,000 acres, averaging $20 per acre. We hit like a Special Forces team, black masks and guns. All leases were bought in bogus names. It may have been the first time any company had deliberately concealed its purchasing patterns on such a large scale over such a long period of time. If the buyers were not recognizably strong, and land was not being blocked up by one entity, the purchases did not seem too threatening to the main players. They could easily be dismissed.

Our landman had to live with comments from competitors: "Hey Jim, how come you're at all the sales and you never buy anything? Canadian Hunter is all talk!" They would have to eat those words—big time.

Six months after our purchases, the price of gas in B.C. soared 50 per cent. If Noranda thought we had anticipated that, we didn't say anything to deny it. That's the way legends are encouraged.

I was studying several different aspects of gas accumulation in western Canada, never knowing which possibilities would pan out or prove futile. The great sand wedge in western Alberta had to be part of a much bigger conception It had been just slightly under the surface of my consciousness since the birth of Hunter. It was what I had tried to describe to Mr. McGee but didn't know yet. I constructed a map of gas shows across the whole region—twice the size of Texas. I'll repeat that: the map was *twice* the size of Texas. (I've never known a Texas geologist who could accept that observation as reality.) Recording the test recoveries of gas in abandoned wells, I carefully noted the formations tested and such details as pressure data and the flows from each test. I also constructed a group of electric-log cross-sections 300 miles long, running east-west, across the basin from eastern Alberta to the foothills. Were there any changes in sand composition or rock porosity, anything that seemed anomalous or curious?

In all of this, I was abetted by three particularly wise men who had arrived in the Hunter realm through an old contact at the Colorado School of Mines in Golden. Professor Bob Weimer—Robert J. Weimer, distinguished field geologist and master educator—was a kind of intellectual godfather of western geology. Most important to me now was his expertise in the Cretaceous sands of the Rocky Mountains.

"Bob, Americans know more about these sands than the fellows in Canada do. What *they* know is Devonian reefs," I told Weimer on the phone in late 1974. "I need somebody who knows the Rockies Cretaceous section to come up here and apply the same rules to the Canadian section." Because there were ten times more wells and correspondingly more production in the U.S. than in Canada, American geologists were far better prepared to understand our situation.

"Larry Meckel is the guy you want," Weimer said. A geologist with Sneider & Meckel Associates, a new consulting company in Houston. "He can go through that Cretaceous section faster than anybody I ever saw."

It was good counsel. Meckel, peering inquisitively at the world through thick horn-rims, was an exceptional exploration geologist with a mind like a machine-gun. Brilliant and fascinated by everything, he was as unassuming as a big kid, given to working in his stocking feet (with holes). His partner, the rotund, laughing Bob Sneider, was a superb earth scientist, as much an engineer as a geologist. He was also extraordinarily analytical, which would prove immensely valuable over the years. They'd hired a couple of employees we came to know well. John Farina was a young engineer of Italian parentage, funny with his self-deprecating humor, gifted with his intensive, quantitative knowledge of petroleum engineering. And the incredible Lloyd Fons, a six-foot-seven, black-browed bear, turned out to be the fastest electric-log analyst in the West.

The two partners had worked together at Shell Oil, a breeding ground for some of the best-trained geologists in the world. Sneider in particular had a fascinating background. Raised in seaside New Jersey, amid plenty of sand but no rocks, he hadn't even considered geology until belatedly switching majors from metallurgical engineering at Rutgers. Serving as a frontline combat engineering officer with the U.S. Army in Korea—where he learned the value of a multi-disciplinary team approach—Bob found time to take two graduate-level correspondence courses in economic geology.

He came home to get his doctorate and went to work for Shell Development Company under the famous research manager, Gus Archie, a powerful name in petrophysics (study of the physical properties of various rock types). Archie's work was the first to demonstrate dramatically that well log measurements were vital in identifying pay zones. And Archie's Equation, christened for him, was seminal in measuring the hydrocarbon saturation of rocks by their various electrical properties. Both of these findings would become important to the future of Canadian Hunter.

Bob Sneider learned well from Gus Archie, but after seventeen years at Shell, he and Larry Meckel decided to start their own consulting firm. It was barely out of the womb when Meckel attended a geological meeting in Wyoming and saw a professor he knew, Bob Weimer, who passed on his name to an oil guy in Canada—me. We quickly flew both partners up to Calgary. Sneider recalls to this day how he and Meckel had rehearsed a speech about the importance of seismic work, using shock waves to define underground formations.

"That's interesting," I told them after they presented their pitch, "but I'm not interested. I'm interested in tight sands."

Immediately, they gave me a new speech about the importance of electric-log evaluation, an area that could be of special relevance to our situation and one in which Sneider had extraordinary expertise. ("Talk about luck," he says now.)

I wrote out a consulting contract that night on a sheet of paper torn from a yellow pad.

I soon visited their office in Houston, where they introduced me to the master of log analysis, Lloyd Fons. One day, Bob and Larry told me, they'd been studying in the Houston well-log library, a public archive of nearly every electric log previously run in that region. They were looking for pay zones in Texas counties that oil companies had bypassed. Fons strolled over, said he knew what they were doing, and mentioned that he specialized in reading such logs. Over three decades, he'd worked as an independent and as an employee of major firms, including Schlumberger, the French-born company that invented electric logs in the year

The astonishing Lloyd Fons, possibly the best—certainly the fastest—log analyst ever.

of my birth. With my blessing, they hired him and he began consulting with us in Calgary.

He was a strange one. His previous bosses, finding him difficult to manage, just let him do what he wanted, embarrassing as it sometimes was. Bob tells of the time Fons was in a Houston restaurant full of Shell people and yelled out to them, "These guys"—Sneider and Meckel—"are so good, they've found more oil than Shell!" Left on his own, he was a magician. He didn't just read electric logs, he devoured them, at a speed that should have earned him a place in the Guinness Book of Records.

Electric logging tools are sophisticated instruments, usually in the shape of a long pipe, slender enough to drop into a new drill hole on a cable that conducts electricity to the tools. The cable reels out like a fishing line from a truck converted into a portable measurement lab on wheels. The tools transmit the data up the cable as wiggly lines on to long strips of paper—the logs—to record salient information including resistivity, self-potential, radioactivity, sonics, magnetics, neutron density. The scope and complexity of the logs mean the average analyst might take a day to evaluate three or four of them thoroughly through myriad computer calculations. Fons was far from average: he came in some days and told us, "Well, John, I think I did 200 yesterday."

Standing at a long table with a stack of logs, he laid all the logs of one well side by side, ran his laser eyes down them in a single sweep, integrating them like a computer, called out the pay zones to a secretary, and dropped the logs into "good" or "bad" piles. At night, he did the mathematical calculations that complete the analysis procedure as he sat in front of a television set watching his beloved NBA Houston Rockets. (A former pro basketball player, he sometimes gave unsolicited coaching advice that was intriguing enough for the local newspapers to report. He's too old for the game now, yet he continues to give free advice on a wide variety of scientific subjects. One of his favorite activities is informing traffic police on duty that their radar equipment is antiquated and inaccurate.) Each morning, he arrived at our office with a package of figures from the previous night showing calculations of pay thicknesses, rock porosities, billions of cubic feet of gas (BCF) per section, estimated flow rates—among others.

In the beginning, I usually asked him, "Lloyd, did you find some gas?"

"Oh boy, I got a bunch of gas."

"How much BCF?"

"I don't know."

"Didn't you even add it up?"

"No," he admitted.

"Well, what part of the province are the wells in?"

A shrug—he was totally uninterested in locating any log on a map.

"Do any of them cluster?"

"John," he said finally, "I don't do stuff like that. You do it a helluva lot better than I do."

It absolutely astounded me that the man's only consuming interest in the project was laying those logs out and identifying the gas layers they showed. He had no curiosity about where they were, how they connected to each other, or how economic they were to produce—he'd get just as excited about finding gas at 18,000 feet, where it was probably worthless, as he did about shows at 3,000 feet.

Originally, I thought we would use him for no more than a few days. But he quickly became our secret weapon. Fons charged us about $1,000 a day but was worth every damn dollar. His operating philosophy was mine: "Those who say it can't be done should not interfere with those who are doing it." A piece of advice so insightful that no one will ever pay any attention to it.

At the time, there were 75,000 abandoned exploratory wells in Canada, which represented 35 billion dollars' worth of geophysical data at current drilling costs. Hard facts that could tell us "yes" or "no" about the presence of oil or gas, solid information that no oil-finder had likely ever used to explore on a regional scale. In the past virtually all electric logs were used only for structure-mapping purposes or evaluating single wells at the conclusion of drilling.

Now, at Canadian Hunter, we were converting a specific-use development tool into a broad reconnaissance exploration method. *Eureka*! This adaptation became a bulldozer, eventually exerting a powerful influence on Canadian exploration, and ultimately on the U.S.

The use of electric logs for exploration may seem like a simple, obvious idea, but the mere fact that it had not been attempted before created a formidable barrier to acceptance. A favorite argument, offered always as a clincher, held that it was a futile exercise to study old logs because the major oil companies would surely never by-pass any significant pay zones in a well. Yet many of the tens of thousands of abandoned wells had been drilled at a time when gas was selling at depressingly low prices and when few gas pipelines existed in western Canada.

The curious fact is that the human mind sees mostly what it's programmed to see. Recognizing that gas was an unprofitable commodity, explorationists not only didn't see it, they had been *trained* not to see it—their companies didn't want to waste money on drillstem tests and completion costs. Shell Crewson, an oldtime well-site geologist for Hudson's Bay Oil and Gas, remembered his days when young geologists were told not to bother with the uphole portions of wells located in western Alberta. They weren't even to visit the site until the drillers had passed through the overlying Cretaceous section, in places up to 10,000 feet thick. Why bother? It could only have gas.

When I began to plot Lloyd Fons' data on a regional map, I found he'd evaluated 5,000 wells across the eastern Alberta shelf, but only about 18 per cent had indications of gas. I placed big dots on all of those. Most were scattered randomly across the shelf without showing any abnormal clustering. They did not suggest large fields. However, there was a group of wells in the western part of the basin that did exhibit very promising characteristics. A hundred of them were in the downdip, deepest part of B.C. and Alberta, a large number of them indicating considerable bypassed gas reserves.

An obvious, eye-catching cluster of these wells was around the little village of Elmworth near Grande Prairie, in Alberta's fertile Peace River region northwest of Edmonton. I arrived there, mentally, in the spring of 1975. It was time to make a contour map of the quantities of gas being identified by Lloyd's log analyses. In exploration, you must periodically accumulate your scattered data, correlate and refine it into cohesion, then step back and see what it's doing. Is it starting to look valuable? Does it have form? Is it pointing somewhere? What procedures will illuminate it? The method is not formulaic. A successful pattern can rarely be brought from another region and laid over the new data. Computers are no use. Only the human mind is sufficiently intricate and ingenious enough to recognize a subtle unity or direction that may serve to integrate the data into some form of consistency. When that happens, you've "found" something. (This explanation may convey little meaning to normal people. It is directed to "finders." They are not normal.)

I knew it was time to analyze because we had started to post data which was clearly in a separate, more significant category than the random, one-layer measurements of gas we had seen in wells coming up from

Saskatchewan, across southern and central Alberta. Now we were seeing thick gas zones in multiple layers. My ears were pointed up. My tail was starting to wag. Although I didn't understand it, I knew I liked it.

In the Grand Prairie area, I drew a rough contour line that enclosed all well spots where the log calculation was greater than 8 billion cubic feet of gas per section. It was a higher number than I'd seen for 900 miles. I narrowed it down with two more contour closures labeled 15 BCF and 25 BCF. I did my contour interpretation of the entire map—which stretched from Saskatchewan to British Columbia and covered a whole wall—in two days. I believe this was the first time a BCF-per-section map over a large area had ever been created from electric-log analyses.

Eureka!

BCF-per-section maps are now used so widely by so many that no one ever stops to consider that they were invented by one geologist in a little company in a little office in Calgary in 1975.

Our mapping of the Cadotte formation at Elmworth seemed to indicate a gas-rich area downdip from the water-saturated portion. It reminded me of a large tight-sand gas trap near Denver called Wattenburg. Meanwhile, Duncan McCowan, a young geologist who'd just joined Hunter, was focusing on the similar Bluesky formation to the south at Gold Creek, aided by the work of Lloyd Fons. Our first maps of bypassed wells at Gold Creek showed indications of an already-sizable reserve of 800 billion cubic feet of gas that other companies had ignored.

The Sneider & Meckel specialists, the Houston Mafia, were moving into high gear with us. They were studying wells drilled back in the 1950s and '60s when the emphasis was on oil. Until now, no one had thought to dig into those old records in search of gas. Since 1938, any company exploring in Alberta had to send copies of its well logs to the Energy Resources Conservation Board, which made them public for $1.50 per computer file. Our evaluation of electric logs drilled by Texaco in the Elmworth area had identified numerous zones of gas saturation. Some of it was conventional reservoir rock, relatively easy to tap, but most of it would have to be stimulated by hydraulic fracturing—fracing at high pressure. The potential of frac technology was becoming plainly evident. Our engineers began a review of formation stimulation, reading everything they could find. I sent them to the U.S. for first-hand observation. We were revving up.

Bob and Larry, who had taught at Shell, took a small group of us (including Lenora and Dave Smith's wife) on a field trip down south to study formations around the Gulf of Mexico. Every field trip I had ever been on was to study rocks. This one was for sand. They led us through a week-long crash course, lecturing us first at their Houston base about how the Gulf region's depositional processes—the way sediments are formed and distributed—might apply to western Canada. Then we went south to Galveston and worked our way eastward along the coast to Louisiana and on to New Orleans. Our guides showed us the physical processes on the surface, such as how deltas and long, onshore bars are created, and trooped us to their office again to apply all our new knowledge to the subsurface rocks back home.

We also had the immense privilege of being lectured to by one of the great sedimentationists of our era, Rufus Leblanc, who had studied the Gulf shoreline for forty years as a Shell research geologist. He is a brilliantly creative scientist and an uproariously funny Coon-Ass who laces his lectures with side-splitting, usually dirty stories about the bayou Frenchmen. After all these years, I still can't decide which I liked better: the science or the jokes.

The trip, the first of many in American settings, was magical. We learned more than you could in a year at graduate school—among other things, that we Hunter guys weren't the sophisticated geologists we thought we were. We studied bays and estuaries, channels and deltas and bars, even jumping into the water and letting our toes feel the sand of a transgression—a migration of the shoreline from a basin onto land. On one dramatic day, we sat above a salt dome in southern Louisiana, gulping soda pop at a small general store, and discussing with mounting excitement the area in northwestern Alberta we were hoping to exploit—Elmworth.

* * *

As my electric-log map of the area had taken shape, my mind was racing for an explanation of the great concentration of gas in the one place it should not be—in a synclinal position, a trough-shaped fold in the rock where the rock layers are concave in an upward direction. By this time, as part of my regional studies, I had constructed east-west cross-sections of logs. They showed the spectacular eastward wedging of the great sand section but failed to show the expected easterly sandstone pinchouts, those stratigraphic petroleum traps which taper out of a reservoir into nonporous rock that seals them in. The log cross-sections did, however, reveal rapidly increasing electrical resistivity—westward and downdip—throughout the entire Cretaceous section in the deeper part of the basin. The Cretaceous sands out on the gentle eastern shelf were clean, porous, and saltwater-bearing with resistivities of only two to three ohms. As the layers in the basin thickened and dipped deeper, the resistivity of the sands rose dramatically. The whole section finally exceeded 200 ohms. The first rule of subsurface exploration: a gas accumulation identifies itself almost always as a sharp increase in resistivity.

For many years, Canadian geologists had observed this phenomenon and argued that it simply meant very tight, highly cemented rocks. I asked our log analysts to consider carefully whether the high resistivity in this basin could mean the entire section was saturated with gas. This possibility, if it even occurred to others, had probably been dismissed as ridiculous. One of those dumb ideas, so easily ignored. But the disbelieving geologists had likely never seen the San Juan Basin in New Mexico, as I had, where gas pervades the whole 5,000-foot Upper Cretaceous section. One of the principal weaknesses of most geologists today is they haven't seen enough territory.

I was also beginning to think San Juan in relation to Elmworth because another set of my maps was showing an intriguing pattern. A map of gas shows indicated a large area on the eastern shelf with small pockets of gas and abundant water. It was quite common to have recoveries of both gas and water from the same test. But in this area of western Alberta, I saw many tests showing gas but no water over a very large area. It was a striking difference. Excitedly, I drew a 400-mile-long, northwest-southeast line that separated the huge, mixed gas-water province of the eastern shelf and the gas-only, downdip part of the basin. The gas was downdip from the water, saturating every streak of porosity in the rock over a vertical section of 12,000 feet!

This map brought sharply to mind one of the most remarkable characteristics of the San Juan Basin accumulation. The gas is in the syncline at the bottom of the basin where there is no water, and goes updip through a gas-water transition zone to fully water-saturated rocks. This is upside-down from, the complete reverse of, the normal gas-on-top-of-water relationship—which was the only situation all the geology textbooks talked about. (As Dr. John Gruner, geology professor at the University of Minnesota and advisor to the Atomic Energy Commission, told me in southern Utah 27 years before, "If you want to be famous, take a well known idea and turn it upside-down." He did that to the vast Mesabi iron-ore deposits in Minnesota and became a legend.)

It was a right-brain moment in my Calgary office. I experienced that flash of intuition that suddenly sorts out numerous random, subconsciously recalled data in your mind into an ordered pattern. Another *eureka!* The flash was accompanied by a powerful, exhilarating sense of understanding and control. I stood on a peak. I *knew*. It may be life's grandest feeling.

From that moment in the summer of 1975, only two years since Canadian Hunter came into being, I recognized one of the largest gas fields in North America. No individual or institution would shake me from that conviction. Yet no geologist, even from the San Juan Basin, had ever described this inverted gas-water situation in the literature as an acknowledged gas-trap mechanism.

When I went back to Bob Weimer for an expert on the San Juan, he suggested an oil-exploration consultant in New Mexico, Elliott Riggs:

"Seems to me I've heard Elliott talk about some kind of crazy idea like this, how the gas is trapped."

"You know," I told Riggs on the phone, "I've got a board of directors in Toronto. I need to show them something scientific about why I've got this crazy idea in Alberta and why I need a lot of money. Can you write me a no-nonsense, summary account of the important facts about the San Juan Basin gas accumulation?"

He could, and did, within a few weeks, sending me perhaps the briefest but best commercial geology report ever written on that key basin. It contains the largest gas field on the continent. I read and re-read Elliott's report and kept envisioning the gigantic gas field we might be sitting on in Alberta. It might even surpass the Milk River field of southeastern Alberta, already one of the largest in Canada. There too, I knew, the porous sands were saturated with water updip but the low-porosity sands downdip were saturated with gas. Once you get a really big idea, and it's right, it starts to scoop up countless scattered observations that previously had no pattern. The sense that it's right floods over you as the facts line up in ordered rows.

My hope of finding such a major field was heretical in the intellectual

"It is likely that the larger pools, in most of the exploration plays, have already been found and exploration effort in the future will be devoted to searching for remaining smaller pools as well as improving the recovery from existing pools".

CANADA GEOL. SURVEY, 1977

The Canadian Geological Survey's famously ignorant condemnation of the future petroleum possibilities of western Canada.

climate of the time. That year, 1975, the Canadian Geological Survey pronounced on the possibility of further gas prospects in the West: "It is likely that the larger pools . . . have already been found and exploration efforts in the future will be devoted to searching for remaining smaller pools." Most of the leading companies, having already reached this conclusion, had moved their exploration crews to the Arctic and the Canadian east coast. Bankers, consultants, industry columnists, and pipeline companies all concurred. A solid wall of negative thinking was in place when I came to the startling conviction that there was an elephantine San Juan-like field in the Elmworth area holding a treasure measured in trillions of cubic feet of gas.

Now all I had to do was prove it. The first step was convincing our moneybags. Jim and I flew to Toronto and laid the massive electric-log maps, covering B.C. and Alberta, on Noranda's long conference table in front of the President, Alf Powis.

In my most portentous manner, I said, "Alf, you are looking at the most valuable set of geophysical maps in Canada today."

As I explained the whole concept, Alf—who wasn't a geologist but was a quick study—grasped the thrust of my spiel. But even he got stuck on the fact that the area we wanted to drill already had 93 dry holes—bypassed gas wells. "You're trying to tell me that a couple of dozen major companies drilled all these wells through a huge gas field and every one of them missed it? I find that very hard to believe."

His Board of Directors found it even more difficult to accept. In the end, though, Powis finally ruled that if we were convinced of our arguments for the field, he would reluctantly go along with us in spite of the dissent.

Our first move was to get Jim Chaput, our landman, to make offers to two major companies to acquire land positions in our prospective area. Our objective was to find good blocks within fifty miles of a gas pipeline. We wanted farmouts—in which a leaseholder assigns part of the lease to another company for exploration or development activity. He came to terms with Texaco for a half-interest in 56,000 acres at Elmworth and with

Atlantic Richfield for 210,000 acres at Gold Creek. The size of those farm-outs tells something about how unfavorably the rest of the industry regarded this region. These ranked among the largest farmouts ever negotiated in Alberta because no one else wanted the land (today, intense competition, which we initiated 25 years ago, makes it nearly impossible to farm out more than 1,500 acres at a time).

In September 1975, we spudded our first well at Elmworth. I was particularly interested in the gas show from a dry hole in the Cadotte formation there. Although we used hydraulic fracturing on the well, it produced only a disappointing, uneconomic flow of gas. It helped to keep repeating the admonition written in old English script on a placard in my office: "Thou shalt not give up!"

A couple of months later, we were all somewhat heartened by the successful retesting of an old well drilled in 1956 to the Halfway formation at Town in northeastern B.C. Lloyd Fons had made a favorable electric-log analysis there, prompting our engineers to ignore the original drillstem-test recovery of just 40 feet of mud. When we boldly made a successful re-entry and frac, the well tested two million cubic feet a day. An encouraging discovery—because it resulted from log analysis in a zone where the previous testing had indicated no gas. Our Hunters were quick to realize Town's significance. Fons's unbelievable ability to speed-scan piles of logs for the merest evidence of hydrocarbons was immediately put into action to survey hundreds of square miles north and south of the well.

By year's end, we had drilled across Alberta and B.C. 47 exploratory and development wells, which brought in five oil wells and 23 gas wells. Our net revenue had increased five-fold over 1974 to boost the company's income to more than $1 million for the first time. Meanwhile, our staff had doubled to 28.

And then in January 1976, after abandoning the first Elmworth well, we spudded in a second one four miles to the north. Our geologists had identified a sedimentary formation called the Falher sands, deeper than the Cadotte, as a possible secondary target. We were sure our farmout agreement with Texaco allowed us to drill another well to the lower depth.

So while not attaching much importance to the Falher sands, we drilled into them to 6,251 feet and recognized some meaningful porosity and a strong sampling of gas. Log analysis indicated gas saturation in the area in every layer of sand from 2,500 to 10,000 feet. A test in Falher sands produced an impressive flow of four million cubic feet per day. We had hit it lucky—how lucky we would soon find out—in a discovery zone I hadn't even been targeting. Against all statistical probability, that well became, after frac, the second-most-prolific hole we ever drilled in the Elmworth field. But that knowledge came much later. Only a few months earlier, the Geological Survey had written off western Canada.

A long time afterward, a Texaco landman told us, "You know, you guys defaulted on our deal. I remember the day we talked about it all afternoon and came within an ace of bouncing you out. If you read that agreement letter, it says that Canadian Hunter will re-enter the old Cadotte well for the purpose of attempting to complete the Cadotte. Then it says if you do and get a producing gas well, you have the right to go ahead and drill option wells. But you never did complete it. When you wrote and said you planned to drill the first option well, we had a lot of talk about disallowing you. But we decided, 'What the hell, there's nothing there anyway.'"

It still gives me an icy chill to recognize that we nearly lost Elmworth before we found it. The field would surely have been discovered by someone, but no one would have ever heard of Canadian Hunter Exploration.

Remember: there is no new idea anywhere, any time, that is readily accepted by everyone. Be not dismayed. New ideas usually start with only one believer. Then a few more. The group increases. Finally, when the idea is in the bank, everyone claims to have invented it.

Shortly before all this, in late 1975, Lenora and I moved in together. These were busy times. In the wake of all the turmoil my leave-taking from Susie had precipitated, it was now time, as Lenora said, to start building memories, not regrets. We promised each other we'd do that.

The Elmsworth discovery well of 1976, preceded by six dry holes that cost a total of $6 million. That's me on the left, age 49, then Bob Sneider, Jim Gray, and Larry Meckel.

CHAPTER ELEVEN

DEEP BASIN

BOB SNEIDER, LARRY MECKEL, AND LLOYD FONS became our teachers, imparting their expertise in electric logs, reservoir engineering, and stratigraphic geology. They brought the advanced technology of Shell Oil to a group of clever, aggressive people who didn't know enough yet to be dangerous. They turned us into killers.

At the time, that wasn't immediately obvious. With great expectations, built on the discovery well at Elmworth, we drilled a third well there—and came up with a very dry hole. The fourth well was a dud, too. And the fifth and sixth. We were getting a little desperate and so were our angels at Noranda. Our program at Elmworth had so far cost $6 million to drill. The Board told Alf to shut us down. I pleaded with him for a seventh well. Every well had been located on a northeast trend. I wanted to go northwest. Alf replied: "The Board will have my head and yours too if you drill another million-dollar dry hole." I didn't flinch. "We've got beach conglomerates," I said. "If they don't go northeast, they've got to go northwest. We got to do this, Alf." He stuck with me. He was not a geologist. He was not an oilman. But he was a brave man. And he had built his career on logic.

We located our seventh well 12 miles from the dry holes but close to a promising old well. I prayed *northwest*. Here, finally, we hit it big again. The well blasted in for 24 million cubic feet of gas per day from the Falher formation. We were ecstatic with excitement. The logs correlated point for point with our first discovery well. The stratigraphic trend was clearly northwesterly. It seems dumb now that the first judgement indicated the trend was to the northeast. Dave Smith and Larry Meckel both went on to a lot of fine work in the early days of Elmworth, but I used to beat up on them for that original misinterpretation.

By March 1976, I recognized that the spread of our acreage from northeastern B.C. to the town of Erith in central Alberta, due west of Edmonton, seemed to be a continuous trend of gas accumulation. As clues, we had the data from the Elmworth discoveries, trend data from localized areas of formations like the Cadotte, and extensive log indications of pervasive gas zones. Gas could be saturating the specific layers of sandstones we were focusing on over this vast region. My cross-sections showed 12,000 feet of strata with gas indications in every sandstone layer. No such thickness of gas had ever been found anywhere before in North America. That was wonderful, but that was also what made it so hard to believe.

The most challenging element of brand-new discovery is not so much comprehending it as having confidence in yourself despite a wall of disbelief. How many grand ideas have been lost and forgotten in doubt?

The Deep Basin. That's what I christened it when drawing the first diagrammatic sketch of the wedge of gas-rich rocks straddling the Alberta-B.C. border. The phrase was designed to catch the attention of our people, to help sell the concept to investors, and eventually to describe it to the general geological community in Canada (although today in the U.S., everybody refers to this kind of accumulation as Basin Centered). In a staff meeting I outlined the trend and declared that from now on Hunter's exploration would "focus on the Deep Basin area from Jedney [in northeast B.C.] to Erith. This is the area of downdip water-sealed gas traps, the area of maximum sand content, and the area of maximum land availability because of previous lack of pipelines and lack of drilling."

By then we had a chief log analyst on staff, Ted Connolly, who'd been doing that job for Imperial Oil and now began hiring the best computer log-analysis group in the Canadian industry. He and his geologist colleagues, Earl Hawkes, Dunc McCowan, and Nick Wemyss, spent weeks painstakingly mapping the total potential of billions of cubic feet of gas per section. They emerged with a wall-wide map of hundreds of electric-log control points. It showed clearly and conclusively a massive concentration of natural gas in a thick grouping of sandstones in front of and parallel to the Rocky Mountain Foothills—a belt several hundred miles long and 60 miles wide straddling the Alberta-B.C. border. In this Deep Basin, as everyone would soon be calling it, we calculated that reserves averaged 17 BCF per section—an immense potential of 440 trillion cubic feet (TCF) of gas. I thought all of this gas would be recoverable. Inadequate engineering experience. Even after I learned to make better estimates, the ultimate recovery number would depend on gas prices and technological advances. But my final number of 30 TCF, worth about $30 billion net at those early prices, would mean, by itself, a 15-year supply of gas for Canadians. It would be the largest gas field ever found in Canada. And it would provide a vital new model for future discoveries. We found Elmworth a quarter-century ago. Fifty years from now, we'll still be producing Elmworth and finding new technology to get still more out of this incredible storehouse.

Our electric-log maps showed us quite clearly where the main volumes of gas would lie. But of equal importance was the concept of the region-spanning trap, as in the San Juan Basin and other capacious fields. We knew theoretically, academically, intellectually that all those widely scattered dry holes, which we analyzed as bypassed gas wells, were part of One Big Field. We were no longer paralyzed by the apprehension that there might be only small, isolated pools separated by large dry areas.

With the drilling of the seventh well (the second gas well), we established another geological concept that confirmed our growing confidence in the basin. Our field operators delivered heavy, cylindrical core samples from Elmworth to Calgary. Jim Gray and I, Dave Smith and Bob Sneider examined them at Core Lab, a petroleum service company specializing in reservoir description. We were focused on the Falher conglomerate—black-and-gray chert pebbles—the main pay where gas had flowed from about 6,500 feet deep. We were like a bunch of kids with new playthings, exclaiming about the size of the pebbles, enthusing about the porosity between them—all of us but Sneider marveling at the cores.

Bob was looking for something else. For many minutes he studied the rock intently with his hand lens, examining every foot of core, carefully, in sequence. Suddenly he snapped his fingers and said, beaming, "Goddamit, you guys, that's beach conglomerate! Pebble beaches. Look how well sorted it is. Look how it coarsens upward. They're not river channels, they're shoreline beach sands. I've seen exactly the same thing in California. These beaches go a long way."

He was telling us that the reservoirs of gas would be miles-wide and very long strips—rather than narrow, winding, and discontinuous channels. He didn't have to explain that a beach trend could hold tremendous reserves. And our two big wells, a dozen miles apart, demonstrated a northwesterly trend. We had discovered our first large field in the Deep Basin.

Our comprehension of the beach environment was a highly critical piece of geologic information. Rival companies considered the Elmworth area a graveyard of broken dreams, writing off the prospects as non-commercial. These multinationals, knowing that the pay zones there were conglomerates, assumed they were river channels. Giant Texaco had all the logs and cores but still did not understand it. They appeared not to know enough about sedimentation to make a proper reading. Sneider had learned how at Shell and his expertise would prove priceless. I was ready to go.

Bob and Larry Meckel were taken aback by my audacity, finding it strange and stressful that I would act so precipitously on preliminary indicators. They had come from a major company where the committee-bound review process would have insisted on finding all the answers to all the questions before acquiring any land. But we did not control the sales. The federal and Alberta governments were fighting over oil revenues, with Ottawa overtaxing windfall profits while the province was raising royalties. So the multinationals were pulling back and leases were cheap, down to as little as $15 an acre.

I was thinking *Blitzkrieg!* We scooped up hundreds of thousands of acres of oil and gas leases through sealed bids at sale after sale.

Our almost-religious zeal placed a serious burden on Alf Powis of Noranda, at a time when his company was facing much-reduced earnings and cash flow and mounting debt. As he later told Peter C. Newman (who recounted the conversation in a profile of me in *The Canadian Establishment*), "we had this Canadian Hunter demanding greater and greater gobs of money and, in my view, if we couldn't find it we were going to blow the opportunity of a lifetime. On the other hand, most of the rest of the industry thought they were nuts. I said to them, if you guys are really right, then the industry has an awful problem."

When it finally seemed prudent to advertise what we had done, this only brought forth a fresh barrage of criticism and derision. A lot of people wished we had never happened. Powis recalled, "If you're a Noranda director and Jack Armstrong [president of Imperial Oil] tells you that Noranda's nuts doing what it is, and Alf Powis sits there at a board meeting and says, 'No, we've really got something here'—who are you going to believe? . . . Obviously you're to believe Armstrong. You should. What do I know about the oil and gas business?"

Powis mused on, still perplexed that he was was doing what he was doing: "I guess it was in 1976, after a long argument with the board, that I finally got them to agree to a $15-million budget for Hunter in 1977. And by the middle of February they'd spent the whole thing on land sales around Elmworth."

In fact, we had already spent the entire budget for 1978 too. Powis looks back on that as one of the most acute embarrassments we ever dealt him — in a long string of them. After our spectacular overrun, the Noranda Board said it wouldn't come up with another dollar. (The Board did not distinguish itself in the early days of Elmworth.) Jim Gray began calling around the country and even overseas for additional financing. "When the field gets muddy," he liked to say, "you just put on longer cleats." Not surprisingly, Big Oil ignored us, as did the industrial companies.

One man's name kept popping up: Gus Van Wielingen of Sulpetro Ltd., a Calgary-based resources company that he'd built into a significant producer and then sold its Alberta land rights to Hudson's Bay Oil and Gas for $102 million. This sophisticated Dutch engineer, a close friend of Alberta Premier Peter Lougheed, understood oil technology and took risks. He listened as Jim poured on the excitement and promised to show him the Deep Basin project if he'd consider a joint venture. Our philosophy was always to make the exploration pitch before discussing the arithmetic. Prospective investors are always impatient to know the terms and, once they have them, can't pay attention to the technology. I did my dog-and-pony show with maps, electric-log readings, and colored pencils. Enthused, Gus agreed to invest $24 million in return for half of any acreage acquired (giving us the other half free). Peter Newman called it "the largest leveraged deal ever made in Canada where no prior acreage was involved." (While Van Wielingen eventually farmed out half his investment to CanDel Oil for $18 million, the remainder would swell 25-fold in value within five years.) His participation reassured Noranda's directors and pleased Alf Powis in particular, who began to think we might be walking on water.

After we went through the money from Gus, Jim made deals with a kaleidoscope of companies, including Canadian Commercial Bank, Capital Bag, and, oddly enough, Gray Beverages, a Vancouver soft-drink distributor.

When we again went cap in hand to Alf, he decided to sell a piece of Hunter to Kerr-Addison Mines—41-per-cent controlled by Noranda—which took 25 per cent of its parent's stake. A prominent brokerage firm advised: "Noranda Mines Ltd. is not allowed to borrow funds for exploration and development in Canadian Hunter. This fact, coupled with Noranda's deteriorating balance sheet (the result of weak base metal markets) and Hunter's insatiable appetite for exploration monies, opened the door for Kerr's participation in a venture which, under different conditions, would not have been available to them or anyone else. We are excited at the potential that this investment offers Kerr over the long term future." A Toronto invesment dealer also introduced us to Klaus Hebben, head man for significant German tax-shelter funds, who had co-financed Petromark, a successful exploration company. When we couldn't agree on the terms of a deal, Hebben went to Alf and, through him, to Kerr-Addison, which charged him $28 million for a ten-per-cent share of its Hunter holdings.

Lenora and I became close friends with Klaus and his partner, Dietrich Von Boetticher. They visited us in Canada and we vacationed with them in Germany, France, and on the Adriatic. They invested a lot of money in some of our projects and we showed them a lot about finding gas. We also learned why German soldiers were so tough.

About that time, we made another of our attempts to get the scientific community on-side and encourage favorable opinions among the regulatory authorities. We invited the Canadian Geological Survey's director of oil and gas reserves assessment and his assistant to an all-day presentation on the geology and reserve potential of Elmworth. At day's end, when everyone was tired and the room was relatively quiet, the director turned to his aide, hand over mouth, and whispered in a too-loud voice, "I sure hope they're not right. It would mean a lot of work for us."

It's perhaps surprising how little the experts shook our confidence. We were true believers. Yet I have to admit there was often a powerful sense of loneliness about our position, along with a fear that we might actually, by the slightest possibility, be wrong. What if the field would not produce as predicted over the long term? We would have spent all those millions in vain. Our careers would surely be ruined. No one would ever trust us again. You can be very smart, and highly trained, but no one can really see under the ground.

We had another sobering experience with engineers from the National Energy Board, the agency regulating Canada's oil, gas, and electrical industries. Realizing they doubted our claims for the Deep Basin, we asked them to our office for a private briefing. Several of us described our proprietary geologic and engineering data which, if publicized, could have led a competitor to potentially hundreds of millions of dollars worth of natural gas. As I told them, "geologists and engineers have a historic tendency to overestimate small deposits and an almost-tragic inability to recognize the size of really big deposits." None of the engineers showed the slightest interest—in fact, one of our severest critics actually dozed off during my talk. And taking our story to the B.C. Department of Energy in Victoria, we were met with the same disregard. After a long afternoon presentation, the provincial minister, his chief geologist, and others thanked us. Then the chief engineer, an old Shell hand, summed up: "All I'll say is I never heard so much bullshit in one afternoon in my life."

If your particular brain structure guides your life out to the edge, then—like Columbus—that's where you will find yourself. Nothing else will do. Those who don't get it may sail in a straight line all the way around to their starting place and still say it's all bullshit.

As I've said, it is an intrinsic part of human nature that new ideas are automatically rejected by almost all recognized experts. Nearly every one of the great inventions of the 19th and 20th centuries (among them the steamboat, wireless, radio, telephone, airplane) were scoffed at. The most advanced minds in science and engineering are just as unreceptive as the uneducated. Almost no one could see the promise of Spindletop, East Texas, Scurry, Prudhoe Bay, Elmworth, Kuwait, or Saudi Arabia. Discovery of new mechanisms, new mineral or oil deposits, new music, new art is always a very steep, uphill battle. How many world-changing concepts have been left behind and forgotten because the thinkers gave up against the pervasive negativitism?

Wallace Pratt, the great explorationist, wrote in 1952:

> A new field in a known trend of successful fields is very desirable but not a major intellectual accomplishment. If Company A doesn't find it Company B surely will. But, a new field in a new trend in a new area, where no oil has ever been found before—that is both a very significant intellectual achievement but also a personal triumph over the multitude of so-called experts who never willingly accept anything new. Searching for a big new field pits you against all the obstacles of science and nature. But, it also pits you against human nature. The former can be overcome by logic and luck. The latter never gives up until it is bulldozed or buried. Then, it claims to have always known the answer.
>
> Where oil is first found, in the final analysis, is in the minds of men. The undiscovered oil field exists only as an idea in the mind of some oil-finder. When no man any longer believes more oil is left to be found, no more oil fields will be discovered, but so long as a single oil-finder remains with a mental vision of a new oil field to cherish, along with freedom and incentive to explore, just so long new oil fields may continue to be discovered.

God graced me with more perception than most about oil, gas, and minerals, the secret riches in hidden places. The confusing thing is that while my perception is quite good, it is not perfect. Unfortunately, I can't tell the difference. No one else can either.

Never mind the stubborn Department of Energy engineer, northeastern British Columbia was a pivotal part of the Deep Basin. We came to know this after a field trip to California Larry Meckel took with his engineer, John Farina, our Dave Smith, and others on our staff. The idea was to study modern and Pleistocene-age conglomerate beaches (dating back between 1.8 million and 10,000 years) which might correspond to the Falher conglomerate trend we were seeing in Alberta. The province's ancient coastline must have looked much like the California coast today with its nearby mountains, pebbly conglomerate beaches, and pounding surf.

Thinking about that trip later, Dave Smith began speculating that if the Falher beaches in Alberta trended northwesterly, then they just might extend 50 miles across undrilled territory to the formation outcrops in the Rockies foothills of northeastern B.C. But what if the trend changed direction? We could look at the rock exposed at the surface along those mountains to seek telltale beach conglomerates somewhere on the north-trending outcrop. This would allow us to project the trend accurately from our last control well in Alberta all the way to the outcrop in British Columbia. This was high-powered exploration thinking. In July 1977 Larry Meckel offered to make the trip with our geologists, Dave Smith and Dunc McCowan. They flew to Fort St. John and took a helicopter southwest across 100 miles of virgin bush to the belt of outcrop. Few geologists had ever explored there in North America's untouched wilderness.

Landing first on Mount Belcourt, they scrambled up a cliff, looked carefully, hammered the rock, and studied it with a hand lens. No luck: wrong shales, wrong sands—continental rock. They flew a few miles north and repeated the process, with the same result. By mid-afternoon, hot and discouraged, thinking maybe the shoreline had turned north and they'd never find it in the outcrop belt, they decided to land one more time on a ledge below, on the massive cliffs of Bullmoose Mountain.

Hallelulujah! Here they found all the right stuff: rounded, sorted, coarsening-upward, stratified beach conglomerate, lying thickly on top of fine-grained foreshore sandstones. Two separate cliffs of conglomerate. Over there in Alberta, seeing those rocks in cores and samples, the shoreline was largely an intellectual concept. Here, in solid rock strung out for miles along the cliffs, it was real.

Meckel called me the minute they landed back in Fort St. John. "John, we found it!"

"Are you sure it was beach?" I asked.

His voice lowering in seriousness, he replied, "John, you could hear the goddam seagulls!" *They were screaming across a hundred million years of time.*

We had it then! Over the next two years we bought 336,000 acres of land in B.C. for $45 million and formed ventures there with other companies. Rarely in the industry's history has so much been bet on an interpretation of stratigraphic geology. It would take us many more years to bring in productive wells there, but now, in our fourth year of operation, we had defined the enormous boundaries of the Deep Basin. We were leading the industry! We were the hottest company in Canada!

We now had a director of research in the person of Dick Wyman, who came from Shell's research division in the U.S. He's worth describing in detail as an example of the kind of people we were fortunate enough to find during our adolescent years. Born a couple of years after me, in the back hills of Tennessee, Dick was raised by his widowed mother in California, where he hunted jackrabbits with a rifle. Although Dick was enamored with the earth sciences, he chose mechanical engineering at college. Then he served with the Strategic Air Command during the Korean War, overseeing the electronics of the Big Boy and Little Boy atomic weapons which happily were never needed. After grad school, he got into Shell's awesome training program, doing everything from roughnecking on a rig to learning about land and legal issues.

By 1956 he felt comfortable in any arm of the company. His first assignment was the west-coast petrophysical department, evaluating well logs (an appropriate bit of background for his eventual work with us). At Shell Development, the highly respected research branch in Houston, he helped appraise and nurture a new tool called the nuclear magnetism resonance (NMR) log. Although even its makers didn't understand its potential, NMR has since become an important tool in the petroleum industry to evaluate reservoirs and determine, among other things, the properties of porous rocks. Moving to New Orleans, Dick became chief of 250 engineers in offshore exploration, where Shell was a leader, drilling ever deeper with new technology. Back in Houston, he headed the petroleum engineering research department before being assigned to implement new high-tech geophysics in Canada by interpreting bright spots on seismic readings indicating the presence of natural gas.

Bob Sneider, who'd worked for him in Houston, insisted Dick meet me while in Calgary. In one of my infrequent appearances in the deep-carpeted, wood-panelled Petroleum Club, we had a weighty philosophical discussion about exploration and my belief in the lesser role of engineers. Dick argued back, adamant about the importance of integrating the geological and engineering disciplines. He returned to Texas and that was the last I saw of him for two years. Then in 1976 Dick wrote a long paper extolling the virtues of exploring tight-sand formations and other alternative sources of natural gas. As he tells it, a subsequent meeting with a Shell Vice-President did not go well. The man actually yawned.

Dick finally let loose: "You said that we must do everything we can to improve our reserves of gas and I think there's a good potential with this!"

"Yeah," the VP said, "I worry about that now and then."

So when approached by Sneider on our behalf not long after, Dick Wyman was ripe pickings. To lure this outstanding scientist of more than two decades' experience, we paraded our technical people before him to demonstrate what we were doing. I guess we communicated our enthusiasm so strongly that he wrote me an excited letter saying he'd work for us for nothing—a statement he later regretted but didn't have to honor when we made him a generous offer.

After finally leaving the oil giant in 1977, Dick said, "I have tried for seven years to get people to understand that tight sands offer the biggest potential for new reserves of gas. I believe that Hunter is the only company in the business which understands that. I want to be part of the action." He was a fine engineer, a good geologist, and one hell of a researcher—a bridge linking our many technical specialties—and the only guy who understood everything we were doing. It was a dream job for his skills and, in the coming years, he took us in several new directions via his knowledge.

* * *

By August 1977 we appeared to be over the financial and emotional hump of building a startup into a real company. When a well at the south end of Elmworth kicked in at a flow rate of 18 million cubic feet a day, the office was jubilant. Jim said, "I guess we can all retire now." We could have, it seemed, on just what we'd found in the past seven days, our most amazing week of exploration success. It began in the B.C. foothills where a joint well, in partnership with British Petroleum, tested the Triassic formation at a roaring 21 million cubic feet a day. Then, in quick succession, we made discoveries at nine other wells in Alberta. That single week, we estimated, may have added half a billion dollars to the value of the company.

But we still needed cold, hard—or warm, soft—anything but hot, ill-gotten—cash. Acquiring more land, drilling scores of wells, kept us on an endless treadmill of fund-raising. In our courting of investors, we soon learned, nothing worked better than taking them out to the field. After a quick plane trip from Calgary to Elmworth, they hopped in a helicopter to fly over our vast field. We pointed out our 20 to 30 rigs drilling down there in the forest between the dim horizons to the north, south, east, and west. With a big smile, I said, "It's all ours!" I reminded everyone aboard that they'd never seen so many square miles. Then the chopper landed beside one of our big gas wells, where we presented "the Sacred Ceremony."

A testing crew had the well hooked up to a flare line directed into a large pit with a high dirt back wall. When all were safely behind the well, my partner gave a John Wayne signal like "Let 'er go, boys!" and they slowly cranked the well open. The gas ignited with a *whump!* The tester continued to crank, calling off the flow numbers from his gauge: "Five million . . . eight million . . . ten . . . twelve . . . fourteen . . . *sixteen million.*" Now, shouting at the top of his lungs: "Is that enough Mr. Masters?" He was coached to indicate clearly that he could keep going, but everyone would be at serious risk.

The ground shook, you could feel it, the noise like a 727 taking off, the heat ferocious (we had them standing so close they'd have to back away), and you could barely hear someone yelling in your ear. After several minutes—long enough to make them think the world was on fire—I waved for a shut-off and the tester cranked it down quickly to a lazy flame, and then there was silence. The dead, unearthly silence of the northern bush, 350 miles north of Calgary. There were coughs, nervous laughs, then typically one of the visitors flashed a wide smile and clapped a Hunter on the back or shook my hand. Finally, pandemonium and joy! Few of them had ever seen Hell tapped into. The scene never failed to have an extraordinary impact, especially on people who'd had a sneaking suspicion the day was going to confirm their worst doubts about our project.

"You have just seen the only practical solar-energy system you will ever see," I told them. "That gas came from the energy of the sun, 100 million years ago, that was transformed by photosynthesis and concentrated into a jillion tons of plant life. It was later buried and chemically altered, by the heat of the earth, into methane gas. I wanted you to come out and see that miracle.

"And just as an added little touch, we wanted to show you that it's not all stored in tight sands. We have some conglomerate reserves about 7,000 feet below us which are among the highest-quality pay zones in all of Canada. A lot of people don't believe this, but now you can say to them, 'Have you ever been up and seen those wells?'"

Each trip, we took home a happy group of potential investors or new supporters. Few of them could doubt any longer.

CHAPTER TWELVE

THE ELMWORTH MIRACLE

THERE WERE MANY MIRACLES at Elmworth, beyond that of transforming plant life into gas. One of the first was the fact that after the headwork of making my original wall-width map from electric-log analyses, it had really taken only two days to analyze the data and find the field. The next was my *eureka!* identification of the upside-down nature of our basin, where the gas was peculiarly located downdip from the water. Yet another: our drilling a second, deeper well beyond the zone we were focused on and discovering gas in the Falher conglomerates below. Perhaps not a miracle but a blessing was the fact that, although our agreement with the people at Texaco hadn't allowed us to drill that discovery well, they decided not to call us on it. Definitely miraculous, to this agnostic, was Bob Sneider's recognition that our conglomerates were actually a beach trend capable of huge reserves—and none of our rivals recognized this. Not even our partner, Texaco. And Larry Meckel's phone call to me in the summer of 1977 that he and Dave Smith had found the same conglomerate beach trend in the mountains of British Columbia, which defined the expanse of the Deep Basin—the largest-ever gas field in Canada.

We had placed a bet and won big. That year we drilled 37 oil wells and 53 gas wells. Our drilling success ratio was an astonishing 84 per cent. We signed the last "take-or-pay" contract TransCanada Pipelines made for many years. They would process and transport all of our gas from 40 townships, beginning in 1979, giving us an assured market to justify the enormous investment in wells. And in the five years since 1972, the price of gas had increased nine-fold. Remember my first estimates. By the end of 1977, Canadian Hunter had almost doubled its staff to fifty-five.

Yet, although Hunter had strode like a giant the past year, we still had to hustle to keep ahead of the competition. The plan was to acquire as much land as possible at the big sales in British Columbia during the winter of 1978—when we'd have the maximum drilling results available and snow in the mountains would prevent rivals from examing the revealing outcrops until the following summer. I wrote Noranda's president a long letter in March:

Dear Alf,

We have 200,000 acres posted [for sale] for April 6. We have got to hit that sale like a ton of bricks...whatever we pay, the land can only increase in value...The April sale is where we have to lay it on the line. That will be our last chance.

In a way, the March sale was good for us. We got the best tract, just barely, and we learned a helluva lesson. In this business, you never stay ahead of the game for long. The rest of the industry is too smart and too rich for any one company to stay out in front.

I must tell you what is beginning to show clearly from the results of the January, February and March sales in Alberta and B.C. First, the strength of the sales is obviously building. Many more companies are bidding on many more tracts. Experienced landmen can sense this at the sales, like brokers at the stock exchange. The hum of business turns into a roar. Our landmen are seeing dozens more men at the sales, carrying bundles of bid envelopes. The per acre price at the last B.C. sale was the highest in history. It did not result from a few spectacular bids, but a solid, healthy price on nearly every tract offered.

We can still buy acreage out on the plains, I am sure. But any acre we can buy in the next six months will never be cheaper. In one year, Alf, this will be a different ball game. It will be dog eat dog, the kind of competition I knew in the U.S. We'll still make money, but it won't be stealing like we've been doing.

In the Deep Basin, we have not yet seen any appreciable competition. I think that means the following: companies are rapidly picking up the log analysis idea, but no one has collected enough information over the whole area to put together the regional picture. This is a conceptual problem. It is impossible to know when it will flash on some widely experienced geologist. He'll be ignorant one day, but in the middle of the night he'll suddenly understand the whole thing. We know that Amoco understands the entire concept in the U.S. Rocky Mountains, but incredibly, they do not yet recognize its application in Canada. They will, sure as hell. Shell should also pick it up soon.

The only thing we can do is speed up acreage buying as fast as possible. Once the big boys are onto the idea, then watch out. They will brush us aside like a fly.

I must tell you in the strongest terms: the incredible opportunity that has been Noranda's is fast disappearing. With the acreage we have now, we are a major company, but we can double this in the next several months. By the end of this year, we may have to be pretty selective about where we try to compete.

At the risk of being terribly presumptuous, I submit that the most important corporate decision you and I may ever make will be how much money we can get for acreage buying in the next six months.

We are blasting ahead on the assumption that somehow you will find the money for us. What is done in the next several months will lay the foundation, huge or only big, for the future company.

Our directive, as we understand it, is to bid heavily at the B.C. sale, even if we go over the budget, and then figure out a solution later, either by bank loans or selling some to a partner. This method is entirely satisfactory to me. We can get back inside the budget later.

I apologize, Alf, for being so 'pushy' about this acreage money. But, in my whole experience, I have only one time previously seen a major exploration move that so clearly needed to be done—with speed and daring and big bucks. The other time was Ambrosia Lake. I laid my career on the line to McGee that it was the right thing to do. I feel the same way about this. The Deep Basin acreage is an absolutely unique opportunity to make a giant gas company.

Let's charge . . .
John

When people later asked if we were wary of charging ahead so dramatically, I responded with a reworking of a wonderful Mark Twain line: "We had the serene confidence which a Christian feels—in four aces."

In early 1978, Jim and I also decided we held a good enough hand to go public with the Deep Basin. Our rationale for finally telling our story was complex. Canada's national energy policy had to change if we ever hoped to market the potentially massive resources of the basin. But first we'd have to overturn the entire scientific community's thinking about gas reserves: the conventional wisdom in Canadian industry, government, and media said the country was running out of gas—the tank would probably run dry within 20 to 30 years. Besides, we realized that our technological and conceptual lead would last only another year and, given Noranda's financial constraints, it seemed unlikely we could buy appreciably more land during that period. Meanwhile, our Board of Directors was nervous about other companies' skepticism of a project in which Noranda had invested such huge sums. More altruistically, Jim Gray and I wanted Canadians to have the benefit of a vast supply of cheap energy to shore up their economy the way North Sea oil had backstopped the British.

For these reasons, both selfish and generous, we decided to tell the world what we'd discovered. The Hunter way was to broadside public and scientific opinion with a coordinated information barrage. We began with a speech titled "A Peek at an Emerging Giant" that Dave Smith gave to the Canadian Society of Petroleum Geologists in May. Outside the local industry, his presentation didn't create much of a stir, but my talk in June did. I delivered my Deep Basin paper to an international conference the Geological Society sponsored in Calgary:

> Geological evidence suggests the probable existence of an enormous gas accumulation trapped in the deepest part of the Alberta syncline . . . it is large enough that it will probably significantly increase Canada's total resource base and have a significant impact on the economy of the country. These large supplies could displace part of Canada's foreign oil requirements and, exported to the United States, could resolve Canada's serious balance-of-payments deficit . . .
>
> Electric-log analyses of most of the wells in the Deep Basin show 84 per cent of them to carry recoverable gas, averaging 17 BCF per section.
>
> The entire Deep Basin area is indicated to contain potential recoverable gas resources of 440 TCF.
>
> Recoverable gas at $2 per mcf (millions per cubic feet) net after royalty may reach 150 TCF.
>
> Such large quantities of gas could have a powerful effect on Canada's national economy in addition to significantly increasing North America's total energy supply.

The speech was a stunning surprise to that standing-room-only audience of knowledgeable geologists. They were especially startled when I showed them the slide of land holdings and announced that all those names on the map were pseudonyms (like Smith or Jones Land Companies)—and the *real owner* of all that acreage was Canadian Hunter Exploration! A geological elder told me afterward, "I have never seen an entire industry fooled right out of their pants." It was surely one of the great days of my life.

Suddenly we were the Little Company That Could. "Noranda's Belief in Elmworth Paid Off," the Toronto *Globe and Mail* headlined. "Gas Find Seen Swelling Canadian Surplus," the *Wall Street Journal* said conservatively. The title of a *Canadian Business* article was more bullish— "Up to our ass in gas"—and the magazine, noting we were the most prominent of Canada's independent gas companies, estimated Hunter was now worth up to $1 billion (it also said "Hunter's success is a clear illustration of the virtues of buying when it takes more courage than dollars"). The message even got out to the general public in a *Reader's Digest* piece, which enthused: "Backing hunches with hard work, two Calgary giant-killers made what may be the biggest gas discovery in Canadian history—a spectacular energy bonus for all of us."

If our approach to competition sounds opportunistic and unfair, we thought of it as guerilla warfare. Hunter was a small company with a limited budget, scared to death that one or more of the majors would wake up and blow us out of the water. We had neither the money nor the muscle to play the game straight up; we had to use all the smoke and mirrors we could find. Since Elmworth, most companies have adopted our tactic when involved in a sequence of sales. Now, reading Alberta's sales results, I believe that most exploration directions are heavily camouflaged.

Summing up, Carl Nickle, the far-sighted publisher of Calgary's *Daily Oil Bulletin*, editorialized: "In our view, there is no longer any doubt but that the Deep Basin concept outlined by John Masters is valid. In fact, the Canadian Hunter team deserves the primary credit for establishing through research and huge risk-capital spending what may well be one of the largest Natural Gas Reserve Basins in the world." Nickel later put his money where his pen was by investing $1.7 million with us just one hour before a land sale.

The Canadian stock markets began to react to the news of more gas where none was supposed to be, and now the majors were paying close attention. Fortunately, I had an astute advisor to consult when one of them came calling. A photograph of the late Mark Millard is among the three portraits I still have hanging in my gallery of heroes. He was a senior advisor at New York's prestigious brokerage Loeb Rhoades & Co. (later Shearson Loeb Rhoades and then Lehman Brothers). Author Peter Foster describes him well as "the very epitome of a Wall Street Financier and one of the leading lights at Loeb Rhoades." He then writes, a little hyperbolically, that his mid-European accent and impeccable manners "somehow remind one of a perhaps more benign version of Count Dracula." Foster tells the story of how Mark had been introduced to me at a dinner party given by Bob Wisener, who ran the Calgary branch of the Walwyn, Stodgell brokerage firm. "Millard was as impressed by Masters as Toronto-based mining giant Noranda had been, and Imperial Oil was to be . . ."

Mark became a dear friend as well as a financial mentor, a man I could call anytime for advice in the investing field, which was as foreign to me as the Navajo language. Amazingly, he never exacted a fee for his counsel, saying that someday I might be able to return the favor (which I happily did). He was one of those advisors whom I turned to when Imperial Oil finally came knocking. We had once approached Imperial to invest in Canadian Hunter; the nation's largest petroleum company diplomatically declined. We couldn't help feeling that the big kahuna of Canadian oil, the mighty subsidiary of Exxon, thought of us as a poor, raw country bumpkin.

All that changed when we signed an agreement with them in August 1978, the largest of its kind ever. As I gleefully recorded in my leather-bound notebook at the time:

> On July 3 [1978], Cal Evans, Imperial's Vice-President of Exploration, called on me in my office (one cannot but be pleased when the largest oil company in the world is sitting in your reception area awaiting your pleasure). He proposed that Imperial would do $60 million of drilling to earn a range of interests at Elmworth. The proposal was terribly complicated. However, in the inevitable later discussions between us, Jim said, 'Why don't we give them ten per cent of the whole company for a lot of money like the Petromark deal?' It was the kind of flash idea which has made us modestly famous. We both sensed instantly it was a winner. In a few more moments we agreed to ask them for $150 million for ten-per-cent interest. That is precisely the amount of study that went into the structuring of the richest farmout deal in Canadian oil history.

In the end, Imperial agreed to spend a total $179 million to drill and complete wells over thirty months in return for 12.5 per cent of our Elmworth holdings and 17.5 per cent of our other acreage. I still have a homemade trophy in my office that some of the Imperial guys presented me to symbolize what they thought we'd done to their company: it's a gilded, bent screwdriver on a stand. *The Financial Post*, Canada's major business newspaper, wrote: "For Noranda, the deal establishes its funding of Canadian Hunter as its shrewdest investment in recent years." Alf Powis sent us a telex from Toronto: "To have achieved this from a standing start five years ago is a truly incredible feat. . . . You and your associates can take enormous and justifiable pride in your accomplishments to date."

Mark Millard had already delivered an exultant message to the Noranda board: "This is a miracle because, when the deserving get what they deserve in this day and age, that is a miracle. Gentlemen, Canadian Hunter's credibility is now absolutely bullet-proof; their reputation has been attested by the largest oil company in the world." Later, to me, Mark said: "Oh, if I could dance, I would. This is so wonderful."

That fall there was a lot of celebrating, if not dancing, after a consulting firm's report on Elmworth to the National Energy Board indicated Hunter gas reserves of 900 billion cubic feet. Boastfully, we ordered T-shirts bearing the optimistic slogan "1,000 T.C.F." — *trillion* feet, no less — and threw a party in the seventh-floor reception area with banners, champagne, shrimp, and great helpings of satisfaction.

Imperial's buy-in turned the tide. Carpers and nay-sayers still remained, but they were being left behind, stranded on the flats, sinking into the mud. We watched with little sympathy as they went down. Canadian Hunter, a small venture virtually unknown to the industry, had sailed in under the noses of 400 other companies and netted a monster.

In 1978 we drilled 116 oil and gas wells, 38 of them exploratory, with a combined success ratio of 85 per cent. Our net revenue exceeded $7 million and we now had ninety-eight hunters working their hearts out — clever, aggressive people who had turned into killers.

The truth is, however, that until the early 1980s, there was still a lot of brinkmanship and seat-of-the-pants flying in our shop. For about three years — 1977-1979 — I guessed pretty closely what our competitors would bid in the land sales that happened almost every month, with values escalating at every sale. I knew this because of the experience of our own wells, the information our scouts gleaned about our rivals' wells, and a keen sense of how the play was developing. But often, after all our experts had exhaustively considered a bid, I'd have a change of heart and the night before a sale call our head landman, Jim Chaput, to alter our offer. Yet on 83 sale parcels during those three years, Hunter won 82. We bought 675,000 acres for $130 million, averaging less than $200 an acre. Landmen later admitted that we were sometimes beating them by only $5 or even $1.75 per acre. I don't hold much with ESP; all I suggest is that you can boost your performance well above normal in anything by really focusing, living and breathing it night and day, and positioning yourself to gather more information than anyone else. We worked very hard at that last element, recognizing which piece of land would give us the critical drilling location to collect the best data to evaluate a future sale.

Those scouting reports of rival wells were vital to us. Before Elmworth, such espionage hadn't been carried out with the same intensity we brought to the game. "You can't steal in Calgary," the murky ethic seemed to state, "but anything goes in the field"—listening in on telephone calls and mobile radios, peering from a distance through binoculars, eavesdropping on roughnecks in a bar, or befriending mud men and drillstem-test crews. One of our electric-log experts, Ron Hietala, likes to hark back to our first office in the field, room 123 in Grande Prairie's Norway Hotel. "When the first land sales happened and the tests were being drilled, there were wire taps on us. So everybody tried to stay away from there while the scouts in the area were trying to steal information back and forth." Our people learned never to call from a motel phone or even a pay phone, unless they were sending deliberately misleading information. We comforted ourselves that we stole only from the rich.

Scouting in the Alberta bushland had its own peculiar problems. One day a scout called our Calgary office from the mobile in his truck. "Wait a second," he began, "I've got to roll up the window."

"What's the matter? Is it cold?"

"Naw, just a bear trying to get in here."

Cold? Sometimes it was 50 below zero.

We had three guys then in the land department who spent $130 million at 29 sales in three years. Think of the most awful goof-up imaginable, and we made it. But like Pauline in peril on the railway tracks as the engine comes hurtling down, we always escaped in the nick of time. Some of these near-misses were so horrendous that they were only confessed to me a decade later. One day, for instance, Gary Aitken left $21 million in certified checks in an envelope on his kitchen table when he caught a plane for a government sale in Victoria. A colleague came to the rescue, picking up the payment, and taking a direct flight that beat Aitken to the B.C. capital.

Once, on the afternoon before a land sale the next day, we still hadn't decided on the amount of our bid for the acreage. Finally, late in the day, one of our people called the manager we dealt with at the Canadian Imperial Bank of Commerce, who asked, "How much do you need?"

"Twenty-five million," he allowed.

"Good lord, you guys, that's me, personally. If the auditors are here tomorrow, I lose my job. I can't do this. You want 25 million, and you haven't got a hundred bucks in the bank?"

After we pleaded and he wouldn't budge, Jim Gray called him. "Mac, what the hell's wrong with that cheap outfit you've got over there? What's the big deal about 25 million bucks? You know we're good for it."

Mac, looking over his shoulder, came through.

Our seemingly whimsical and free-wheeling approach to operations in those years relied on the superiority of our people and the confidence they developed working in teams. Our young purchasing manager, Gerald Schultz, supervised acquisition of all the iron necessary to supply 20 drilling rigs. Just two weeks on the job, he placed an order for $27 million of pipe and then, recalling the formal policies at his previous job, he had second thoughts and decided to check with Jim: "Does it bother you that I just signed a purchase order for $27 million?"

"No."

"Do I need to have these approved by anyone else?"

"No. I don't know anything about pipe, and I doubt if anyone else does. Isn't that what you do?"

"Yup—I guess. . . . What if there's a problem?" he wondered.

"It's your ass, not mine," Jim said. "Is that fair?"

"I can live with that."

Schultz got to know Jim Boyd, our completions man, who had run more than a thousand hydraulic fractures of wells in his 17 years at Halliburton, one of the world's major suppliers to the petroleum industries. "Let's have a meeting," Boyd suggested. That meant their discussion had now turned formal. "You know those valves that have handles like this?" he asked, showing and telling.

"Yeah — WKMs."

"I like those. Let's not buy anything else."

And so the Canadian Hunter policy on valves was established.

Our men and women stretched themselves thin. Out in the field during 1980, as an example, we had 10 service rigs — the truck-mounted equipment brought in to complete a well and improve production. Jim Boyd stick-handled reports and gave operating instructions to all of those rigs for 340 nights in a row. During the day, he designed the fracs — with a calculator, but no secretary. Almost single-handedly, he invented the fracturing procedures at Elmworth, learning how to frac conglomerates by being right on the spot in the control trucks. He showed the industry how you can take good wells flowing gas at 10 million cubic feet per day and hammer them up to 25 mmcfd. No one had ever done that before as standard operating practice. The rule had been, "If it's a good well, don't mess with it."

As the new decade began, we started to solidify the great teams that distinguished Hunter from our competitors. My introduction of team organization into our technical procedures was instrumental in our success. The classic structure of a petroleum-exploration company was top-down hierarchical, split into geophysical, engineering, geology, land, and accounting groups. Orders went down and results went up. VPs or senior managers amassed the data from the various departments and created the technical picture on which they made decisions. I realized early on that managers don't know nearly as much about geology and geophysics as the guys doing the job. The old system of trading that information at the top was clumsy and inadequate because the problems could be solved better at a much lower level. Yet geologists typically didn't talk to engineers (in many companies, they weren't even introduced). And geophysicists were actively discouraged from wandering into geologists' offices to check a map — and seldom had the benefit of a working geologist suggesting, "That probably isn't steep dip; the wells tell you there's a lot of parallel faulting in there." But if they had worked together, as in our teams, they could have modified and improved their interpretations early in the process. However, none of our rivals did it that way.

Denise Woofter, a confident skiing whiz who'd taken an oil-geology course I taught at the University of Calgary, joined us as a 22-year-old geologist in 1981. All these years later, she remembers the Hunter team approach as deeply democratic. "When I think of Canadian Hunter right now," she says, sitting in her charming house in Calgary, "I think about the people before the geology. And the recognition that success wasn't one person's. It may sound clichéd, but as a geologist you never said 'it's my play'—it was 'our well, our play'. And anyone who ever said 'my play' didn't last very long. There was always an engineer behind you—or with you, I should say. We as staff recognized that it worked." Denise was one of my stars who spoke with deep knowledge of our company.

As I said in a commentary to the staff, we built teams to solve specific problems—and upon fixing them, a team dissolved, to be re-formed into other active teams. I didn't want one team to have a separate existence, a protected life of its own. So each specialist might work in two or three teams, being a manager in one, a member in another. The teams reported to me, I helped them with personnel problems, and was always involved in final reviews and conclusions. This system doubled or tripled our technical output, improved quality, pushed responsibility down the line, and expanded each individual's understanding of the larger process to which he or she was contributing. Canadian Hunter truly introduced this team approach in the oil business and our friend, Bob Sneider, promulgated it widely. The idea didn't merely work well for us. It virtually revolutionized the organizational structure of the exploration and development industry. From time to time, I've seen a well-worn quotation of mine repeated at petroleum conferences: "In tomorrow's complex technology, you cannot put individuals up against well-integrated teams. It is a no-contest situation."

A physical symbol of what we'd created within the company was our roof garden. In the late 1970s our burgeoning operation moved into seven

A typical Canadian Hunter exploration meeting, with me in the background.

floors of offices at 4th Avenue and 4th Street, in Calgary's very core. The penthouse garden, built at a cost of $50,000, was designed to offer a pleasant and relaxing place for lunch with its cedar decking and lawn chairs ringed by trees, shrubs, and flowers. Some colleagues wondered how we could justify such an expenditure. I'd already thought out the answer: "This roof garden will be the company's meeting place. It will belong to everyone, not just one department or another. This is where everyone will get their strongest sense of working together in one unified group. The spirit will be harmonious, and it will be prideful, because no other company in town has anything like it. The money is irrelevant. The spirit is everything."

And it was.

CHAPTER THIRTEEN

FAMILIES

ALL OF THIS CORPORATE SUCCESS was unfolding against a backdrop of great joy for Lenora and me—and then, with devastating suddenness, great personal tragedy. We were living in an apartment in Calgary, when on August 1, 1977, our first son was born. His mother, who'd walked a couple of miles a day to the end of her pregnancy, was in good shape, determined to have a perfect baby. Robert Lantz—his middle name honoring my first mentor—was a big, healthy, strong-willed platinum blond ("angel's hair," his mother called it). For a long time before his birth, Lenora had all Robbie's clothes ready and waiting, folded perfectly in a drawer. I always knew she wanted a child to fulfill herself as a woman and, although fifty years old at the time, I was pleased for her and for us. Over the past couple of years we had been planning—and were soon to move into—a dramatically designed home outside the city where we could raise our child in the fresh foothills air.

Meanwhile, I was teaching a course at the University of Calgary a couple of times a week, introducing students to the real world of petroleum geology. My department head was shocked at the work I made for myself by assigning each of them a term paper on a different topic. As the old truism has it, I was learning more than they did while boning up on arcane areas of the subject that had eluded me in my own education. After reading a textbook about the relatively new science of geochemistry, I had its author—a sophisticated professor, Dietrich H. Welte—fly over from Germany to consult with Canadian Hunter.

As I taught college kids, ran a growing, aggresive exploration company, and became a new father, my life seemed full of youth and promise.

Then less than two weeks after Lenora gave birth to Robbie, our whole world changed. I was still legally married to Susie, who continued to refuse me a divorce. I think the only solution to her situation she could countenance was for me to apologize and return to the marriage. In the years after I left, she'd gone into a heartbreaking decline. Trying, and failing, to muster the will to take courses at university and look for a job, she retreated into herself—and into alcohol, which must have made her feel all the more alone. Although never a drinker, she began spending too much time with a woman neighbor who became a drinking companion. Susie's mother had suffered from mental problems that instutitionalized her and now the daughter sank into deep depression. At one point, Barbie had to commit her to a psychiatric ward. Susie received shock therapy, which apparently helped briefly. She made attempts to quit drinking, but a kind neighbor named Al reported later that whenever he stopped in to check on her, she was invariably drunk.

Then on Saturday, August 13—our son Alan's seventeenth birthday—the neighbor came to visit again. He found Susie slumped over in her car, in the garage, with the engine running. She was gone. Perhaps this was the only escape she could finally achieve.

I was off on a field trip, so Jim Gray came to our door and told Lenora in person. Luckily, her parents were there to see the new baby and helped her try to deal with the horrific news. I wept too after hearing it, crushed with grief at the loss of a once-vivacious woman whom so many people had loved, whom I had loved in the beginning. In the days that followed, I asked my secretary, Debbie Morrice, to help with funeral details; when she came to my home, I couldn't stop crying. And, for a time, I felt the unavoidable guilt: what terrible thing should I do to myself to compensate for her death? Or should I just go away and never come back? Arthur Miller, the playwright, once wrote: "A suicide kills two people . . . that's what it's for!" But with my devotion to Lenora and our new son, and my love of my three other kids, I couldn't afford to wallow in any dramatic act of contrition.

The older children reacted individually, in their fashion. Ever since I'd left Susie, Chuck had been a support to me, as well as his mother, and continued to be in his sober-minded manner. Barbie, with her profound sensitivity, was less forgiving in her rage against her mother's death; she told me plainly that she needed time alone to deal with it. While it was years before we talked in any depth, when we did—before she had children of her own—we came to a kind of peace. Alan, though, was still a high-school student, had still been at home with Susie, and he took her suicide the hardest. Reluctantly, he came to live with Lenora and me for less than six months before moving out to the acreage of a friend's family outside Calgary. My heart ached with the realization that I hadn't seen him often enough during his crucial mid-teens. And, like Barbie, Alan avoided me for a few years. Intellectually, I understood their anger and their need for distance, but even the temporary loss of them in my life was painful.

My mother's long-ago warning about marriage had resurfaced: "I'm not telling you how to live your life, but the decisions you make in that regard are very serious." Several months after Susie died, my mother acknowledged that it takes two people to end a relationship. "I always felt you must have been at fault," she admitted to me. "I was like everybody else, believing that Susie was only sweet—but I'm beginning to see she could be pretty stubborn." Her words, if not offering absolution, were at least compassionate, understanding.

* * *

A corporate family is a complement to, not a substitute for, your own. But it is one of life's bonuses if you can help create an atmosphere in your workplace that reflects the finest familial qualities. Eric Hoffer, the American social philosopher, said *esprit de corps*, that intangible concept, comes from a sense of pride and a sense of family. During our first decade, Hunter's *esprit* was tangible and forceful. There was pride that we were performing so well and the industry was talking about us. And a family atmosphere because, despite our accelerating growth, we were all such good friends at the office and took pains to include spouses in our unusually successful company activities. Along with the usual office parties and all-day picnics, the company had golf tournaments, Christmas balls, ski weekends (and each year a week of powder skiing at a remote B.C. lodge), even geology field trips, think-tank sessions at Banff, and tours to Elmworth. We routinely hired employees' children to do meaningful work for us in the summer (along with many geology students, several of whom came to work for us after graduating). No employee was ever fully integrated into the Hunter team unless his or her family was involved; most spouses thought of us as their company too. For instance, we leased four ski cabins at Banff for everyone to use during the winter. "Healthy body, healthy mind," as my secretary, Debbie Morrice, said. "Work hard, play hard."

The depth of the bonding sprang from the qualities of the people who came together at Canadian Hunter. We purposefully went after the best, both in technical and personal terms, and by attracting the cream from other companies we came to be called Canadian Rustlers.

A typical catch was Ron Hietala. Blond-haired, kindly son of a grain farmer, he'd worked on drilling rigs in western Alberta before taking earth sciences at a community college, graduating at the top of the class. He was very smart. The year we started Hunter, he wound up as a wellsite geologist for Imperial Oil around the province and in the Arctic gas fields in the Mackenzie River delta. Hietala became a specialist in computerized well-log interpretation in which Imperial was a technical leader. In 1976, his log-analyst mentor, Ted Connolly, left Imperial for Hunter when he became unhappy at how little the seismic-dependent Imperial was applying his log analysis to exploration. His protégé had no intention of following him to work for a small independent like us. Then Hietala attended an Exxon geology school in Houston where Bob Sneider was guest-lecturing on the value of teamwork among the industry's various disciplines. Afterward, discussing the consulting work he was doing with Connolly at Hunter, Bob excited Ron into applying to us. As most often happened then, both Jim Gray and I interviewed Hietala, who was impressed with our passionate belief in the Deep Basin.

We lured him too with our profit-sharing plan for the early group of vice-presidents and senior managers, offering net-profit pieces from the 12.5-per-cent pie we'd negotiated for ourselves at Noranda. Eventually, we gave away about half of our share in incentives—which collectively could total many millions of dollars a year. Other employees who came later got bonuses based on individual performance, with points awarded for years of service and level of salary. Most of these people would do anything I asked of them without bitching about it, even working 15 hours a day if necessary, and spending a lot of time away from home in brief bursts of corporate hyperactivity. Our philosophy, ahead of its time in the industry, was simple: people are motivated by a financial reward beyond salary—by anticipating something remunerative at the end of the tunnel—in return for expending that extra effort. Most employees can count just as well as their bosses. A salary survey of 102 petroleum companies in the early 1980s showed that in 80 per cent of the job categories, the top Hunter employee was either the first- or second-highest-paid person in the Canadian industry. And we had a more extensive profit-sharing/bonus scheme than any other company, more perks in recreation allowances and days off, and less bureaucratic hassle.

Hietala also liked the overall Hunter environment. Reminiscing not long ago, he recalled our Think Tanks at resorts like Jasper where families could enjoy the outdoors, the golf links and lakeside barbecues, while husbands or wives brainstormed about current challenges and future directions. Jim and I listened hard to them and tried to instill our conviction that all of them were crucial to the success of the enterprise. In an effort to build their confidence in the company, we would even have our chief financial officer open up our books to give specific confidential numbers about how Hunter was doing. A memo I sent to participants in 1984 sums up not only the evolving mood of those sessions but also the corporate flavor in general:

> I have had discussions with several of you concerning the subject matter of the Think Tank weekend. There is a general concern that we do not deal with weighty enough matters and various suggestions have been made to increase the effectiveness of the meeting.
>
> This is a meeting to which we have grown accustomed to inviting about 30 participants. Planned or not, we sacrificed its ability to be a real thinking session. However, it has evolved into a very meaningful social occasion, the only time we can get together as a small unit in the way we did when we were young. Each time we have had the meeting, I think the feeling at the end has always been one of renewal. Everyone is surprised and pleased at the comfortable feeling of satisfaction that we all gain from being together and talking together about our problems and our hopes.
>
> I don't think it is terribly important that we do not reach momentous decisions. It is enough if we confirm a mutual harmony. At times, in fact, the meeting has illuminated problems of disharmony and served to bring those situations closer to solution. . . .

Ron, who has a marvellous technical mind, soon took charge of our log analysis. I relied on him to make sense of reservoir fluids and properties, read rock porosity, permeability, and water saturation to identify pay zones and make recommendations about whether to drill a million-dollar well or back off. The only time he blindsided me was the day he and Jay Christensen showed up with their hair permed into tight curls. I thought it was a joke, but no, their wives had convinced them to do the deed, which I tried to overlook as a temporary lapse of sanity in these two smart guys.

Hietala left Hunter two years after I did and has since formed his own exploration company in Calgary. Still keeping in touch, he says his home office has a copy of a plaque we displayed in the coffee room at Hunter with this defining message, signed by Jim and me: "You can easily judge the character of others by how they treat those who can do nothing for them or to them."

His fellow curlyhead, Jay, was another of our high-quality individuals. After doing such a good initial job for us with heavy oil at Lloydminster, he moved into head office. At first, he temporarily replaced our Production Vice-President, a man of limited vision who'd bristled at working with our American consultants, Sneider & Meckel Associates, and with Dick Wyman. I was fed up with the VP for unfairly attacking outstanding colleagues and finally told him he'd have to leave. Although he had a close relationship with a VP at Noranda, Alf Powis backed me up in firing him. Jay Christensen, on the other hand, was positive and open-minded, a temperament not entirely common in the engineering fraternity.

During the late 1970s, Jay had helped me repay my debt to Mark Millard, the Loeb-Rhoades specialist who'd mentored me through many a financial deal without recompense. It happened that Bob Blair, the aggressive President of Alberta Gas Trunk Line (AGTL), was in the middle of a battle with the federal government's Petro-Canada and billionaire Armand Hammer's Occidental Petroleum. Blair wanted to take over Wyoming-based Husky Oil and its huge heavy-oil operations in Alberta. Of course, as Husky's one-time production manager, Jay Christensen was a terrific source of background information. Mark, advising Blair, called me: "John, you said you'd make any of your people available to us. I wonder if you'd send Jay Christensen down to New York for a couple of days." He couldn't tell even me, a friend, why he wanted him there. But as Peter Foster writes in *The Blue-Eyed Shieks*: "When Christensen walked into Millard's office, he was stunned to see the team from Alberta Gas, which swore him to secrecy and then proceeded to quiz him. They found out enough to realize that heavy oil could be a good investment . . ." In what became the nation's biggest takeover fight, Bob Blair won control of Husky.

Jay was the most all-around oilman I knew and when he stepped aside for another production VP, he stayed on with Hunter. I relied on his mature counsel to help solve virtually any problem we faced in the field. I'd wander into his office, shut the door, put my feet up on his desk, and ask away. When his son joined us later as a budding geologist, young Rod and I always seemed to speak the same language—although he had to learn some of the vocabulary the hard way, as he admitted to me in a letter after visiting in Denver not long ago:

> One of the things that continues to be foremost in my mind was a note that I received from you after a quarterly update meeting with Alf Powis, etc. from Noranda. I was a young geologist trying to impress— and spent my fifteen minutes trying to bamboozle the retinue from Toronto with my geological vocabulary. A couple of days later, I received a handwritten note from you on a legal-size foolscap page. The letter was your constructive criticism of that performance. (I still have the page.) In essence, you gently reminded me that in any meeting you have to gauge the audience. If an audience is comprised of geologists and geophysicists—then the technical jargon is fine. However, if your audience is comprised of business-oriented individuals, then the presentation should be geared for what they understand. I have taken that advice to heart [as an independent consulting geologist in Calgary], and now feel that my presentation skills are excellent. I have had corroborating comments from others to that same effect.

Al Dillabough took over from Jay as VP, Production, one of the three most important jobs in the company. He was another star we stole from Shell (at one point, there was a sign in the covered, elevated walkway that linked

Shell's building with ours that read: "Tunnel of No Return"). Dillabough, a handsome, charming senior reservoir engineer—touted as the best in town—had been a well-paid manager of production in a company that produced more natural gas than any other. Bob Sneider, who recruited him for us, got a lot of heat from Shell Canada which had been grooming Dillabough to be its President. He brought good technical skills and professional understanding of big-project management with sizable staffs and drilling rigs by the dozen. In hindsight, I identified one of his drawbacks as a tendency to spend the way he had at Shell, hiring more and more staff as the majors do. "We've got all the people we can afford," I had to tell him. Frankly, I always had more spiritual connection with the exploration personnel and let Jim oversee the production team.

My partner and I continued to evolve a working relationship, he as Executive VP, I as President and CEO, which I explained to our people in a commentary on a management-consulting study we commissioned in the mid-1980s: "I am good at exploration, managing people, and problem-solving. Jim is good at PR, representing the company to outsiders, new contacts, and is amazingly quick at picking up on new problems, such as gas marketing . . . He is the one whom all the politicians and most of the Presidents go to when they want to make contact with Canadian Hunter. Inside the company, I am generally perceived to have the dominant role because I attend the meetings, hear the presentations, make the decisions, etc."

My commentary also spelled out the task-force, team approach we took with our key exploration, production, research, land, and finance people:

> If we have a problem that requires input from all these people, we get together and thrash out the problem. However, and this is an important difference, if the problem only requires the input from three of the people we just get the three together. Things get done faster that way. In addition, our meetings have the flexibility of being open to any other member of the company who has significant information

186   SECRET RICHES

> to give. Therefore, the important company decisions are not only made by the top executives but are made by the best-informed people in the company whoever they may be. And they are made quickly. This is a decision-making structure which, while it cannot be set down clearly on a chart and will not be found in business-school textbooks, works remarkably well at Canadian Hunter and makes us the envy of the industry for our rapid, accurate decision-making.

Jim and I usually teamed up to lure the top people to join Hunter. In the case of Al Dillabough, for example, we met him at lunch a couple of times, invited him to the office, went to his home and met his family, and after a few more meetings decided to marry him. Nick Wemyss, a bright, young gas-finder, typifies another approach we took to hiring. The lean, fair-haired son of a Scottish refinery engineer, actually born in an oil refinery in Singapore, Wemyss studied mostly mining geology at the University of Toronto. Switching his focus, he went to work for Gulf Oil as an exploration geologist, seeking heavy-oil fields on the prairies and oil discoveries in the Arctic. Later, he dealt in light oil for Dennison Mines in Turkey, Africa, and South America and for a small oil company drilling in northwest Alberta but teetering on bankruptcy. Approaching Wemyss, we asked him to make a formal presentation to his peers in various disciplines at Hunter—which became a standard operating procedure for new contacts. Trial by fire.

Nick described the work he'd been doing and responded to a barrage of questions that tested his knowledge and commitment. As he realized after joining us, the people at Hunter had to have a high degree of creativity and faith in their projects—the talentless and the timid need not apply. At the time, though, he felt vulnerable about the presentation process because we were asking him for what amounted to proprietary information about an area he knew we were also working; in this case, it didn't matter because his company was going out of business.

As with Nick Wemyss, every new hire presented a serious problem of investigation, analysis, then the waltz, finally the resolution of differences, and the reality of adjustment. We worked at it; the new people worked at it. Our hiring practices were the key to Hunter's success. Ron Hietala recalls my telling him repeatedly: "Don't screw that up. Don't jump just because you have to fill a space with a warm body." His memory is that the process was gruelling and the demands on a new employee continued in the following few months: "I want to make sure you know 50 people's names here in the next two weeks and a hundred in six weeks," I insisted. "And I'll come back to you and see how many you do know." It was the first step in really making your new colleagues realize they were joining a family, a team.

Debbie Morrice, who took over from Lenora as my assistant, was responsible for pre-screening all the support staff, the other secretaries and clerks, before the managers could even meet them. A handsome lady whose husband, Jim, worked for us in the land department, Debbie had learned about the business working for a couple of oil companies in Calgary. "You and Jim probably hired me because I was cute and friendly," she later said in her husky voice. "You were lucky I was as smart as I am"—and she was. She also jokes that she never had to learn shorthand because, in my academic manner, I dictated letters so slowly. She and Patti Donaldson, another executive secretary we hired, were fun and bubbly but relentlessly business-like when necessary. Debbie may have been the first secretary in town to have a company pay her membership in the Calgary Professional Club (at a time when women couldn't join the more conservative Petroleum Club). Once, when her husband and a geologist returned from a long out-of-town project, we flew the two couples to Disneyland with their families. And when she left Hunter to become a mother in 1980, we gave her a car as a thank-you gift.

During her time with us, Debbie often stayed after work with Jim and me to discuss ways to deepen the family feeling in the company. One idea was *The Hunter Forum*, organized by another superstar secretary. Audrey Newcommon, raised on an Alberta farm, had a big shock of blonde hair, a wide smile, and a face and hands that were long and elegant. After she threatened to quit because of a chauvinistic boss, I convinced her to stay and edit the monthly publication. Of course, it ran the usual reports of social events and photos of new employees. But it also featured accounts of trips as exotic as Jay Christensen's to a remote oilfield in China ("Small children would point at us and laugh") or as domestic as secretary Libby Smith's to a drilling rig: "He kept talking about 'beaches and bars.' At first I thought, 'Rick, you party animal you!' It was later that I discovered he was speaking about the formations below the earth's surface." A cartoon called "Conversations on the Seventh Floor" chronicled Jim and me discussing weighty matters: "What's the Stampede damage this year, Jim?" "Better than last year, John." The *Forum* served the vital role of offering everyone a sense of equivalency; the people chronicled assumed an importance that bore no relationship to their position at work. After each issue was circulated, you could hear a paper clip drop in the building.

Another of Audrey's jobs was to take a newcomer around the offices to make initial introductions, a process that eventually took an entire day. When she took over someone, they were took. She performed so many tasks that epitomized Hunter—for instance, organizing the Santa Claus program to deliver educational toys to employees' homes and our United Way campaign, in which we had 98-per-cent involvement, the highest of any Calgary oil company for several years' running. Even today, long after leaving, Audrey will hark back to those days and say of someone she admired, "He was a real Hunter." So was she.

And so was Gordon Brown, although he was never on staff. Gordon was the lawyer Jim and I used while at Kerr-McGee in Calgary. At Canadian Hunter, we always included him and his dear wife in holiday parties and weekend retreats. Like a lot of good people around the company, he was the son of a farmer. A few years younger than me, he was a friend first, then a legal consultant, and helped me through times of personal trouble, including Susie's death. Fine-featured, a dapper dresser, he was that rare professional who wrote and spoke lucidly, often using his eloquent hands to make a point. Gordon was a partner in the prominent Bennett Jones firm, founded by a Canadian prime minister, R.B. Bennett, and much later employing the former Alberta premier Peter Lougheed. Unlike some of his other clients at Mobil and Imperial Oil, we started out small with him. He thought of me as a determined and sometimes difficult customer. Ignoring his strong advice against using "Canadian" in our name because Hunter would have to be federally incorporated, I insisted we were going to be a Canada-first company and wanted to wave the flag—even though I wasn't yet a Canadian citizen.

For all his skill in language, avoiding the labyrinth of legalese, Gordon was lousy at mathematics; somehow that portion of his left brain had been excised. "Gordon," I said more than once, "you don't know your ass about numbers"—which could have been a problem as he helped us negotiate our initial profit-sharing with Noranda and our agreement with Imperial Oil. When his secretary called one Christmastime to ask what he might like as a gift, I said, "That man could use a calculator," and that's what he got. The Imperial deal may have been the only time he and I ever had words. When I saw the size of his bill—for admittedly complex bargaining—I walked across the street and demanded, "What the hell's this all about?" In embarrassment, he explained that a large law firm like his has committees that decide the fee for a major case and he had a responsibility to honor their decision. I was still ticked off, but Gordon Brown was too valuable an ally to lose. He steered Hunter—*Canadian* Hunter and the American spinoff we later launched—through often-troubled waters without ever letting us founder in negotiations with the numerous companies doing business with us.

Once early on, when Hunter was seeking tax-write-off funds from German investors, Gordon and I flew to Munich and Berlin. I hadn't traveled overseas before and his heart sank when he saw I'd booked tourist-class fares. But I spent so much time arguing with the airline staff about taking my long, bazooka-like map tube on board with me that they upgraded us to first-class. He still laughs that the luxury of it all so impressed me that I changed our economy seats and flew home in high style. On that German trip, I confided to Gordon about my affair with Lenora and even showed him a picture of her I was carrying. He advised me about a colleague who handled divorce.

* * *

In November 1977 Lenora and I got married in a simple ceremony in Calgary and the next day moved with our new son into our new home in the country. All these positive changes in our life helped distract us a bit from the shock of Susie's death. By now I knew Lenora's strengths, which only grew as we began raising a family. She has the grit of her mother, who was the youngest of five children of a Low German farmer in Manyberries, Alberta. Hilda was brought up by a stern, frugal stepmother in a house heated by coal her Dad mined and a bed warmed with a hot brick. At 18 she began sorting and packing at a bottle plant in a suburb of nearby Medicine Hat where she met an ex-soldier, Don Johnson—"he was a handsome bugger," she's told me in the same soft voice as Lenora's. They married and had their daughter and then a son, Les. Lenora was a little treasure, Hilda remembers, easy to raise, and ran with a good crowd as a tall and beautiful high-school student. I look at mother and daughter now and realize the rich genes that have been passed on: in her seventies, Hilda still actively golfs, occasionally bowls, plays darts at the Legion, and after her husband's death a few years ago is seeing his brother-in-law— "a good-looking hunk."

Lenora has her Mom's energy, as she demonstrated in the months leading up to our marriage and move. Over many weekends we explored the countryside around Calgary, looking for a piece of land for our dream house. She'd recently had back surgery for a disk she ruptured when we were deep-powder skiing. Despite her injury, she gamely accompanied me one day when we stopped the car on a ridge in the foothills overlooking the Bow River, one of the great Canadian waterways, and walked down to the end of a road where a new development was rising. After hiking farther along the river on my own, I came back and said, like Brigham Young coming upon the site of Salt Lake City, "This is the place." We bought 20 acres near an area called Springbank, 20 minutes out of Calgary, and hired the best architect in town. Bill Boucock conceived a stunning cedar-brick-and-glass residence of four storeys and 4,000 square feet along the Bow perched as close to the river cliff as possible. We wanted an indoor garden, an open curved staircase, a bridge—and, as we told him, a view with a roof on it. As it turned out, we also got a view from a circular observatory atop the house. The centerpiece of the house was a conversation pit and fireplace with a lofty redbrick hearth—an extension of a brick exterior wall. Adjoining the living room was a skylit atrium lush with leafy trees and bougainvillea. Overhead, a bridge linked the master bedroom to the main winding stairway. Windows two storeys tall wrapped around most of the house to drink in the views of aspen, fir, and river. It was a glorious place to raise a family and it was a warm, beautiful house.

And it was a place that helped lead Lenora to her real faith. Her parents had raised her as an Anglican, but on the day Robbie turned four, she accepted a neighbor's invitation to attend a Billy Graham crusade at a stadium in Calgary. She was among 16,000 people singing hymns under the stars and, when the charismatic evangelical leader began to speak, felt a stirring in her heart. On the bus ride home, the woman who'd taken her to the meeting cried as she described a past of drugs and drinking. Lenora was so moved that tears poured like rivers down her cheeks. She was still emotionally raw from Susie's death and, as she confesses now, was open to a faith that might bring the joy she saw in the people at the crusade. That night Lenora sat in a big leather chair below a skylight, and told herself, "I don't know what these people have got, but whatever it is, I want it." She wrote a letter with that message and left it on the kitchen table for me to find. After reading it, I went to her with tears in my eyes, saying, "If this is what you want, I'm behind you." Although remaining a skeptic, I supported her need for a strong faith.

Lenora and I soon had a second son and, with his arrival, a second home. We had it built in 1983, the year Jimmy was born. The house went up on the shore of Kootenay Lake, amid the Selkirk peaks in British Columbia. We were powder-skiing there—Lenora, as always, floating faultlessly down Meadow Mountain like a leaf—when we stopped to look across at the valley. "John," she said, "we ought to buy a piece of this." Here our sons could ski in the surrounding mountains, play ping-pong

Lenora, getting in the Cat to ski on the mountains, where there was no better female skier.

and volleyball, and swim, sail, and wind-surf from their own front yard. All of us could wallow in the four-season wonder of the Kootenays.

We bought three lots along the lakeshore and had Bill Boucock design a magnificent log house in the subtly shaped form of a cross. A walkway rings the upper floor where all the bedrooms look down on a voluminous, wall-less living area with a soaring ceiling. It feels like a half-scale secular cathedral in the woods. A master local builder named Chris Temple directed a small, specially picked crew in handcrafting it of golden trunks of larch they cut on Howser Ridge. They were so proud of their work that when the plumber and electrician arrived, the workmen—shirtless, carrying chain saws—said they'd put their lives into the house and warned the new guys not to screw it up. We put a plaque on a wall recording all their names and invited everyone who'd helped build the place to a housewarming party. We began flying out from Calgary almost every weekend. One Sunday afternoon, there was a knock on the door and one of the crew asked if he could show his wife and kids his handiwork.

I told Lenora we couldn't have another child because I couldn't afford another house. Jimmy was six years younger than his brother; his mother was thirty-five and I was—well, even older. Another blond with penetrating blue eyes, James Mark (named in part for my dear New York friend, Mark Millard) was three weeks late and had a heart murmur that kept him in hospital for another week. Afterward, he was a fit little guy. To tell the truth, I hadn't been as delighted this time when Lenora announced her pregnancy. But Jimmy was lovable from birth and she found him as sweet-dispositioned and easy to raise as she'd been for her Mom. Robbie was more strong-willed, born to rule. Although he had a kind nature, from the

Lenora and our boys, Robbie and Jim, Christmas 1991.

beginning he didn't want to submit even to diaper changes and his independent nature surfaced later as he preferred solo sports to being on a team. Teaching him to ski when he was four, I foolishly untied a training rope from his waist too soon and he instantly took off down the hill, hit a mogul, and broke his little leg. Within a couple of years he was a crack skier, the envy of the hill.

Jimmy, who always wanted to be an NHL star, was elected captain of his hockey team at nine. When I asked if he'd voted for himself, he said, "I couldn't do that."

"Well, who did you vote for?"

"The guy who didn't have a chance."

The two brothers were close. Jimmy wanted to emulate what Robbie did, although they were as competitive as my brother and I were, in everything from foot races to roller hockey, the one sport in which Jimmy could beat him.

Early on, the boys learned to avoid doing two things to me: stepping on my sensitive toes, which sparked unspeakable language, and waking me from a sound sleep. One morning a long time later, I barked at Jimmy for bugging me: "You don't cut me any slack." To which he replied: "Dad, I've given you fifteen years to get perfect and you still come up a little short." I'd get back by waking him at 6:30 a.m., saying "I thought you were up." His typical retort: "I thought I was, too." Aside from such minor run-ins, the boys and I had a loving relationship from the start, despite my age. Sometimes, when a new friend asked them discreetly about the gap in years between their Mom and me, they gave him a brush-off answer—"My Dad kind of robbed the cradle"—and thought no more of it.

Lenora has recently read a book called *The Two Sides of Love* which describes people in terms of animal traits. She compares Rob to a fun-loving, detail-avoiding otter. Jim is more beaver—orderly and analytical. Lenora thinks of herself as a golden retriever. She calls me her lion (whoever heard of a real lion who belonged to anyone?).

But from the first, I saw her own beaver-like qualities, especially when we traveled. Lenora proved to be a great companion on our many trips around the continent and abroad. She could be counted on to know the schedule, the exchange rate, what people were saying, where we should go. Observing her on the road, I always had the warm feeling that I really *liked* this person. In all our years together, I've never had that awful sensation of estrangement that can strike in the close confines of a journey: "What am I doing with her here?" I knew exactly why we were anywhere together. That was especially true on our first grand tour in Asia.

CHAPTER FOURTEEN

CHECKERED CHINA

HERE I WAS IN BEIJING, having a sumptuous dinner with China's vice-minister in charge of petroleum, when he asked me what I thought of Canada's new state-owned oil company, Petro-Canada. My immediate, instinctive response was to stick out my tongue and let out a loud raspberry. All of his underlings at the table burst into surprised laughter. It was October 1980, I was supposedly taking a holiday from the past seven years of company-building—and still I couldn't escape from the business 8,000 miles away. As I told the vice-minister diplomatically through an interpreter, big government-owned companies may work well in socialist countries like his, but in North America they were the worst performers, and Petro-Can was a particular disgrace.

That scene was a peculiar confluence of two of the most notable events in my life at the beginning of that eventful decade. Back home, the Canadian government had decided to leap into the petroleum business with both feet and was trying to explain its action with another foot in its mouth. Furious at this federal interference in an already heavily regulated private industry, I was primed to return to Calgary where I would take on the government. But not before I continued my fascinating exploration of a nation that had just spent the past four years recovering from the excesses of another heavy-handed regime—and its Great Proletarian Cultural Revolution. Now, Chairman Mao was dead, his Gang of Four was history, and capitalism was creeping in here at the same time it appeared to be retreating in my adopted country.

Lenora and I were visiting China in the company of dear friends, Tai Ng and his wife, Annette, both born in Hong Kong. His family had a Chinese-medicine business there as well as in Canton before the Communist takeover in 1949 when the Mao government forced them to leave. At a tender 16, he left home for Australia to get an applied-physics diploma and then moved to Canada for a master's degree in theoretical physics and a Ph.D. in geophysics at the University of British Columbia. Graduating, he went to work for Shell and had joined Canadian Hunter only two years before as our first geophysicist. At university in Vancouver, he'd met and fallen in love with Annette who was, as she puts it, "the youngest of more than ten siblings, each born in a different province of China." Energetic as well as intelligent, she took a sociology degree in Hong Kong before coming to Canada and studying at night to be a certified general accountant while working full days as a librarian. This brilliant, highly educated couple had an only daughter, Won, whom they lavished with love and care. Brimming with cleverness, integrity, and a generosity of spirit, she would eventually spend two summers working for Canadian Hunter in research geochemistry under Hans von der Dick, a German scientist known for his rigorous standards.

Tai and I had come to know a couple of Chinese geologists teaching at the University of Calgary, where I was lecturing, and on returning home Tai kept up the connection. He was a scholar of all things Chinese and the differences and the complements of his homeland and the West. Every few years the Ngs return to China and this time insisted we join them for a three-week tour with the added bonus of meetings with some of the country's leading energy poobahs. Tai was one of my best friends at Hunter, a shy scholarly type, but one of our premier scientists. Annette is serenity itself, with a wonderful smile and a low, soothing voice. They proved to be perfect travelling companions: intelligent, fair-minded, respectful of their surroundings, and invariably cheerful. Lenora, too, was the eternal good sport—supportive, observant, and organized, she likes her comfort and is thrilled with elegance, but can graciously do without.

We flew to Hong Kong, seething with people and money, and after two days on to Canton, which had not yet become the showcase of China's open-door economy. Four translators met us at the airport—one spoke only Russian, another only Spanish, and a third from Beijing who knew English and would be with us throughout our stay. After a drive through drab streets, several hours of banqueting, and warm professions of friendship, we flew on to Shanghai. Another deputation of four, including a Professor Wang, packed us into cars that twisted through dark streets and thousands of cyclists and pedestrians to our huge hotel complex encircling a treed courtyard. There, in the best lodging in the city, we gathered with our hosts in our sprawling suite, complete with a living room and a conference room. Dr. Wang, a geologist, had worked in Russia and was forced to spend three years laboring in the Chinese countryside during Mao's Revolution. I explained my theory of gas downdip from water and gave him a copy of the paper I'd done for the American Association of Petroleum Geologists. He was so excited, he trembled.

Our week in Shanghai was a blur of industrial exhibitions, bonsai gardens, the fantastic athleticism of Chinese acrobats, and a dazzling Peking Opera performance, which was an incomprehensible kaleidoscope of brilliant ancient costumes, swirling figures, flashing swords, and bursts of smoke and fire. I thought it must offer locals a pleasant sensory experience after the canvas of blue and grey that pervades the city. Lenora had an exhilarating visit to 300 pre-school kids in a nursery brimming with songs and excited, black-eyed little huggers. We'd arranged to see Chinese physicians in Shanghai. Mine could do nothing for the arthritis in my

Everywhere in Beijing, the streets are jammed with people.

Lenora and Annette visit 300 kids at a Shanghai nursery.

Aloing with the Chinese, we gape at the 4,000-mile-long Great Wall.

football-wracked knee but did send me to a practitioner of massage therapy called Tui Na. The strong masseur laid into the back of my leg for a week; by the fourth day I was walking up long flights of stairs with no problem. Lenora's doctor examined her back, injured while skiing with me, and prescribed acupuncture—seven needles, two inches deep, ten minutes in the small of her back, which left her feeling much improved.

One day I spoke to a geological society and a polite, intense student body in a shabby lecture hall at Tongji University. The themes were an introduction to geochemistry, a subject in which I too was a novice, and advice on how to organize their marine geology. Throughout our stay, we kept hearing how education was only reviving after its devaluation during the Revolution.

What struck us in this teeming city of ten million, astonishingly loud with honking horns, was the seeming peacefulness of the population. None of the soldiers we saw was armed; the only police were directing traffic. Doors in the hotel were left unlocked, as were bicycles on the street, often with raincoats slung over their bars. Nowhere in the world had we ever been drawn so instantly to a mass of good-natured, patient people and nowhere were there more pretty girls, sunny and natural. Regardless, a hundred men sometimes ringed Lenora on the sidewalk just to view this beautiful Caucasian woman.

In another lecture, I described the Deep Basin in two hours of talk and translation, impressing an audience of supposedly experienced oilmen with the idea that large gas fields might remain undiscovered. Tai, the geophysicist, spoke on the technologies of different methods of exploration. During a three-hour question period, I got the impression that none of them sounded like good general geologists, nor seemed to have a clue about finding oil. In the 4th century, the Chinese had drilled oil wells down to 800 feet with bits attached to bamboo poles and they were among the first to use petroleum for heating. At the time of our visit, China had a couple of giant onshore oil fields which had produced since the early 1960s. Although the energy ministry employed tens of thousands, I knew the industry was mired in the Dark Ages, as many of our questioners were quick to confirm. The Chinese of today don't use much oil; it was only a half-dozen years ago that they'd seen any need to start importing it. However, they did show an enormous eagerness to learn, even if their culture emphasized specialists over freer-thinking generalists.

Our guides took us out of town to the famous gardens of Soochow and Wuxi—Little Shanghai—one of the nation's major tourist spots, yet primitive by any Western standard. Many men were pulling wheeled carts of rock, sand, produce. One stayed in my memory: lugging a heavy cartload over an arched canal bridge, he had a pulling rope around his chest, and leaned almost horizontally, sweat streaming from him, every muscle straining. Hundreds of people walked by, no one offering to push; it would have been so easy if someone had pushed.

The host on our lake-boat tour was the head of the provincial Friendship Association, a thin, driven guy of about 40, with a mere six years of formal education but a thoughtful, outspoken manner. Jin Xun said China's problem was that of all socialist countries: how to select leadership. The old leaders didn't want to step down and there was no competitive process to choose new ones. I replied that an effective system must allow the freedom to succeed and fail—even a hotel serving the public here couldn't fire anyone.

Our conversation was devoid of ideological barriers; Jin was only seeking solutions. I argued for less planning, letting Canton loose to become another Hong Kong. But Tai interjected to point out that this society didn't want money and progress at the expense of its principles and ideals. I bowed to that. After a lunch that was one of the great meals of our lives—freshwater crab, whole fish in sweet sauce, hot tiny shrimp, slivers of duck, the best roast chicken ever—Jin reassured Tai about his ancestral home: "Do not worry about your Mother. She is poor but your brothers will take care of her." Tai, who seemed torn between his life in the West and his loyalty to China, was deeply touched. I promised Jin a subscription to one of my favorite newspapers, the capitalistic yet compassionate *Christian Science Monitor*, which I knew he'd devour.

Flying on to Beijing in a Boeing 707, we and the Ngs arrived at a modern-looking but nearly deserted terminal and drove into the city along a road thick with black Flying Pigeon bicycles and dotted with mules pulling wagons. At the time only about twenty people in Beijing owned private cars (by the end of the 1990s, there was one car for every five bikes). Construction erupted everywhere, workers up on bamboo scaffolding, men hauling gravel with carts, women doing dirty jobs like street-sweeping. What we learned later was that a parallel city lay underground: a series of nuclear-bomb shelters dug by hand and explosives over ten years in the form of tunnels with kitchens and clinics that could house all the eight million people of Beijing. Our best interpreter, Li-Li, a moon-faced woman in her mid-20s, had helped dig a shelter below her university for two to four weeks a year over three years. Like the ancient Great Wall, which we also visited, the tunnels were an amazing testament to how this people could be mobilized to move heaven and earth to defend against the barbarian. I couldn't imagine the U.S. ever accepting a system of underground shelters in answer to a nuclear threat; the instinctive American response would be to build more missiles and blow up the enemy first—and if our own people go too, so be it. I don't know if the United States will persist into the far future, but it's clear that China will.

After a brief sojourn in one of the world's worst tourist hotels, we were relocated to a small, charming inn where the toilets worked and young women collected the laundry every morning. Tai and I soon met in another foreigners' hotel with government petroleum geologists. The encounter was a disaster—no questions, no interest. In Shanghai, we'd been treated as saviors; maybe we'd just hit a dry hole. The next day, we attacked another group, this time with the Deep Basin. Good old Elmworth, it never fails: the geologists could hardly stop talking among themselves about several similar-looking basins in China. They showed me a geologic map of the country marked with oil and gas fields and a clumsy electric well log that was virtually unusable. I had the strong impression that, given this lack of necessary data, their interpretations were likely primitive.

Their superiors were less backward, as we discovered a couple of days later meeting with China's Vice-Minister of Petroleum. By this time, Tai and I had become geological celebrities, exciting our hosts with our ideas and the possibility of sending men to train at Canadian Hunter (which unfortunately never happened because of Chinese bureaucracy). Present were the head of an energy research institute, the ministry's chief geologist, and a severe little woman in charge of "foreign affairs." The Vice-Minister was a thoroughly impressive fellow, a little too slick-looking with dark glasses but bearing his authority gracefully. He plied us with good questions and displayed a deep knowledge of the oil business. At dinner that evening, he pointed at black 100-year-old eggs on the table and said, "They are good source rocks" (he obviously understood organic material and thermal evolution).

Describing a huge gas blowout, an uncontrolled well still flowing 70 million cubic feet a day from the remote Tarim basin, he laughed and said they'd drilled three relief wells, all of which missed the original hole. When everyone at the table saw him laugh, they laughed too. In the West, no one would be laughing; so many heads would have rolled for such incompetence that no one would have even smiled. I helpfully suggested a famous team of wild-well fighters in Houston who might be able to cap it. He was indifferent. His ministry had an incredible 10,000 geologists and he admitted how hard it was to remember the names of even his 40 chief geologists. At one point, bless him, he asked me about Petro-Canada. I torpedoed the Canadian government's oil company in the nicest way I could.

Just how much the Chinese respected us hit home in a later session with Qiu Li Yue, the Vice-Premier of Energy. We met him in the Great Hall of the People, on the edge of the world's largest urban square, Tian'anmen, which would one day symbolize China's iron fist on its people. The Great Hall, justifying its name with its nearly half-mile length, went up in an astonishing ten months to house the National People's Congress and commemorate the tenth anniversary of the People's

In the Great Hall of the People, I'm standing beside Qui Li Tue, the Vice-Premier of energy who lost an arm fighting during the Great March.

Republic in 1959. Its banquet hall seats 5,000 people, an auditorium nearly twice as many. Our gang of four, entering through the big bronze doors, was ushered into the most elegant room we'd ever seen, adorned with landscape and floral paintings, tapestries, and live pines. Lenora and Annette sat a little less conspicuously in the semi-circle while Tai and I flanked Qiu Li Yue. An old revolutionary general with one arm missing, he'd been on the Great March and fought Chiang Kai-shek. The Vice-Premier spoke of the contributions our talks were making to his people and discussed oil exploration in mostly philosophical terms. Our smoothly translated conversation grew more animated as I started to debate him politely. When he said Chinese petroleum technology was as good as ours in Canada, I openly disagreed.

Thinking I didn't understand him, he repeated it again, louder. "Mr. Vice-Premier, I respectfully disagree with you."

Disbelieving, he asked his interpreter, "What did he say?" The interpreters told us afterward they were horrified we'd argued with him.

I persisted in making my point that China wasn't as technologically advanced as North America in this area and could profitably learn from associating with us. At first, he was offended enough to remark, "In China, no one disputes a minister." But as our conversation continued, he finally said, in English, "I like you!" The interpreter damn near fell out of his chair. Qiu Li Yue enjoyed the dialogue so much that he kept raising controversial matters to hear what I had to say. Eventually, Tai joined in with some specific suggestions that might enhance the Chinese petroleum industry. Our audience with the Vice-Premier, scheduled for 30 minutes, lasted nearly two hours. He invited us back to China at any time, at their expense, and practically pleaded with me to let Tai return soon.

During our time in Beijing, Lenora and I went cycling one morning, visited the intricately detailed wooden buildings on the 200 acres of the walled Forbidden City—and after nearly three weeks of Chinese food, I finally tracked down a hamburger at a Beijing hotel. (A decade later, three McDonald's restaurants in China would set global records for opening-day sales.) Throughout, we'd tried to hand out small gifts like scissors or fountain pens, which were declined as a matter of political honor. But when I offered geologists copies of a book by the American petroleum guru A.I. Levorsen, they knew his name well and couldn't bear to decline. I wondered what they'd think of Levorsen's opinion of the bureaucratic tasks that governments and big companies force a geologist to do: necessary as these are, he'd written back in 1943, "they are not directly concerned with the thing which he can do best and which is of greatest importance to the petroleum industry, and that is the discovery of new oil fields."

Perhaps the Chinese wouldn't really understand. Leaving their country, I realized how difficult it was for the worldly, skeptical westerner to comprehend how bureaucracy-ridden and suggestible the Chinese appeared.

If their leaders said "Jump!", they responded, "How high, comrade?" They could turn from the Cultural Revolution to pragmatic socialism, from burning books to revering technology, in a flash.

Now I was going back to Canada to keep on doing things that North Americans do better than anyone else—if we can just keep our eyes on the ball. And side-step the accountants.

CHAPTER FIFTEEN

GOING SOUTH

ON OCTOBER 28, 1980, two days before we flew home from China, Canadian Energy Minister Marc Lalonde introduced the National Energy Program as part of the Liberal government's new budget. The idea behind the accursed NEP was to boost both federal control and Canadian ownership of our industry and supposedly to shield all Canadians from rising oil prices. The weapons were broadswords such as price controls and federal taxes on oil and gas production, resulting in even more state control of petroleum companies. In the mid-1970s, just two years after Canadian Hunter's birth, Prime Minister Pierre Elliott Trudeau's government had already imposed a Crown corporation on us, the shameful Petro-Canada. Petro-Can had wide powers to explore and develop energy supplies, import oil, do R&D, and even create a nationwide chain of service stations in competition with private companies—all with the advantage of having a state sugar daddy. Ottawa rubbed our faces in it by appointing a non-oilman as president, Bill Hopper, who didn't know squat about exploration or operations.

And now the NEP. I was red-faced furious about what amounted to the highway robbery of western Canadian companies. The issues were many and maddening: trampling on the rights of the provinces to control their own natural resources; courting the majority of voters in Ontario and Quebec by keeping petroleum prices low while sticking it to the West again; damaging the prairie economies by crippling an entire industry.

The jetlag had just ebbed when I came out swinging. A week after touchdown, I lifted off on the front page of *The Globe and Mail*'s business section. The lead story, with a photo of Jim and me in the Elmworth field, described Canadian Hunter as "one of the brightest stars on the Canadian exploration scene" before quoting me at full volume: "In a single stroke, the federal Government took away one-third of the value of this company and one-third of my personal assets. We are so outraged that if we could move physically to the United States, we would almost do it." Pointing to Ottawa's plan to use the NEP as a tool to help Canadian companies take over their foreign-owned rivals operating in Canada, I told the national newspaper, "It's the filthiest thing I have ever heard of . . . it makes me sick to think of going around town trying to figure out who has been hurt the most and trying to buy them out. It's like the Nazis sending Brownshirts out to break the windows for the looters."

Well, it hit the fan—especially that last comment and the headline on the article that shouted: "Canadian Hunter shifting to U.S. in wake of budget." Intemperate words perhaps, but understandable given that I'd recently returned from a nation where the state's strong hand had begotten an epically ineffecient, bureaucracy-bound petroleum industry. And that I'd just been on the phone with Alf Powis who said an Ottawa official had called, wondering whether the NEP's thrust could help a company like Noranda pick off a few-foreign-owned subsidiaries—to which I responded: "That's the shittiest thing I've ever heard." I told Alf I'd talked to a Jewish friend who fled Germany before the war and suggested a Nazi parallel to me.

Here we are, all of the 300 Hunters, in 1985, with Jim and me up on the bridge.

But the fact was, we and our industry colleagues were now looking south of the border, intending to vote with our feet. Within a month, the first stories surfaced about the lines of oil rigs heading to the friendler U.S.: 120 well-drilling contracts in Alberta had already been cancelled since the NEP announcement and more than sixty rigs were on their way out of the country. Almost every independent with the money to fly to Houston said the hell with Alberta, they weren't going to drill there anymore. No wonder the famous bumper sticker soon began appearing on cars across the province: "Let the eastern bastards freeze in the dark." Fortunately, we had a brilliant premier, Peter Lougheed, who would fight the feds for us. I was quoted at the time as saying, in my best Churchillian tones: "Lougheed's enemy is my enemy. Lougheed's friend is my friend. Without Lougheed's strength, Lougheed's balance,

Lougheed's confidence, Alberta would have been lost a long time ago."

Marc Lalonde was not my friend. The federal minister seemed aggrieved mostly by my comparing his government to Brownshirts. But in a counter-punch, he referred to me as "Masters, or whatever his name is" and, using further dismissive, insulting language, said I'd made millions off the citizens of this country, incorrectly claimed I'd been in Canada for thirty years—try just over thirteen years, Marc—and hadn't had the wit or taken the trouble to become a Canadian.

Some powerful allies quickly took up my case and replied to the politician. A guest columnist in the leading business daily, *The Financial Post*, an oil and gas analyst for a big Canadian brokerage firm, reflected the angry mood in Alberta by describing the "rather distasteful fracas" between Lalonde and me:

> After Masters equated the government Canadianization policy with some of the tactics used by the Nazis to drive Jewish shopkeepers out of their shops, Lalonde launched a particularly nasty—and uninformed—attack against Masters in the midst of a prepared speech. In Calgary, certainly, the attack crystallized the feeling of anger and alienation here perhaps more than [any other] single event.
>
> Lalonde summarily dismissed Masters' remarkable gas-finding contributions to Canada by claiming that he had become a millionaire on the backs of the Canadian people, and worse still, that he hadn't bothered to become a Canadian citizen after living here for 30 years. This attack would have been offensive even if Lalonde had gotten his figures straight. Masters has lived in Canada for only 14 years, and has had an application in [for] Canadian citizenship for the past four of those years. And up to six years ago, he worked for a U.S.-owned company that had a policy of moving people around, so applying for Canadian citizenship under those circumstances would have been pointless.
>
> Most disturbing, however, was that Lalonde obviously thinks Masters' lack of Canadian citizenship is more important than the fact

that Masters and his team, Canadian Hunter, have probably made the biggest contribution to Canada's energy security in the past 10 years. That's through the Deep Basin natural-gas discovery which conservatively could contain 60 trillion cubic feet of natural gas.

I wanted to become a Canadian but actually postponed the deed for a couple more years simply because I didn't want some eastern politician blackmailing me. Meanwhile, my fellow Calgarians made me a local hero. It got so that when Lenora and I walked into a restaurant, all the diners stood and applauded . One guy came over to say, "John, I wish I had the guts to say what you did." But after Lalonde and I traded more insults, there came a phone call from his personal secretary in Ottawa, saying something like "Mr. Lalonde would like to settle this down. We believe that the altercation between you and Mr. Lalonde has gone far enough and we think it would be in the interests of the country and the oil business for you and him to call a truce and end the invective."

"Well, why doesn't Mr. Lalonde call me?"

The secretary gulped and said, "He's a very busy man. He asked me to call you and see your reaction to this."

"You tell Mr. Lalonde that if he wants to talk to me, I'll be glad to take his call and hear what he has to say. You want a commitment from me and I'm not getting any kind of a personal commitment from him."

What I did get was another call from Lalonde's assistant reassuring me that the minister really did want to put a halt to our slanging match and would offer placating words in the media if I'd do the same. I agreed so provincial politicians could negotiate with Ottawa in calmer waters. Peter Lougheed did sail into battle for us, wringing less-onerous terms from the feds in what I saw as their attempt to commit an organized massacre of our industry through the National Energy Pogrom.

By then, Lalonde had been proved grievously wrong in his overall philosophy. Instead of oil prices soaring as he and his government had predicted, they sank like a drilling bit in 1981-82 as the global oil industry faced its worst crisis of over-production and plumetting prices in half a century. Suddenly the arguments for tighter federal controls and a state oil company carrying out government policy became spurious. In response to the price drop, Petro-Canada pulled back on many of its frontier projects and fired 2,000 employees. In 1984, Brian Mulroney's Conservative government began privatizing the company and dismantling the NEP—ending the benighted experiment in economic engineering. Today, under knowledgeable hands, a revamped Petro-Can has gained the respect of the industry.

In the end, the after-shocks of the National Energy Program were strong and lingering. It increased the West's feelings of alienation and led to the creation of western-based separatist groups, indirectly inspiring the Reform Party, which then became the Canadian Alliance—the official opposition party in Parliament. The rancor lingers even today. More than two decades later, a columnist for *The Globe and Mail* can routinely hark back to the NEP and its "punitive taxes to loot Alberta's energy industry for the benefit of petroleum-free provinces."

At the time, we had to put our money where my mouth was and act on our belief that the government policy would be a disaster for most of the industry. That meant accelerating our plans to move into the United States by creating a company called American Hunter Exploration Ltd.

The idea was to seek tight gas-bearing sands in various areas across the U.S. We began with several wells in California and southwest Wyoming. Typical of our luck was the limited success in the Pinedale anticline play in Wyoming's Green River Basin. This 90-square-mile structure had been drilled as far back as 1939, but its low-permeability Tertiary and Upper Cretaceous sandstones produced little. And although we did bring in one producing well of several drilled, the expensive techniques required to complete it didn't make the project economical to pursue. Two decades later, long after we abandoned it, Pinedale would emerge as the state's next giant gas field.

We had opened an office in Denver and, for a time, had another in Houston to explore onshore Gulf Coast prospects. But my first mistake was trying to run the operation from Canada. By the mid-1980s, everyone at Canadian Hunter knew that our American operation was failing. In commenting on a management-consulting study we commissioned at the time, I raised the question that our people were asking themselves: "Why is Hunter keeping an operation that's only eating money?":

> Now, this is a good question and it's one I get from Noranda. For starters, let me admit that we have had a sorry exploration record in the U.S. That is my fault because originally I thought we could do the job with Canadian-experienced people. Now we've got first-class, U.S.-experienced people in both Houston and Denver. Although it is difficult to find reserves in the U.S., once found, they are extraordinarily more profitable than in Canada, especially gas. Finally, economics in Canada are good now, thanks to changes by the present [Conservative] government, but the Liberals and the NDP will be back, sure as the sun rises, and we want some income in the U.S. to balance that evil day. Let me put it this way: your jobs have a lot more long-term security if we have U.S. income.

Blindly hopeful words, because my second—and biggest—mistake had been thinking that pedigree was necessarily the be-all in choosing distinguished American executives to run our U.S. operations. What we did was hire mostly chiefs but few Indians. Consulting to us were five former high-powered Vice-Presidents of Exploration from Chevron, Exxon, Shell, Unocal, and Consolidated Gas who started a small independent petroleum company in Houston. As I bragged to the Wyoming Geological Society in 1989, "they were instrumental in the discoveries of giant fields in Alaska, the Michigan Basin reefs, Monterey fields off California, Norphlett sands in Mobile Bay, deep-water structures in the Gulf of Mexico . . ." As I later discovered, they'd been good at their jobs maybe twenty years ago, with big staffs to back them up as managers. Now, when it came to selecting one gas play over another for us, they simply didn't perform.

After closing the Denver office, we reopened it in 1990 with half a dozen geologists to pursue three other major plays. Two of them used horizontal drilling: one in the San Juan Basin of New Mexico and Colorado was a viable commercial project, the other in the Austin Chalk of central Texas was mediocre. And the results of our continuing work in North Dakota's Williston Basin were miserable. The staff had no focus and no sense of the Big Picture.

One of the few stars I employed in the U.S. was an operations engineer and petrophysicist named Monte Fryt. Like me, he climbed mountains; unlike me, he was serious about his avocation, ascending the highest peak in South America and North America's highest, Mount McKinley in Alaska. For a decade he'd worked as a field engineer for Schlumberger, the global oilfield-services company. Fryt was known as Dr. Death because of his reputation for evaluating oil and gas plays from the petrophysical and reservoir standpoints and rejecting most of them on technical or economic grounds. He was one of those rare birds who saw electric logs as a tool to evaluate an individual petroleum prospect, not merely a way of correlating one well to another across a field or basin.

While our Denver office was shuttered temporarily, American Hunter operated out of Monte Fryt's base above Duffy's Restaurant in Denver. After relaunching in the city with our offices downtown, we called on his talents fully, providing all the money required to drill new prospects. Where we failed was in not supporting him with enough staff. As he's reminded me since, "It was such a small group generating plays for the whole U.S.. There was no focus—it was a scattergun approach. And the staff here weren't thinking big enough." Because I didn't visit Denver often enough, the people there had to come to Calgary to do their reviews of prospects every couple of months. I simply wasn't paying enough attention.

Unfortunately, it took a decade and $60 million worth of failed exploration programs before I comprehended this depressing fact and in 1991 closed the Denver operation, our last outpost in the U.S.

G. Warfield—Skip—Hobbs is a veteran geologist who founded Ammonite Resources, an international petroleum-consulting company. In a paper called "Strategies for Success in Oil and Gas Exploration," he pretty well nailed what we did to ourselves in our American venture. Mentioning our team of VPs from the majors, he pointed out there was "plenty of leadership and experience." So what the heck happened? "The company followed others in high-risk plays without the creativity and thoroughness that was required. Canadian Hunter apparently failed to employ the strategies that had been so successful in Canada."

Some good things did emerge out of our American experience. Dick Wyman, Canadian Hunter's research director, had long since persuaded us to adopt a specialized technology using the high-powered binocular microscope to view rock cuttings from a well. It allowed us to measure porosity, permeability, and other petrophysical charactertistics that identify productive formations. In our Calgary headquarters, Dick formed a group of technicians called the Rock Lookers, colloquially named so they didn't threaten our college-educated staff. We had to infiltrate them into our procedures for evaluating wells because of aggressive resistance from a particularly anti-anything-new group of engineers who'd amassed strength during the company's formative years. Bob Sneider, who had learned from the immortal Gus Archie at Shell, trained two of the the key Rock Lookers in Houston—Howard King and Kathy Stolper. Both of them worked for American Hunter there in a lab designed to evaluate the prospects originating out of our Denver office.

Howie, a Saskatchewan electrician's son, had studied engineering at two different universities without graduating from either. Despite lacking a degree, he joined Chevron in Calgary, where he took night courses in geology and worked for a paleontologist, whom he convinced to buy a microscope so Howie could explore the mineralogy of rocks. He later ran the geological lab at the local office of Amoco and eventually wound up in the engineering department of the Alberta Energy Conservation Board—where he was bored, no longer looking at the rocks he loved. We hired Howie for his uncanny ability to observe cuttings and add his own ideas to their analysis; he became our King of the Rocks. Typically, after one to two years' training, we had a mock ceremony for him and others in the group to receive a pair of pilot-style wings as members of the Order of the Holy Rock.

King, a feisty, vigorous little guy, became so important to us that we often referred to him as a geologist. Other companies seldom focused on the porosity/permeability in rocks that allowed them to transmit fluids like gas and water. Our people could examine cuttings from any well in the core-storage warehouse in Calgary and identify the clays, cement, mineralogy, permeability, and other characteristics that might lead to overlooked hydrocarbon plays.

One day King came to me with a worried look. "John, the engineers are ready to plug 1-26 [a well at Elmworth]. They think the Falher is no good. It does look poor on logs. But, John, under the 'scope that conglomerate is very permeable. That's a helluva well. And those porks are going to plug it!"

"Goddam it, Howie, your methods are unproven. No one has ever made a completion decision against log interpretation on your kind of data. You want to spend $200,000 on what you see in a microscope?"

"Yeah."

"Howie, it'll be your neck, you know. The engineers will want you killed if that well is dry."

"John, kill me if it's no good. But that well is going to be a boomer. I can *see* the permeability. It's full of holes. It's gonna *blow*!"

"Okay, we'll do it. This is going to test the microscopes!"

We did it. Howie was right as hell: that well came roaring in like a volcano. A week later I took all the rockhounds to lunch where I reviewed the incident and then said, "You guys aren't Rock Lookers anymore. You are Canadian Hunter petrographers. You are honest-to-god scientists. I don't want anyone to use that Rock Looker name again."

They stood on their chairs and cheered. We were recognizing them as professional gas-finders in the best damn petroleum company in Canada. While our rivals relied on seismic records, the science of petrography—in combination with subtle readings of pressure records from drillstem tests—became our secret weapon. Petrography describes and classifies rocks by careful miscroscopic description. No other company really knew how to use it, none had the trained specialists.

Howie King later spent three years in American Hunter's small Houston office and visited every basin in North America to broaden his knowledge. He then trained all our petrographers—among them Kathy Stolper. With her light-brown hair framing big brown eyes in a heart-shaped face, her slight frame and soft voice, Kathy is a gem of a lady and a superior scientist. This quiet Texan in her early 20s came to do joe-job technical work at our rock lab in Houston. She recalls a jovial and impassioned Howie having so much fun with rocks that she kept badgering him to peek at what he was seeing under the microscope. Wow! she thought, learning to recognize such telltale signs as how a rock breaks—flat like a piece of glass or with a rough surface that implied more porosity and permeability. Meanwhile, Bob Sneider—who'd developed our rock-classification system—took Kathy under his wing, pointing her to scientific papers that would broaden her knowledge and sending her to work with Lorraine Dryuff, one of our petrographers in Denver. While Kathy had joined American Hunter with only a high-school degree, she went on to earn a bachelor's degree in geophysics and geology as the first in her family to attend college. I became devoted to her because of her expertise and sheer goodness as a person, especially when she came to work for me again years later.

One of American Hunter's scientists in Houston was Tai Ng, our geophysicist and my friend. He'd asked me to move him there from Calgary, where his knowledge of seismic waves wasn't particularly useful in Alberta's

Deep Basin. For a couple of years he worked with the data from a local seismic company in an attempt to generate American plays, but when we closed the Texas office in 1986, Tai quit in frustration and moved to Toronto. Soon he was commuting from there to both Calgary and Houston, where we were still following up on one of his prospects, a field with a few gas wells. Finally, he rejoined us at head office as manager of geophysical research. In that role he was a key member of a team—with people from Noranda and a Calgary computer company—developing software to handle cumbersome seismic data at the individual workstation level. Initially funded for about $10,000, this powerful seismic-interpretation program called Seis-X swept the western Canadian industry and earned us royalties from users in the Canadian petroleum industry for years.

Along with the continuing miracle of the original Elmworth field, we were having smaller successes in western Canada throughout the late 1980s. Denise Woofter, still in her 20s, did some good geology in the forest of the Kakwa area of west-central Alberta. She was working on a test of the first prospect she could call her own. Encouraged but still unsure of its potential, she ordered a drillstem test one weekend. Because Denise had a family commitment, the wellsite geologist agreed to call her with the results in a code they'd conceived to foil competitors who might be tapping the phone. The call came and Denise thought, "Oh, shoot! It didn't work out." Monday morning, she arrived at the office to review the real data, which indicated that in fact the well *had* tested for oil. She'd got the code wrong. Getting the good news, I rushed into her office, gave her a hug, and said "Congratulations, you're an oilfinder"—my highest praise.

And she was, later working with a team to exploit the Brassey oil field in northeast British Columbia. It began production only two years after discovery (a short time in the B.C. wilderness) and delivered its millionth barrel only seven months later. (When Brassey's first well came in, it blew out the drilling rig and burned for a month.) For me, the real kick was that Denise had become a true Hunter, actively teaming with geophysicists and engineers to bring in the wells. So actively that the account she and geophysicist John MacGillivray wrote about their collaboration earned them the Society of Petroleum Engineers award for best paper of the year.

Denise Woofter never felt gender was an issue at Hunter. Among many other female geologists we hired over the years was Gay Jervey, the wife of our Vice-President of Exploration. While Mac was somewhat reclusive, Gay was a good-looking blonde who communicated easily, but—like her husband—she was nose to the grindstone. Coming out of a hard-rock mining background, she trained at Imperial Oil. In 1984 I'd chosen her to review two dozen wells that had been plugged dry around Bullmoose Mountain in B.C. during our early days six years before. Gay assembled a team with a stratigrapher, an electric-log analyst, a petrographer, a drill-stem analyst, a hydrodynamics specialist, and a completion engineer—we were going to do it the Imperial way. They rigorously evaluated all the wells Hunter and other companies had drilled in this westernmost edge of the Deep Basin. In her final review, Gay reported that, using our more advanced current methods, many of the wells could have produced commercially—with a potential reserve of several trillion cubic feet of gas.

We brought in BP America as a partner in a deal that would allow them to earn a 50-per-cent interest by spending $400 million. Again, as with Imperial Oil and Elmworth, Hunter made one of the biggest farmout agreements in Canadian petroleum history. The twist this time was that we'd been bargaining with land that mostly still belonged to the Crown. As Noranda's Alf Powis said later, "You guys must be the world's greatest salesmen. Nothing is that sure." Luckily, the beach conglomerates we drilled were beautifully porous right at the B.C. border and saved our skin. To give Gay Jervey credit, that's exactly what she'd expected. She later became our manager of geology in B.C., overseeing a tightly knit team.

Another of our young geologists was maturing well. Nick Wemyss had been leading us into a prospect called Ring Border north of Fort St. John, B.C., near the boundary with Alberta. It was in the Montney sand, deeper and older than our Elmworth pays. He lived and breathed that prospect, at one meeting suggesting what seemed like an over-optimistic estimate of the gas reserves for the formation. Sensing that Nick was exaggerating the numbers to justify a bid to acquire land there—and with the sale only two days away in mid-1988—I ordered him and our more skeptical engineer, Murray Grigg, to re-evaluate, non-stop, all the data. What with our losses in the U.S., and Noranda's increasing pressure to trim our sails, I had to be more cautious. Exhausted from no sleep, but just in time, Nick told me the reserve estimate was indeed overstated in his eagerness to tie up the play.

Barely in time, we cut our bids way down to $7 million on about 50,000 acres. Our bid procedure was called "sly bidding." There were five tracts. We spread the whole bid over those five tracts in the first stage. If we were outbid on anything, we would bid the whole amount on four tracts in the second stage. And there was a third stage. We were bumped once but took everything else on the second bid. We still spent $7 million and we were warned that someone else was on to our play. It was Texaco. We beat them that time, but the game was not over. We were up against a company several hundred times bigger than we were. The only thing we could do that Texaco couldn't was move like lightning. Over the years, we caused Texaco a lot more trouble than they did us.

Nick had initially proposed bidding $25 million. I thought it was even farther out of line when our lower bid won the acreage. My memory of this whole event—involving half a dozen key players, a large bid meeting with at least a dozen experts, a mass of geological and engineering data, millions of dollars, only two days to the sale—is rather fuzzy. But Nick tells me that after we got the sale results, everyone happy, he absolutely ecstatic, I called him to my office. He expected a big pat on the back. I told him he was fired for having so badly misread the bidding competition. It's hard for me to understand now how I could have been so ugly. I have no memory of it. Nick says the event was burned into his mind. I suspect I was reacting to the growing pressure Noranda was putting on me to be careful, cut costs, go slow.

Nick's boss was Mac Jervey—Old Stonewall. He said, "Just hang low for a while, go home, come back tomorrow, and let's play this out." Again, my memory of this has been erased. I do know that I fired only about a dozen people in my years at Hunter. Usually, I was finished with them. I saw to it that they cleared out their desks and left that afternoon. It was always done decisively. Nick stayed—and stayed—and I never said anything more to him about going. My indelible impression of Nick, my lasting memory over the years, is that he was one of my best. Some young guys go upward and then flatten out. Some turn downward. A few keep going up. Those trajectories are very hard to anticipate. Nick had plenty of reason to turn down. I suspect he didn't want to leave his big field and probably wanted to show me I had screwed up. He won both of those. We're very good friends again. We've walked across hot coals together.

It was late in the same year, around Christmas. Still no drilling because we had to wait for freeze-up. Nick had become interested in Dorsett, a small company with a number of wells in the Ring Border area. For tax reasons, they had to establish some cash flow before year-end. They wanted an offer by December 26. Nick and three other Hunter horses went to Dorsett's office that day, studied all their well data all day long, made their calculations, decided on $11 million, and called Jim Gray that night. I was skiing in B.C., completely out of touch. Jim said go for it. The next day, we made a formal offer by letter. On December 28, Dorsett accepted. Nick was chewing his fingernails: $11 million was a lot of money way up there in northern B.C. He didn't know whether I'd cheer him or scalp him.

Texaco was right behind us, but they couldn't get their management together over Christmas week. We outran them again. In the oil business, professionals don't tell lies about you for pulling off something like that. Texaco invited us to lunch.

Instead of running races with us, Texaco decided to join us. They had more land in the play than we did. Big companies always held big blocks of land wherever we decided to explore. We were agreeable to a deal, but it took another month to negotiate. It had become early February 1989. We had only three weeks before break-up. Do we drill a joint well with Texaco in the middle of the prospect or go to the edge, outside the Texaco deal, and evaluate a large block of 100% land? Well, of course, Nicks wanted to go for the trophy. I know where he learned that. We moved the rig in, drilled, logged, got the pay zone, and tested it. I was in Jim's office. Nick walked in. He looked happy.

"What did you get?"

"I've got the log and test. It looks like a good well. We're golden."

I started roaring with laughter. "Ah, Nick, I knew you could do it all the time. You did it, man, you did it!"

Nick thinks it's funny now. He didn't then.

The Montney sand, and an additional pay, the Bluesky, eventually were measured to contain 650 BCF net to Hunter from a total reserve of 1,100 BCF. That's 1.1 trillion cubic feet—a major gas field. There aren't many of those. It was Hunter's second-largest field, not as big as Elmworth but bigger than hundreds of other Canadian fields.

Very few exploration geologists ever find anything—over their whole careers. Those who do find gas or oil rarely find anything big. One trillion cubic feet is only found, statistically, once in a thousand wildcats. Nick Wemyss found his trophy. What a glorious life this is for a hunter—who hits.

Nick earned his spurs. I'm afraid I done him wrong, but now he's my compadre.

CHAPTER SIXTEEN

ENDINGS

BY 1990 ALAN HAD ABSORBED THE BODY BLOW of his mother's death, although Susie's suicide must have left an emotional wound that would never heal. By then, he and I had re-established a relationship that for a few dispiriting years had been interrupted while he came to grips with his anger and despair. During that time he'd become an extraordinary young man, intrepid and idealistic. His sense of adventure had taken him, during a year off school, to Israel, India, Nepal, and Tibet, where he suffered from some of the same high-altitude sickness I encountered in my mountain-climbing. Alan stood six-two, blond and handsome, friendly and powerful. His charm and intelligence attracted Alison Prowse, an absolute queen of a young woman. Studying nursing at the University of Alberta, she was smart and sweet-natured, three years his junior and about half his size. In the summer of 1983, they met as beginner adults in Jasper where Alison was running a hostel and Alan, at 23, was the youngest warden in Parks Canada's national service.

Alan, a horse warden roaming Jasper Park in 1988, age 27.

They were smitten with each other. She found Alan more worldly and mature, having had to grow up so fast during his teens. He was articulate and self-assured, attracting good people with his sincerity and kindliness. But he also had a melancholy about him. Alison knew he was fundamentally an introvert who needed to recharge in privacy. That was like me, as was his passion for skiing (but not hiking) and his habit of heading for bed as early as 9 p.m. Alison and I are alike in our love of reading; I can't keep up with her in her love for others. Returning to UBC after their first summer, Alan wrote her regularly, including this poignant passage: "As I was walking over here from Poli-Sci, I thought of something you had said in your last letter. That *I* was not *yours* and that I am still a free bird. Well, I accept that, but what occurred to me was that I really would like to be *yours*. Yea, I would."

He soon was. They began living together while he worked as a regional forester in several national parks in Alberta. In 1987 they trekked in China and Nepal, seeing some of the same places he and Chuck had been on their separate climbs. A year later Alan and Alison were married and moved to the Kootenays, where he was assigned to develop new techniques for evaluating a fire-history study of Columbia Lake. This combined his love of computers, the outdoors, and fire. She worked as a public-health nurse and they planned to have children — after doing a stint with CUSO, a Canadian non-government international development organization.

They signed up to work in Bolivia, nicknamed the Tibet of South America for its massive Andean ranges. The newly democratic nation was emerging from military coups and hyper-inflation. It wanted to borrow Alan's computer skills for reforestation on the fringe of the Amazon jungle, where logging companies had destroyed hundreds of thousands of acres of rainforest. As a nurse, his wife would provide health care in a remote region of the country. They left in April 1990 to learn Spanish and local customs and found a place to live in a "definitely Third World" town called Trinidad, as he reported in a letter to Canada: "This morning (after torrential rains last night), we walked to the office along some torn up streets (they're fixing the sewers) and I thought that this is what the battle of Hue must have been like in Viet Nam during the Tet Offense; mud, grey, garbage, mud, drizzle, festering open sewers, mud, more rain, etc. But, having said that, we actually like the place!"

Soon Alison had to return home for six weeks to be with a younger brother ill with cancer. As he recovered, she planned to fly to La Paz, where Alan would be attending a forestry conference. The snow-crested Illimani, the highest mountain overlooking any major city in the world, looms 11,000 feet above Bolivia's political capital, which itself lies at an elevation of 12,000.

As we learned later, Alan had begun feeling symptoms of high-altitude sickness almost upon his arrival in La Paz. In his hotel room during the night of July 22, his brain filled with fluid and he died of a cerebral edema, quietly, almost like falling asleep with hypothermia in a snowbank. No sign. No cry.

His colleagues missed him the next day at the conference. Not until that night did they get a key and enter his room to find him, dead. They then called Alison, who flew to Miami and browbeat an airline into squeezing her on a flight to Bolivia. I tried and failed to get a last-minute ticket to join her there. Alone, she handled all the details of identifying Alan and bringing him back home to Canada.

The program at his funeral service in Canmore, Alberta, remembered that "Foremost, Alan was compassionate. He was also a gentle, genial, yet intense fellow who loved outdoor adventure in hang gliders, ultralights, back country travel, and above all else, deep powder downhill skiing. At that, he was a magician." I skied with Alan almost every year from the time he was four; he passed me when he was 14 to become one of the most beautiful skiers I've ever seen. As son, brother, husband, and friend, he brimmed with a personal magic. Alan had a perfect life ahead of him, with a perfect wife, and it was snuffed out so inexplicably. All these long

Alan–climber, horseman, deep-snow skier, before his death in Bolivia at 29.

years later, thinking of him as I do so often, I recall the words of Margaret Duncan Brown, who homesteaded a sheep ranch in Colorado and ran it by herself: "Some things are painful enough that you remember. Some things are so painful you never forget." And she never had any children.

It seemed like the Masters men were cursed. First, my father dying of an intracerebral hemorrhage, now Alan of an edema to the brain. And in between, in the late 1980s, I'd started experiencing strange symptoms after travelling by airplane. When I deplaned, the change in air pressure caused me to lose my balance. At first it wasn't a real problem, but increasingly I began to stumble, trip over my own feet, and have to catch myself from falling. Lenora remembers forcing me to sit down after seeing me weave as I walked down the ramp; once she watched me run faster and faster up a ramp, trying to stay upright, until I collapsed. Then one day in the Calgary airport, Jim Gray was with me in a long corridor when I blacked out and fell flat on my face. Jim helped me up and said, "John, I don't give a damn what you think you're doing tomorrow, you're going to see Otto and find out what the hell this is all about."

Dr. Otto Spika was my doctor, fellow skier, and friend. After examining me and ordering a magnetic resonance imaging test, he said, "You have a tumor. It's right up here"—tapping my head. "We're going to get you to the hospital." Later, in his Austrian accent, he explained his embarrassment at missing some early signs. I had a meningioma, a non-cancerous tumor of the cells of the membrane covering the brain. If it becomes too big, it can cause mental deterioration much like dementia. Some of my colleagues have since confessed they'd seen me show puzzling symptoms. Nick Wemyss recalls a feeling in the office that something wasn't right with me for a while, that I was moody and having memory lapses. Monte Fryt, our American Hunter consultant, observed the occasional lapse in my focus of attention during a meeting.

A neighbor who'd had a meningioma visited me to describe the delicate operation and the critical recovery period, which he said might keep me away from the office for six months or more. Concerned as I was, there was barely time to worry: the specialist, Dr. Terry Miles, had to remove the tumor as soon as possible. I was in surgery for twelve hours. The growth he cut out was larger than a golf ball. Lenora says that when they brought me out on a stretcher, I lifted my bandaged head and said, "Piece of cake!" I thought I'd been there only two or three hours. She had been there all day, and collapsed in tears. Within a week, I was out of hospital and a month later was back at the office. It pleases me very much to have made an almost miraculously rapid recovery. My right brain has been working fine ever since. I never had much of a left brain.

But meanwhile, not wanting to miss the Christmas party, I convinced Lenora—against my doctor's advice—to let me dress up in a Santa Claus costume and sit in a room at the Westin Hotel while the party went on. Later, she delivered a message I'd written for the 600 Hunter people and their spouses in the ballroom. As Lenora was telling them how we appreciated their love and best wishes, I entered the ballroom "Ho-ho-ho'ing" in my Santa suit and pulled off my beard and hat to reveal my shaved head. Nick Wemyss remembers the mood of the party had been somber because of my surgery. When I revealed myself, he says, even some of the men began crying and hugging one another. It was a beautiful moment in my life.

Another heartening moment happened a year after Alan died, at a point when I needed comforting words. One day in September 1991, Carmen Morris, an experienced accounting supervisor for our drilling and completions, stopped in at my office. "I know you're going through a lot of pressure," he said. "I wanted to thank you for all the good and grace you have given to me and so many others." Finally, after we talked, he said. "I hope you have the peace of God." It made even this old unbeliever cry.

His comments were well-timed. Within a couple of months, I would be speaking to a petroleum conference in Calgary about the state of the industry: "I cannot remember in 40 years seeing it so shaken and demoralized. It is worse now, I think, than in the days of the infamous National Energy Policy. That calamity seemed to have some sort of solution mixed up in it because you knew who to hate . . ." The price of natural gas, Canadian Hunter's lifeblood, had been heading downward during the last decade and would soon dip below a dollar per thousand cubic feet—half what it was five years earlier. At the time, Hunter earned 80 per cent of its revenues from gas. And like the rest of the industry, we were cutting staff in our first large-scale layoffs in 18 years of operation: 25 per cent of our 300 employees. Along with those who lost their jobs, Jim and I were devastated, as I told the conference:

> We have hated every single step in the whole complicated procedure although we have involved ourselves throughout, trying as hard as we could to put heart and gratitude and appreciation into a process which is intrinsically cold and cruel. . . .
>
> At last, accepting 77 terminations, we tried to accomplish those as graciously, as personally, as privately, and as generously as we could. We guided some of our people into setting up private businesses from which they could provide consulting services to us, retained some of them part-time, provided professional outplacement consultants for everyone, and provided them with a severance package designed to respond to their years of service, age, and skill level. Wherever we had a reasonable choice, we tried to penalize the company instead of the person. Because it is our fault, not theirs. . . .You see, these men and women are family to us. They are competent, hard-working, wonderful human beings who have children and problems and bills to pay and hearts and souls.

What I didn't know at the time was that I was among those who would soon be leaving. Canadian Hunter, self-confident after nearly two decades of success, had just moved into a tall brown obelisk of a new building with an imposing glass-sheathed entranceway at 5th Street and 5th Avenue. Jim and I commissioned a self-referential sculpture for the lobby that portrayed a couple of 19th-century explorers shooting the rapids through rocks, their canoe rearing up at a dangerous-looking tilt—yet you just know they'll survive and get to shore safely. As it turned out, only one of us would.

Even before the drastic downturn in the petroleum economy, my partner and I had come through a painful period that tested our loyalties. In 1980, Dick Wyman came to Jim and me with his research on the use of natural gas to fuel vehicles around the world. He'd found that practical technology existed to convert the engines of cars and trucks to run on non-toxic, safe, less-polluting compressed natural gas (CNG), which could increase engine life and reduce maintenance. Not only that, a driver could switch from natural gas to gasoline, if necessary, while driving in dual-fuelled vehicles. The Italians had been using CNG for forty years; 300,000 of their vehicles were operating on it now. World oil prices were threatening to spiral upward—many analysts forecast $80 US a barrel, up from the current $30. The cost of gasoline in North America would, of course, go up just as fast.

Why not, Dick suggested, get into the natural-gas conversion business in Canada? Every financial analyst in North America confidently predicted a continually widening spread between the price of gasoline and that of natural gas.

My partner and I bought the logic and, with our research director, created a company we called CNG Fuel Systems Limited. As Chairman, we chose a friend of Jim, a former federal cabinet minister, Judd Buchanan. He could help us lobby governments to propel the project with new regulations and incentives. One of the few good things to come out of Canada's National Energy Program of 1980 was the federal government's acknowledgement of CNG's potential as an important motor fuel and the promise of financing to foster its development.

During most of that decade, we labored at developing the technology and building the company. We had an expensive infrastructure of conversion stations from B.C. to Quebec, turning ordinary cars and trucks into dual-fuel vehicles by installing lightweight yet strong CNG cylinders of aluminum wrapped in fiberglass at an average cost of $2,000. But the promised price peaks never materialized; by 1990 a barrel of oil had dropped below $22. Eventually, it dropped below $10. We hadn't factored in what Saudi Arabia was going to do in production to protect its market share. The recognition that we didn't know what we were doing began to dawn. The flood of people we expected to convert to alternative fuel was just a trickle. By then we had invested millions in CNG Fuel Systems and needed to share the risk. Jim found a buyer in Bob Blair, Chairman of Nova, the Alberta corporation that had battled Petrocan to take over Husky Oil in the late 1970s. The deal was simple: after Nova had matched our investment, further expenditures would be 50-50.

Blair soon realized we were neophytes in this business and took over its direction, bringing in his own people while retaining us on the board. But even his own experts couldn't buck the reality of collapsing oil prices. In a meeting of serious people, in somber mood, Blair pointed out that petroleum prices were going south. "John, we're really sorry," he said contritely. "You guys lost so much money. I really regret the way this has worked out." His side lost corporate funds. We lost personal money. Big difference.

I hadn't expected him to apologize. Believing we had done it ourselves, I replied, "Listen, that's just the way the ball bounced. We came into it with our heads up and it didn't work out. It's just like drilling oil wells: sometimes you drill dry holes and it's nobody's fault."

He was dumbfounded: "I thought this was going to be the hardest day of my life. I'm just astounded that you're taking this attitude."

Much of the money that Jim and I had built up through our share of Canadian Hunter went into CNG Fuel Systems. I estimate my personal loss approached $20 million. But I'd made that money so easily that losing it didn't seem a desperate, irreversible calamity. I really had the feeling we could make it all back again. My mentor, Dean McGee, told me long ago, "I guess the reason I go on making money is that it's the only way we've got of keeping score."

I never expected that, all of a sudden, the score would be so low.

In September 1992, I turned 65. A few months before that milestone, a couple of Noranda executives came to Calgary for their periodic review of Canadian Hunter. By that time Noranda's major shareholder was Edper-Brascan, a huge Canadian-based multinational conglomerate and merchant bank controlled by the Bronfman family, whose fortune was founded in the liquor business. Alf Powis, my old ally, no longer had much leverage at Noranda. The visiting corporate honchos told me the company was exercising its rule that everyone, including presidents, must retire at 65. And there was no one willing and powerful enough to make an exception for me. The baton would be passed on to Jim Gray.

As Gordon Brown, my lawyer and friend, says of corporate loyalties, "Lick up, kick down."

The new financial people in Toronto did not understand the basic precept that producing oil and gas companies must constantly renew their supplies. Edper was now subjecting Hunter to continual review. In their judgement, finding new gas fields was history; the company's business was producing existing gas wells in the most economical manner. You didn't need to drill a bunch of wildcats in an aggressive, widespread program that could never promise solid results at year's end. What's all this about drilling dry holes? they wanted to know. The entire decision-making structure and corporate personality was taking on an eastern, bottom-line mindset—and I was the one guy who could block this shift. They knew I would. I had to go.

By letting me go, they could virtually eliminate the costs of new exploration as well as research and development, which I propelled and mother-henned from the top. R&D should be a life-force of any resource company, as it had been at Hunter. Admittedly, my search for new prospects occasionally took us down bizarre pathways. You don't find oil and gas fields without dry holes. Edison had a hundred failures before he finally made a successful light bulb. These are meaningful arguments to people who explore. But most people don't explore, don't know how to explore, and have absolutely no intention of doing anything that risky. There was no hope for the new Canadian Hunter. I knew that instantly.

As I digested the painful new realities, I allowed myself the satisfaction of reflecting on the advances in exploration science our little company was responsible for in 20 glorious, tumultuous years.

First, let me list the early ones which were so important to the industry as a whole:

1. Team organization was inordinately successful and has been widely adopted by the oil industry and many other businesses.

2. Bypassed wells identified by electric log analysis was hugely productive in Canada and is making its way into the U.S.

3. Advanced microscopic analysis of drill cuttings, a technology much used in the early years of petroleum geology, was revived and significantly improved by Canadian Hunter specialists to a point that it is an essential adjunct to maximal electric log interpretation.

4. Recognition by microscope of abundant shows of methane gas still retained in low permeability cuttings as old as 30 years is a vital technique in today's search for gas in low-quality reservoirs.

5. Measurement by microscope of "m"(the porosity exponent) is an important factor in the Archie Equation which measures gas saturation in a reservoir, thereby separating productive wells from dry holes.

6. Most important of all was the formulation of the Deep Basin theory of gas trapping or, as described in the U.S., Basin Center

trapping. In 1979, and again in 1984, I published in the petroleum geology literature the first descriptions of this style of accumulation, essentially reversing the main rules of anticlinal or buoyancy trapping which had dominated petroleum exploration in the U.S. for 85 years and still dominates U.S. offshore and all foreign exploration. To sum up, my theory says that in low-porosity/low-permeability reservoirs (which is all we have now in onshore U.S.) gas, and oil too, are trapped not in anticlinal arches but in synclinal downfolds and are held there not by their buoyancy on top of water, but by the backpressure of updip water. This creates what I describe as the upside-down trap.

The above insights into petroleum exploration all came out of experience and thinking at Canadian Hunter. The Basin Center theory received a big push from insight that Elliott Riggs in the San Juan Basin of New Mexico had before I discovered Elmworth. He was using the concept to explore in the San Juan. I used it in Alberta, formulated a complete appraisal, and presented it to the geologic profession in its principal scientific publication. By the rules, I get the credit. Elliott should have half the applause. It was Dr. Dietrich Welte, a professor emeritus at Germany's Aachen Technical University and founder of Integrated Exploration Systems of Houston and Germany, who insisted that I write the paper and to whom I am forever indebted for that counsel.

We had other research successes as well as exploratory ones. Soil-gas direct detection was a method we developed. Based on R&D begun outside of North America, it was a way of collecting and analyzing small quantities of natural gas from soil at a depth of about a yard to identify underlying gas deposits several thousand feet deep. While we knew it had great promise, most of our geologists pooh-poohed the technique because it was outside their scope of knowledge. It was the brainchild of our Research Director, Dick Wyman, and our geochemist, Hans von der Dick, among others. Some of the people who pursued it at Hunter eventually bought the analytical process from us and founded ChemTerra International Consultants. Today the Calgary-based company continues to help major oil companies explore for gas as well as monitor industrial pollution in other industries.

One of our professional associates, the great electric log analyst Lloyd Fons, developed a surface temperature procedure for recognizing underlying hydrocarbon deposits. The method has enormous potential and will assuredly be responsible for a host of new fields.

Another long-time associate, Bob Sneider, developed log-analysis and bypassed pay evaluation into a powerful exploratory tool in the Gulf Coast and West Texas, where he was enormously successful. He earned a Sidney Powers Award, the Association of Petroleum Geologists' highest honor, in 2001 (a quarter-century after Dean McGee received his). Bob still consults free for us because we can't afford him anymore.

Larry Meckel, another of our stars, has for many years been a senior consultant to Pemex, Mexico's state-owned oil and gas giant. I have no doubt that the clever ideas from Sneider and Meckel, which enriched Canadian geology, are now guiding Pemex to Mexican oil fields.

But for Noranda's new executives in 1992, all this—the on-going R&D and fresh exploration for new fields—might as well have been happening on the other side of the moon. They didn't understand it and no longer wanted it. John Masters was history at the company he'd co-founded nearly two decades earlier. Canadian Hunter was now playing swallow the leader. I was hurt, disappointed—and disbelieving.

What comforted me in my worst moments was the knowledge that I was leaving a legacy, a track record not only as an explorationist but as the President of a company that had set the standard for our peers in the petroleum industry—and for Canadian companies generally. Bernice Ramsden-Wood, who was the elegant-looking, people-loving manager of our records center, likes to reminisce about the culture shock she felt when joining us from the banking world in 1990: "I'd never been in a company where everyone was treated like an equal, no matter your pay level or skill level. The fridge in the kitchen was full of food and there was fruit on the counter that belonged to everybody on the floor. You could take off for a two-hour lunch and nobody would say anything because they knew you wouldn't abuse it. On your birthday there'd be a gift—a rose in a bowl, chocolates, or a plant. When I reorganized our huge microfiche library on and off over four and a half months, several geologists came and thanked me. Mike Downey [Vice-President of Exploration] once said: 'Has anybody ever told you how much we appreciate what you're doing?' I thought I'd died and gone to heaven."

When Canada's *Financial Post* published a book called *100 Best Companies to Work For in Canada*, Hunter still retained much of the spirit that had created a working environment celebrated across the country. At the time they surveyed us in 1989, we had 330 non-union employees and a $200-million capital spending program.

The book was a compilation of Canada's best employers, based on questionnaires and interviews with management consultants, business-school professors, journalists, company employees and managers, and even corporate competitors. Not only were the three *Post* authors looking for tangible qualities such as benefits and job security but also the more subjective ones of job satisfaction and personal-development possibilities. They placed Hunter in a section called The Pace Setters: "These are the leaders—dynamic, trend-setting companies, always striving to be innovative in their management techniques."

They rated us "excellent" in pay, atmosphere, job satisfaction, and personal development. We got "very good" for benefits and communications, "good" for job security, and "average" for promotion (because people just didn't want to leave, so openings were limited). But research for the *Post* book had been done in 1989, which is just about when my influence in the company was starting to wane. What the authors captured, then, was the Canadian Hunter that I'd helped to shape. After I left three years later, as so many of my colleagues have since told me, it was a lesser place in reflecting most of those qualities the researchers had credited to us.

As a tribute to the people who shared in building one of the best

Endings 239

Canadian companies, here—for the record, a snapshot frozen in time—is what they said about us then:

> Clocks, prominent in the lobby at Canadian Hunter's office, hint at attitudes within. One (set normally) is labeled "Calgary Time." Alongside it, another (five minutes fast) is identified as "Canadian Hunter Time." A sign tells employees: "Stay Ahead."
>
> Canadian Hunter thinks of itself as being smarter than the competition. It hires the best people and rewards them handsomely. Pay is outstanding even by the historically generous standards of the oil patch, and some of the benefits have a surreal quality to them.
>
> President John Masters boasts so proudly about the excellence of his workforce that he provokes a question about encouraging elitism. His response is quick: Certainly he encourages elitism—he even preaches it. And if outsiders sometimes think he hypes the capabilities of his people too much, he is not apologetic.
>
> He quotes the Roman poet Virgil who wrote 2,000 years ago: "They can be because they think they can."
>
> The employee handbook sets a rather self-satisfied tone: "You have been hired to find and produce oil and gas fields. Nothing is more essential to our lives. We welcome you into an exciting company which has a different style than you may be accustomed to.
>
> "We have chosen you because, from the many who apply to us, we think you are outstanding. We hire only the best. We want you to work with us and we want you to join our family. At Canadian Hunter you will feel an atmosphere of accomplishment. We are doing a big job developing energy, and we are serious about it.
>
> "Every day, all of us are trying to make real progress. We help each other and we'll help you. We are all friends. Many of us are highly skilled and we have great respect for each others' talents and experience . . . When someone asks you where you work, you may be forgiven a little inner smile when you say 'Canadian Hunter.'"
>
> Hunter is decidedly different. Masters and Executive Vice-President

Jim Gray, both geologists, who founded the company, have put their personal stamp on it to a degree rarely encountered in Canadian business. Their free-wheeling, entrepreneurial style isn't what one would expect to find in a wholly owned subsidiary of a multinational resource giant.

The two men are given great freedom to run their own show and they thank Noranda for it. The names of the two senior executives crop up endlessly in conversations with employees: "John and Jim like to do this . . . John and Jim believe . . ." Employees said they find it hard to imagine what Canadian Hunter would be like without these two very strong personalities at the helm. Some even worry about it a bit.

Hunter is remarkably free of bureaucracy, and individual initiative is encouraged, even expected. Says one junior employee: "We are expected to think." For many who have spent time in regimented, hierarchical companies, being expected to think and offer suggestions is unexpectedly refreshing. Even better is that their ideas are actually listened to and acted upon.

Many employees said they were performing duties that normally would be reserved for people much higher up the command ladder in other oil companies. There's a small staff turnover (3.3% in 1989), resulting in limited opportunities for promotion. This doesn't seem to trouble employees, however, who find a flat management structure to their liking.

Managers said their job satisfaction and rewards came in the opportunity to work closely in teams with other professional disciplines and to champion projects. The chance to seek professional excellence was in itself a major reward,

There are more tangible rewards, too, in the high pay scales. Clerical/secretarial staff are being paid [at] about the 80th or 85th percentile for the industry, which Masters feels comfortable with. Some professional salaries are over the 140th percentile. A "soft landing" is currently in progress to bring them down a little—perhaps to the 120th percentile.

Exceptional effort is recognized in several ways. Department managers can provide small dinner parties or time off for their workers. Senior officials may authorize trips for an employee or spouse, or up to a month's bonus pay. High achievers among the lower salaried employees sometimes get a leather pouch with 50 gold dollars. More significant achievements—such as the discovery of a new oil field—are rewarded by a net profit interest in the field, which could reach a value exceeding $1 million.

Masters and Gray have a personal arrangement with Noranda under which they share 12.5% of the net profit from Hunter's oil and gas fields once exploration and development costs have been repaid. This share of earnings ranges from $10 million to $15 million a year.

The two executives give away half of this to about 75 people in the company to reward them for the part they have played in hydrocarbon discoveries. These rewards are structured to keep top talent at Hunter. To ensure this, there is a delay before entitlements are vested, and anyone leaving Hunter forfeits half the award.

Masters says the scheme has been very effective in sharing the wealth of the company with a lot of people. "I'd say we probably have more millionaires in Canadian Hunter than any other company in town."

Masters says he believes Hunter employees perform at perhaps 95% of their potential, compared with 40% to 50% of potential achieved by workers in big oil companies around Calgary. His own staff also feels this is an accurate statement.

New employees, no matter how junior, are taken around and introduced to everybody. They will already have had about half a dozen interviews before they were hired, and will have met Masters who sees all newcomers. He reserves, and occasionally exercises, the right of veto on new hirings.

The atmosphere at Canadian Hunter is open and friendly. Employees feel free to talk to Masters and Gray and chat casually about business and social activities, and everyone is expected to know the names of all their co-workers. This was easy a few years ago when Hunter was smaller, but today it requires effort. New employees are advised to learn the names of 50 fellow workers a week until they have got them all down pat.

Hunter places great emphasis on team work, and it reinforces team building with a range of outside social and sporting activities, fully paid or generously subsidized by the company. Not surprisingly for a company in the high-risk oil and gas exploration business, these include such hazardous activities as kayaking, ice climbing, rock climbing, mountain biking and so on.

Vacations are generous. Most professionals get six weeks off after five years. In addition, employees get six Fridays off each year, and the company closes down between Christmas and New Year. Plus there's a sports day and the annual skiing trip.

The benefits seem endless: subsidized YMCA membership, an annual $100 allowance for meals and accommodation in nearby parks, education assistance, a $38-a-month transportation allowance, and kitchens stocked with tea, coffee, bread for toast, jam, and muffins. Hunter also offers a stock savings plan, to which it adds 30¢ for every $1 invested by employees in Noranda shares.

No wonder Hunter employees smile a lot.

Jim Gray stayed on as President until he turned 65, when he was named Chairman. Steve Savidant, who was Chief Financial Officer, became President and Chief Executive. It is fair to say that Canadian Hunter nose-dived after I was replaced in 1992. In a few years, Noranda returned their ownership to the shareholders. In seven years, Edper sold out their interest for a small amount. In the last few years of the '90s, Hunter re-acquired its focus and went back to developing the big fields I had found. Then the American giant, Burlington, bought the whole company for $3.3 billion as the "match made in heaven." Obviously, there was a huge difference in the valuation put on my company by the Edper-

Noranda financial management versus the fourth-ranked major in U.S. oil and gas, Burlington.

Hunter's last decade—the scramble for power and prestige by the newly anointed, the disgraceful treatment of myself and many of my former loyalists, and the final hand-over to an American major—was a sorry chapter for Canadian nationalism and personal ethics. My lesson was that no matter what you develop in a company by way of pride, *esprit de corps*, and fellowship, it cannot stand against authority and the thirst for advancement. Once those motivations are let loose, goodwill crumbles. We had a wonderful run for 20 years. We revitalized Canada's oil business, returned it from the frontiers to Alberta, and augmented the nation's reserves. We made careers and productive lives for several hundred good people. The foundation was goodwill and smart exploration. It was too idealistic. It did not take full account of power. My mistake.

It may be likened to wild animals who hunt in packs as we do—like wolves. There is order and teamwork as long as the leader is strong. But if he's wounded, survival of the pack demands his termination. There is no place for him any longer. I have an uncomfortable feeling that human packs are subject to the same primitive, instinctual blood thirst, the urge for survival. I believe the sudden, abrupt, heartless break with past connections, the complete termination of loyalty, comradeship, and concern, its replacement with nearly brutal contention for the power positions—all of that, so suddenly, speaks of some pre-human instinctual behavior. Once understood, it can be digested without much harm.

CHAPTER SEVENTEEN

STARTING OVER

WHEN I WAS FORCED TO RETIRE in September 1992, the new management allowed me to keep an office at Canadian Hunter. At first it was private quarters with a secretary. After a few months, I was moved down a couple of floors to a smaller space, with a shared secretary, and later was relocated even further below the executive suite. I'd assumed the powers-that-be would want to retain me as a specialist advisor. But no one invited me to meetings nor gave me access to correspondence. Some people even avoided speaking to me in the hall. After nine months, I left the building and took an office nearby. Essentially, I had no further commerce with the company I built.

I had no damn desire to retire—and, after my losses in the aborted natural-gas-conversion scheme, didn't have enough cash cushion to endow my young wife and family. As I noted in my journal about this time (and these may be someone else's words), "Don't retire. You still may be

My last gasp, an elegant retirement party with members of my family; in the front row Lenora, Jimmy, Alison; in back Robbie, Barbie, and her husband, Bill.

living, and breathing, and eating, but you will have halted something, and it is very important instead to keep this thing going in you for as long as you can." But looking for prospects to start all over again in Calgary resulted in nothing but numerous dead ends—dry holes. My daughter, Barbie, was now married to Bill Davis, a landman who'd worked at Hunter. I briefly considered going into the oil and gas business with him until we jockeyed about who'd preside over the company.

Maybe Denver, my old hunting grounds, would be more welcoming. Although I was loath to leave the warm and welcoming country of

Canada, maybe I could launch a new exploration company in my native land and keep this *thing* going in me.

That year the National Petroleum Council reported the potential for natural gas was promising: "The United States has a vast and diverse natural gas resource base and estimates of recoverable portions continue to grow with production experience and technological advances. . . . Natural gas is an abundant domestic resource and can be produced and delivered at prices that allow both expansion of the market and continued development of the resource." My brother, Chuck, was chief of the World Energy Project at the U.S. Geological Survey which had recently estimated American reserves of undiscovered gas were third in size only to Russia's and Iran's.

Just the information this old oil and gas guy wanted to hear.

But by September 1993 I had passed through six months of hell. I'd tried to do two monumental things, to no avail: sell a large, promising gas play in western Colorado and find a financial backer to support my proposed company. I must have talked to fifty separate groups about the twin goals. That month I met with the legendary Phil Anschutz, a reclusive Denver billionaire, one of the richest men in America. Anschutz had made his fortune in oil during the 1970s, in railroads a decade later, and went on to buy professional sports teams, including the NHL's Los Angeles Kings. Apparently, I was what he wanted at the time. When we met at his office, he was trying to get away for a quick trip to China. Within an hour, he said he wanted me to run his oil company. I walked with him to his car in the parkade and by the time he climbed behind the wheel, I was President of Anschutz Oil.

"Looking back," I wrote defensively in my journal, "I think my problem was I was too good for all the other contacts and they sensed subconsciously the disparity. They could not feel a natural harmony—which, added to their natural hesitation, fear of risks, caution, etc. put every one of them in a negative position. All of them were good people—but pretty average.

"Phil is a different breed. He is smart and he is a driver. I believe he sensed a harmony of abilities. That is the only logic I can see to explain how he could make up his mind in 60 minutes.

"I have almost the same deal I had with Noranda. Salary, interest, complete financial backing!"

My optimism, as it turned out, was misplaced. That first day was also the last day I had a satisfactory meeting with Phil. He assumed I'd left Canadian Hunter with a pocketful of confidential deals I could now exploit. Of course, I didn't have any list of secret prospects to bring to his table from my former employer. Monte Fryt, who became a consultant to Anschutz Oil, believes Phil simply wanted a big name to get back into the petroleum industry with a bang. There were only five explorationists in the office, including Gerry Loucks, the sophisticated geologist whom I'd hired long ago for Kerr-McGee in Calgary. Given our size, we certainly launched an ambitious program, which ranged from the Gulf Coast to North Dakota's Williston Basin, as well as gas wells in Lake Erie and southwest Wyoming. The company also went international trying to develop gas plays in northern Germany, Spain, Switzerland, and even Bulgaria. But in the end, Phil wouldn't let me do anything useful, by my standards. He didn't want sophisticated evaluations of plays and strategies about operations. Instead, I was to fly overseas and spend a few weeks nailing down a good deal in a foreign country—efforts that would have been foolish in their unreality.

As I was despairing about my future—what the hell do I do now?— my newly retired brother wrote me a warm letter of encouragement:

Dear John,

> Well, I suppose you do what you have always done. Go find some more oil and gas where others have feared or neglected to tread. Now, I appreciate that in fact we do deal with an exhaustible resource but those are my words and you have more than once demonstrated a fertility for oil and gas in unexpected places. To do that, in years past, it

was your custom to spend more Saturdays at the shop than other folks and though at this time you might indeed expect a reward, not a kick in the butt, a little bad luck can force a change in plans and hard work never deterred you. I appreciate that it is easy to preach from my rocking chair but there is no question about the reputation of "oil finder" that you have built over the years and you indeed have the capacity to make the downer times go away. As they say in the Nike ads, "just do it." . . .

John, I'm sorry to hear, at this time in your life, that a hitch seems to have developed in your remarkable career but it's only a hitch, and your history just screams out to the world that you will turn things around for Anschutz exploration. I appreciate your confiding your concerns with me and though the solution to your problem lies on your back please know that you have some cheering supporters in the crowd and that in some way we can and will help.

With our love and very best regards,
Brother Chuck

Charles Day—Chuck—Masters died just three years later, at the age of 70, of a brain tumor. Again, it felt as if the family curse had resurfaced. The U.S. Geological Survey's director, Charles G. Groat, said of his chief of energy resources: "Our country and our science are enormously indebted to him for his exceptional contributions." I remain indebted to my brother for his love and support. His letter is a treasure in my journal of thoughts and memories.

As Monte Fryt recalls about my stint at Anschutz Oil, "it was a clash of titans"—and after three years, Phil Anschutz won. Of course, he had all the cards.

One of the positive experiences to emerge from my time there was the place I found to resettle the family. In the beginning, I spent alternative weeks in Calgary but finally insisted on living full-time in Denver and reluctantly selling our beautiful country house back in Calgary. In the early summer of 1994, I spent every weekend touring the area south of Denver searching for a pleasant roost. I told my real-estate broker I wanted three bedrooms, a fireplace, porch, isolation—and a view. He hoped that meant a house with a library, spa, and maid's quarters in an upscale neighborhood with manicured lawns, mighty trees, and a winding driveway. I saw so many storybook, golden-laned homes that a mere drive past would elicit a disappointed "This isn't it."

Finally, the realtor took me to what he described as a little rental house out in the country, half-way up a mountain, surrounded by forty acres of trees. South of Denver, on the road to Colorado Springs, the land begins to change. In thirty miles you see Castle Rock rising like a medieval stone citadel on a hill with an attractive little community at its foot. From there, for another 20 miles, the countryside takes on the butte and mesa and pine-forest glory of a John Wayne movie.

We drove across a cattle guard (good start), up a long, winding dirt road through big Ponderosa pines well up the east flank of Dawson Butte (no lawns, no mansions, no strollers). The road ended at a small garage beside a small, nondescript brown house beneath a tall Ponderosa. To the south was a full view of Pikes Peak, the first landmark pioneers on the wagon trains could see 150 years ago after long, hot months on the bare prairie. This day it was adorned with early snow and backed by a blue Colorado sky.

I was standing on a hillside two thousand feet above mile-high Denver, which presides over a vast brown pool table called the Great Plains. Here, up the slope of Dawson Butte, you're on the eastern edge of the Rocky Mountains, which extend west for a thousand miles to the Pacific, and north-south 20,000 miles from Alaska to Antarctica. Rising three miles above sea level, they contain oil, gas, gold, silver, timber, water, and the history of the earth. A good place for a geologist to be.

"I'll take it," I said immediately.

"For God's sake, you haven't even been in it."

"It'll be a house with a kitchen and windows showing Pikes Peak. We'll have a place to sleep and a place for books. Oh yeah, it's got a fireplace and a porch. And we'll get a big dog. I know I'm going to like it."

After a five-minute walkabout, I rented it. A preacher-comedian friend of ours named Jim Peters calls it "the Clampett Mansion." Our 12-year-old son, Jim, took one look at the tiny bedroom he was inheriting, thought of the big and beautiful one he'd left behind outside Calgary, and cried. But I liked the house and the mountain and Lenora and I began planning to buy the property someday to build a new home here. Jim likes it fine now.

In 1997, after leaving Anschutz Oil, I became Executive Vice-President of Julander Energy Company in Denver—leaping directly from the frying pan of Phil into the fire of the Julanders, brothers Fred and Robert and their father, Weldon. Again, they wanted to trade on my name in the industry. Friends have long warned me that my initial open acceptance of new people and new ideas can sometimes backfire badly. Yet I prefer to believe that most humans are basically decent and I don't want to live behind a wall of doubt and suspicion, making people prove they're ethical before granting them space. Having said that, my relationship with the Julanders was completely unsatisfactory, laced with misunderstanding that prevented me from engaging in any productive exploration. The atmosphere was so stifling that I was forgetting faster than I was learning. My couple of years there were a complete waste of my time, setting back my career and my life.

The only pluses during that experience were three of the people I worked with there who would soon be back in my life full-time. One of them was Kathy Stolper, who had matured so much as a petrographer since her early days at American Hunter. Don Johnson was a drilling engineer who became my operations manager for a year as we developed a deep gas play in the Sand Wash Basin of Wyoming. And it was through

Julander that I met Alan O'Hare, a smart and personable graduate of the University of Wyoming who had the most sophisticated appreciation of reservoir and development engineering of anyone I'd known in the oil business.

Alan had worked as a reservoir engineer for Texaco in North Dakota and manager of more than $100 million worth of producing property acquisitions for Ladd Petroleum in Denver. In 1981 he started his own company to explore more than two million acres of Indian reservation in Montana and then recovered the original investment of $7 million by selling half the business to the AT&T Pension Fund. But financing for exploration on frontier land was drying up and eventually the company closed down. He turned to corporate consulting on energy for clients such as Dow Chemical and International Paper, among other Fortune 500 companies.

One client was Frontier Resources out of Chicago, run by John Burns in Denver. Alan was hired to review and attract funding for a project to acquire large blocks of land and drill $10-million wells in what would be a multi-billion-dollar deal. We'd encountered one another earlier when I was at Julander and Frontier considered a play I was presenting to prospective partners. His roots in Laramie, Wyoming, showed up in the cowboy boots and Levi's he habitually wore. His strong-featured face topped with silvering hair radiated intelligence. His calming baritone voice had the West in it. I liked him immediately.

When Burns learned I was no longer with Julander, he asked me to join him as head geologist. Alan, still a consultant, was the organization's chief operating officer. I brought in two of my cohorts, Kathy Stolper as petrographer and Dick Wyman as a technical advisor on engineering. The original catalyst for the project was a U.S. Geological Survey geologist who was aggressive and dogmatic and had no sense of the business, nor even the geological aspects of the equation. He shouted in meetings, and to shut him up Alan and I eventually broadsided him with so much incontrovertible technical data that he had to stop hollering and listen. In one tense afternoon, we demonstrated that his theory about why a particular field in North Dakota produced the way it did was nonsense.

I introduced John Burns to the Alberta Energy Company and the two made a deal for AEC to operate our big project. The provincial government had founded AEC in 1973, the year we started Canadian Hunter, and it was now a major oil and gas corporation. Alberta Energy/Frontier drilled one very expensive well to 12,000 feet and turned it into a horizontal well. We tested once, unsuccessfully, tried to get back in the vertical for another test, failed, and abandoned the well after a lot of money. Unfortunately, the play had become too expensive to continue.

Frontier decided to wind up its operations. Suddenly, Alan O'Hare was sprung free to seek other opportunities. After working for others for the last many years, I wanted to run my own company again—and who better to partner with than this smart, articulate, sober engineer with nearly three decades' experience? I told him we should try to transpose the success Hunter had in Canada to the U.S., where our kind of science had never been applied with any scope. He liked the idea of joining forces, seeing me as a Big-Picture explorer who loves the hunt. He calls me "an armwaver." More congenially, I call him my right hand, my left brain, and my wholehearted partner. We work in harmony, although Alan jokes, "When we do have a disagreement, we talk about it for a long time, then I cave in and it's all over." That's the kind of story you get from someone who doesn't cave in very often.

In 2000 we founded a small startup in Denver called DDX, which stands for Direct Detection Experts. Its guiding principle was that many potentially successful American wells have been bypassed because electrical-logging technology was less advanced, well-stimulation methods were less effective, pipelines weren't available, gas prices were very low—and a host of other reasons that were plausible at the time. Every industry has a set of procedures that are high-tech and effective. But those same industries also have various time-honored procedures that are out of date and no longer maximally effective. This is because, I think, most humans get tired of going full speed all the time. When you're in a new suit, behind a big desk, in an ornate office, with a great view of the city, it's hard for most people to know at what speed you're going. Whatever the basic, underlying cause, I recognized years ago in Canada that most companies seldom re-examined dry holes. Canadian Hunter had developed direct detection to identify just such bypassed wells. Now DDX would re-study $100 billion of freely available well cuttings at the U.S. Geological Survey in Denver using log analysis, microscopic examination of well cuttings, and drillstem tests, all integrated with geologic, engineering, and economic appraisals. In western Canada, of course, the concept had been extraordinarily successful for Hunter in recognizing more than 200 bypassed wells and discovering three major gas fields—including the biggest in the country, the miraculous Elmworth.

Let's consider that number for another moment: $100 billion represents one of the largest troves of vital, but free, information available anywhere in the world on oil, gas, or mineral resources. It is hardly used. It lies in thousands of boxes on shelves in dusty warehouses. It is Isaiah's "treasures hidden in the darkness, secret riches."

Direct detection, we knew, had become the cheapest, most efficient exploratory method available in onshore North America. It's so much easier to find things other people overlooked because they were thinking with different sets of rules in the 1960s or even the 1980s. I love using all the information they left behind in log libraries and sample warehouses because we get it all free and they aren't interested in it anymore. No interest—no competition. Don't try to outmuscle the major companies; you've got to learn to run around them.

We gathered a lean, keen group of veterans to work with us. Some of them acted as consultants, including Don Johnson, the operations manager from Julander; Dick Wyman, Hunter's former research director; fast-thinking Larry Meckel, a superb regional geologist; and the brilliant Bob Sneider, who comes willingly whenever we need his experience and creative mind to analyze a major challenge. Since his long-ago days consulting to Hunter, Bob now ranks among the world's leading experts on reservoir performance. He's the guy that Exxon called when it needed better answers on Alaska's gigantic Prudhoe Bay oil play, the guy the

Chinese National Oil Company asked to counsel them on the vast Tarim Basin.

We have David Smith, a prominent land consultant in Denver, to direct our leasing. Company advisors Marlan Downey and John Floyd came to us after distinguished careers in Shell, Atlantic Richfield, and International Paper. Another ex-Shell man who has just joined us is John T. Smith, top technical advisor to the past Shell President, Mac McAdams. Steve Holditch ran Holditch Consultants for many years and is now a senior technical advisor to Schlumberger.

Lloyd Fons now works for us as a part-time consultant on electric logs. This is comforting because he's probably the best, and fastest, log analyst in the world. Kathy Stolper, the great microscope specialist, is back with me, along with her husband, Bob, a geologic technician. They operate from their home in Denver, where they raise their five children, including premature triplets with continuing medical problems that still require hospital time. In an ordinary company, Kathy might not have a job because of the time demands of her kids. But Alan and I wanted DDX to have the same environment as Hunter did, where we could make room and cut a lot of slack for someone with Kathy's extraordinary skills.

We also accommodated our office manager, Noelani Bevill, when she went on maternity leave recently but wanted to come back to work as soon as possible. She'd worked at Frontier Resources, where she was such a clever and versatile jill-of-all-trades that we had no hesitation about hiring her. While she was having her baby, we brought in Jessica Klimek, who just happened to be Alan's niece and my son Rob's girlfriend. He has good taste: she has a delicate frame, long, dark-blonde hair, and a lovely oval face that readily bursts into smiles ("I love to laugh," she says). Jessie stayed on when Noelani returned, but not because of the family connections. Although she didn't attend college, she is just so darn smart, left-brained organized, and sweet of heart that she reminds me of the young women who worked at Canadian Hunter. Born in Wyoming, she moved with her mom and airline-mechanic stepdad to seven different towns. Her mother was an inspiration, becoming a doctor of chiropractic in her 40s.

Jessie has her spirit: she'd prefer a job digging in the dirt to doing the office work she performs so well. "That's one reason I don't like girls—they never do anything fun," she has confessed. Jessie later joined Robbie in Florida, where he planned to go into commercial flight training.

DDX has a simple game plan. In Canada, the techniques we developed for improved, as well as entirely new, down-hole interpretation of dry holes were murderously effective. Many companies in Canada tried, with varying success, to duplicate our methods. There is much more by-pass exploration to be done in Canada but, thanks in large part to the enormous impetus derived from Elmworth, the Canadian industry is still operating at a high pitch. Lease access is very tight and very expensive. In contrast, while leasing in U.S. gas areas has been increasing significantly, prices are not yet half as high as in Canada and several large, favorable areas have still seen no activity at all.

At DDX we have continued to perfect methodology we used with Hunter in Canada. This is not the proper forum to describe all our specific technology. Most of it has already been referred to in summary form.

The most important exploration technology available to the industry consists of two primary procedures. One is the array of different down-hole logs which include self-potential, electrical resistivity, gamma ray, neutron-density, sonic, microlog, and so on. The second is the whole panoply of reflection seismic techniques. Both systems were introduced about 1930 and have been constantly modified and improved, becoming simultaneously ever more accurate and expensive. There will always be wells to log and a demand for ever-increasing accuracy of measurement. But seismic is a different matter. Sound waves are generated at the surface, pass downward through the rock layers, and are reflected back by some of the layers. The time of the round-trip passage is recorded at the surface. The process permits measurement of the depth of a reflecting layer at any number of chosen points on the surface. This was the single, greatest technological breakthrough in the history of the oil business. It enabled us to map the position and shape of the anticlinal arches which have been for the last 85 years the principal oil traps that fuel our modern, motorized economy. Without the seismograph, we would have run out of oil by now. No trucks, no cars, no airplanes, little heat, little electricity, less food, for fewer people. A far, far different world.

The seismograph is still the pre-eminent tool for locating oil and gas fields in the offshore and in most foreign areas. But practically all the anticlines large enough to hold significant fields have already been found in onshore U.S. Of this, there is no question. Furthermore, definitive scientific studies are in full agreement that about half the future oil and gas reserves on the North American continent are in onshore U.S. and Canada. The clear-cut implication of this conclusion is that to satisfy America's constantly growing demand for petroleum, we must learn how to explore effectively on land for fields not located on anticlines. We call these stratigraphic traps; they could also be called non-anticlinal or non-structural traps.

A reality of petroleum transport is that oil can be shipped anywhere in the world by tanker. Hence, our oil supplies are not in jeopardy except by war. But gas travels by pipeline and pipelines don't work under 15,000 feet of ocean depth because you can't fix leaks. Someday, maybe. But now, no way.

So, to meet our enormously growing gas demand (predicted to double in 20 years), we absolutely must tap into the non-anticlinal gas reserves of onshore U.S. and Canada. That is a tall order because our petroleum industry is designed around the seismograph as the primary engine of discovery. In proved gas reserves, we now have about 10 years of supply. This will be added to, of course, by offshore Gulf of Mexico discoveries, but we are obviously working with a short supply. The only reason the newspapers and TV aren't crying loudly about this imminent catastrophe is it's a little too technical for their audiences, as well as the commentators themselves. (To start with, they wonder what's the difference between gas and gasoline?)

DDX's potential for a successful and profitable business is related to two fundamental economic factors: (1) there will be ever-increasing demand for gas, hence rising gas prices in the near future and continuing for a long time, and (2) DDX has almost exclusive understanding of several critical geological-evaluation techniques which will carry us to a leading role in the new exploration that must be used to find the new, non-anticlinal gas reserves on this continent.

These new techniques are most happily employed in areas where you can hold all the leases for little money. Although those areas do exist in the U.S., they are in short supply. Some of the large areas of good potential are held tightly at high cost. But there are also large areas held not so tightly and at lower cost.

The beauty of being a big company is you can blast your way into any area regardless of cost. Of course, you have to know where to go.

The beauty of being DDX is you don't have to have it all to make a handsome return on investment. And we know where to go!

The reality is that nearly a quarter of a continent lies unexplored for the new Basin Center fields that trap dowdip from water and are essentially invisible to seismic. California is leased. Montana, Wyoming, Colorado, eastern Utah, and New Mexico are leased. But that leaves a north-south belt 1,000 miles long from the Canadian border to Mexico and 450 miles wide from the Sierra Nevada to the Overthrust. This vast region has been explored only locally in the Paleozoic—enough, however, to identify enormous thicknesses in local basins. The region has been almost ignored through 5,000 to 10,000 feet of Tertiary-basin sediments. These beds have enough evidence of reservoir, source, and gas shows (according to U.S. Geological Survey reports) that no experienced explorationist can say they have been adequately evaluated. The total Tertiary sedimentary area of the Great Basin is about equal to the total Tertiary-basin area of the Rocky Mountains. I don't propose that the western Tertiary area is better than the eastern, but obviously the eastern part is now largely leased. The western half is largely open. And there are 1,900 miles of gas pipelines traversing the eastern, western, northern, and southern margins of the Nevada Great Basin. Half of that huge area is within 50 miles of a pipeline. So the company that leases the acreage belts 50 miles on both sides of the pipelines—and also selects by well control the most promising acreage of the next 50 miles—wll dominate the play in Nevada-Utah and surrounding areas through federal units and development contracts.

This is plainly a gigantic opportunity. When the industry as a whole finally responds, as inevitably it will, the entire Great Basin will be leased very cheaply as rapidly as were the basins of Wyoming. When that happens, the game will be all but over. He who owns the land wins the game.

I have been very fortunate to drill a number of successful and important discovery wells. But I have also drilled a number of disappointing dry holes. I've come to believe those have a role in your life. If every well you drilled was a great success, how could you continue to feel connected to the human race? Logic would require you to think of yourself as somehow chosen, exalted. I no longer sink into despondency with a dry hole. I've learned to treat it as the price of admission. Looking around me at a crowd of 70,000 people at a football game, I think, *I didn't find one last week, but no one here has ever found one. I've done a lot better than that—and I'll keep on doing a lot better.*

Truly, I don't aspire to displace Exxon-Mobil. That's too much trouble. My desires are to find some large fields and set the pattern for the whole U.S. industry to find the reserves necessary to meet a truly dangerous energy shortage. We must be aware that the gas-reserve and consumption numbers are alarming. If they are recognized soon, before Basin Center exploration has begun in earnest, there will be the usual media panic. This will be followed by a congressional effort to put the government in charge of exploration. The results would be like Congress taking charge of health care by replacing the doctors. In our vast democracy, we are always on the verge of making a major mistake by majority rule. Winston Churchill said our political system is the worst imaginable—until compared with every other system.

The immortal Wallace Pratt said in 1951, "The record demonstrates that, as oil-finders, we have persistently underestimated the amount of oil and gas that have been stored up in the earth's crust. We have been too conservative always."

However, if gas supplies cannot be found to meet demand and we learn that Basin Center exploration fails to solve the shortage—then, yes, we've got a problem. But even then, it's not the end of the world. Just let people get rich who can find the answers. We have enormous supplies of coal; clean it up. Or we have unlimited supplies of burnable hydrogen in ocean water; learn how to separate it economically and flow it through our existing gas-pipeline network. Our economic system is designed to respond to challenges. But we have to keep the political system from interfering.

My purpose—in what some people insist on describing disparagingly as my "declining years"—will continue to be remote, new-field, new-basin exploration for gas. That is a promise.

Frederick the Great preached "audacity, audacity, always audacity."

I am composed in my mind that I make these great efforts for the purpose of my own family, first—but also for the purpose of America, which guides the world and must retain the economic strength to do so for the ultimate benefit of all, including the Arab nations.

CHAPTER EIGHTEEN

ONE MORE MOUNTAIN

IN EARLY 2002 AN OLD FRIEND OF MY SON ALAN and some forestry officers invited me and my family on a hike to the Burgess Shale high in the Canadian Rockies. The Shale is a protected UNESCO World Heritage Site near the eastern border of British Columbia in Yoho National Park. Here is the most significant collection of perfectly preserved Cambrian fossils ever discovered, offering a peek into strange sea-life forms that existed 500 million years ago. For me as a scientist, this trove of fossils is fascinating because of the several clues they offer about the nature of evolution. But the possibility of a trek to view them in a quarry on a ridge between mountaintops had more personal significance.

In the Cree language, Yoho denotes "awe," a fitting word for this magnificent setting of glacier-dug valleys and lofty peaks. The park epitomizes the environment that Alan had lived in and loved as a young forester and park ranger. A long dozen years had passed since my son's death, and the invitation—to be guided miles up a very steep mountainside to see one of the world's natural wonders—seemed timely and irresistible.

Alan's friend, Tony Fogarassi, had a good, although ulterior motive in getting me up there. A Vancouver lawyer who'd first studied petroleum geology, Tony was a director of the Yoho-Burgess Shale Foundation, a non-profit educational organization intent on exposing the public to the earth sciences, particularly geology and paleontology. His idea was to have me endow a Foundation scholarship in Alan's memory. As a first step, my loved ones and I could experience the drama of a steep, twelve-mile hike past waterfalls and wildflowers to a viewing of fossils as diverse as the large, dangerous-looking *Anomalocaris* and the worm-like *Pikaia*, an extraordinarily old ancestor.

And so here I was, on an overcast early morning in September, surrounded by many of the people who were so important in my life. It seemed a good time to take quiet note of how far they had come in their own lives.

Jim, who at 19 was like a six-foot-one cornstalk, had just finished his freshman year at Pepperdine University, a top-ranked independent Christian college amid the Santa Monica Mountains in Malibu, California. In a few weeks he would be on his way to the University of Heidelberg where resident Pepperdine faculty offer fifty selected students a year of humanities, religious studies, and German. Everything about the university was thrilling Jim; I can't remember feeling that same spirit of enthusiasm about Yale. About the only trouble ever to cloud his young life happened recently when police in Wyoming caught him driving 115 miles an hour, roughed him up, and threw him in jail overnight. I told him OK, but if it ever happened again, we'd leave him there.

His handsome big brother (although now somewhat smaller than Jim) was a role model in speeding. Rob has always liked to drive fast, perhaps inspired by his boyhood hero, Chuck Yeager. Reading the autobiography of the first pilot to break the sound barrier, Robbie determined to become a pilot and earned his flying licence at 17. He was now back from three years of flight school and academics at Embry-Riddle Aeronautical

University in Florida. At the end of the current term of brush-up studies at community college, he planned to give into the seductions of flight and become a corporate pilot.

He and Jessie Klimek were together in Yoho, looking very much in love. They share adventures in flying, parachuting, mountain biking, kayaking, and probably several other misadventures they haven't told me about. I am proud of Robbie for being smart enough to choose someone like her. And I suspect that for Lenora, who doesn't have her own daughter, Jessie has filled that place in her heart.

My daughter wasn't with us. At the last minute, Barbie had phoned with the upsetting news that her knees—in rotten shape from hard skiing—were behaving so badly that she couldn't manage the sharp inclines of the Burgess trail. Given the shape of my own joints, I sympathized. In her late 40s, Barbie is an admirable lady: wife, mother, and accomplished artist who in recent years had also taken up the violin to play for fun. She has a bachelor of education with a major in art from the University of Alberta. Now Barbie is painting large and highly detailed yet evocative canvases of landscapes and portraits in oil, selling almost everything she produces. There's a serenity in her work, as there is in her face; her smile lights up everyone.

She and Bill Davis have three fine children: Zachary, 21 at that time; Caroline, who in her late teens looks and acts like my mother; and Georgina, the youngest at 14. Zach was their family's representative for our trek, a pleasing and dependable companion on the trail. He has become as serene and complete a personality as his mother. Best all-around junior cyclist in Alberta, provincial champion debater twice during junior high, and more recently a philosophy major who'd broadened his studies in Alberta with a course of Indian philosophy in Calcutta. Zach confessed to me he had the Masters urge for mountaineering; the previous year he'd done thirty days of ice-climbing. Brave. Tough. Charming. I was tickled that he chose to join us.

Unfortunately, my son Chuck had to pass up this tribute to his brother for a reason as sound as his sister's. Wildfires raging west of Denver all summer had forced hundreds of people out of their homes in Durango and came within four houses of destroying the one where Chuck lives with his wife, Jean. It was well worth saving. Their home surpasses the merely elegant or artistic by being a modest but expressive statement of their values and experiences and adventures. I can't name another house that has impressed me as much. This was a second marriage for both; Jeannie, for whom I have a real fondness, has two grown-up children, while Chuck is childless. He's a serious-minded, independent individual, much happier practising as a pathologist than he was as a GP.

Eldest son Chuck, a doctor in Durango, and a high climber, Grand Canyon kayaker, and deep-snow skier.

Fortunately, Alan's wife, Alison — all five-foot-three of her — had come from Creston, B.C., with the new man in her life, David Drennan. Deciding to move in with him many years ago, she'd phoned me, seeking my blessing. "Alison," I replied, "I love you almost as much as Alan did. I like

Dave very much and I want your happiness above everything else." At 38, Alison was a walking joy machine. After Alan's death, she took her master's in nursing and now counsels youths on probation and caregivers of people with development disabilities. She and Barbie are very close friends who have painted together, sometimes for a week at a time.

The others in our group included Tony Fogarassi and his wife, Blair Lockhart, a former geologist who also became a lawyer. Don Fivey is a consulting geologist from Calgary who'd grown up with Alan and was there simply because Alan was there in spirit. Chuck LaFortune and his remarkable son, Levi, are year-round residents of our home in the Kootenays along with wife and mother Kimberly and two other kids. Levi never stopped asking questions. "I finally got him figured out," I told his Dad. "This kid is actually a college graduate masquerading as a nine-year-old."

And, of course, there was Lenora. Since her transformational experience at the Billy Graham Crusade, her faith has only deepened. In Calgary she'd attended a charismatic Christian centre and now she is a member of New Life Church in Colorado Springs. It calls itself the smallest big church in the country with 8,700 members who seem to have the closeness of a family when they meet throughout the week as well on Sundays. As I understand it, they believe in making simple moments and activities throughout the day an offering of worship. They base their faith strongly on the Scriptures and reach out to others with an active ministry. The philosophy seems to suit my wife, who in the words of her friend Wendy Leigh is "generous of heart, an embracing person who can love unconditionally." Her beliefs have led her to such disparate places as Israel and Quebec on behalf of her faith. Not long ago, Lenora flew to Mozambique to help at an orphanage run by an American couple, Rolland and Heidi Baker of Iris Ministries. With 20 friends from a church in Sylvan Lake, Alberta, she took medical supplies to the impoverished, war-wracked African country and spent more than a week among 70 orphans. She painted dormitories, sewed curtains, and played with the children, hugging them as much as she could.

When she came home, Lenora told me, "The thing I'll never forget is waking up early the first morning just as the sun was coming up and the birds were singing. And then the children started to sing. The dormitories were all around us and they were getting ready for school. They were harmonizing and pouring out with all their hearts and their singing would just build and build until it sounded like a heavenly choir."

In spite of my continuing skepticism of religion, her faith has touched me in many ways. Some nights, when I can't fall asleep because of my concerns about the future, she'll take my hand and together we'll recite the 23rd Psalm: "The Lord is my shepherd; I shall not want. He maketh me to lie down in green pastures: he leadeth me beside the still waters. He restoreth my soul: he leadeth me in the paths of righteousness. . ." And the words most often do comfort me and help me sleep. (Lenora does not fully buy the story that I sometimes need help in my rest; she claims I'm out cold in 30 seconds.)

Where was I in my own life on this late-summer day, as we all prepared to hike to the Burgess Shale? Both mind and body needed some work. I'd seen a specialist recently to check worrying symptoms that sometimes affected my memory and was now awaiting more tests and a fuller diagnosis. Couldn't do much about that. And on the physical side, I knew that my 74-year-old legs and hips had passed their best-before expiry date. To compensate, I was walking as much as possible and continuing my active exercise regime—working out three times a week with Scott Clark, Robbie's friend and roommate and our family's personal trainer. Scott is a well-muscled, strong-jawed coal miner's son from Ohio, a terrific young man who has been studying psychology with the goal of becoming a family counsellor. Two years ago I was limping around a track, holding on to the rail. Now after working out with Scott three times a week, walking as fast as I can, lifting weights, I see tangible gains in my mobility and strength. Would they be enough to take me on this ten-hour, 12-mile trek?

We took off from the Takakkaw Falls trailhead. Our leader was Randle Robertson, the tall, silver-haired executive director of the Yoho-Burgess Shale Foundation. He'd been a park warden here for 20 years and had fond recollections of working with Alan in the early 1980s. I took a deep breath and said quietly "We're all here in memory of Alan to hike in one of the most beautiful parks in the world. I'm sure we'll remember him every step of the way."

There was some irony about this trek, I pointed out. "Alan would be proud to see his family hiking in the mountains, although when he was five and went on our hikes every weekend throughout the summer, he hated the whole procedure. All the way up the mountain and all the way back down, he complained bitterly. It wasn't until I invented the Bear Scare that he began to hike with pleasure. That involved me and Alan running up the trail a few hundred feet to hide behind a tree. When the rest caught up, we'd leap out roaring so ferociously that the whole family was terrified. We then laughed up the trail again and repeated the exercise. We found that this system successfully propelled him up the mountain and back down to the car. Amazingly, this worked hike after hike—until he finally got to the age where he no longer needed the Bear Scare. I suppose you might say that we prepared Alan for the Forest Service. . . . Okay, let's do this hike."

Except for three more rangers who caught up with us on their day off to reminisce about their time with Alan, he was remembered in silence as we clambered up twisting switchbacks and steep trails. In compensation, we had awesome vistas of vast glaciers and ice cliffs, endless forests, and a pleasant sky that didn't cook us badly but didn't rain on us either.

Along the way, I was telling Tony Forgarassi and Don Fivey, the geologist, the war stories about how Trudeau and Lalonde had yanked the oil industry around during the days of the National Energy Program. I examined rocks on the trail and jousted with Randle Robertson over geological

> **THE ELEVENTH COMMANDMENT**
> # Thou Shalt Not Give Up
> **JOHN 4: 22**

The Eleventh Commandment has been a principle throughout my life.

points. By mid-afternoon, my pace began to flag and as we approached the final stretch, about 800 feet straight up, I knew my hip was giving out, if not my knees. Lenora, who has this wonderful gift of becoming 12 months younger with each passing year, held my hand, leading me in the path of righteousness when I was tempted to lie down in green pastures.

Finally, as we neared an outcrop overlooking Emerald Lake, she announced: "John, you better stop. I'm going to sit down on this trail and not let you get by."

But I badly wanted to see the Burgess Shale and its spectacular assemblage of brachiopods and trilobites. My life's motto has been "Thou shalt not give up."

But don't be a damn fool about it.

If I didn't go on, Lenora wouldn't see the Shale either. The only difficult part of this hike for her was helping me.

John, you've got to know when to turn around.

I was angry at my body, disappointed in myself.

"*It is time to be old,*" Ralph Waldo Emerson wrote, "*to take in sail.*"

I stopped and sat with Lenora while the young people went on up to the quarry. When they returned, we began the descent, which soon proved harder than the climb for me. Lenora asked Randle if they could call in a helicopter. There just happened to be one in the vicinity and, in what seemed like a reprise of my adventure in the Grand Tetons 40 years earlier, I came down the mountain in a chopper.

As we landed, I couldn't help feeling my body had betrayed me. But if I had to trim my sails, turn around on the trail when I absolutely had to, and try not be a damn fool about it, I still wasn't licked.

Ambrosia Lake.

Ship Shoal.

Dineh-bi-Keyah.

Canadian Hunter.

Keg River Gething.

Elmworth and the Deep Basin.

Ring Border.

One more coming. At least one.

So far, my life has been a glorious adventure, embracing both triumph and tragedy. I've been a geologist for 50-plus years but never worked a day in my life. All that time, I've been completely absorbed in searching for the secret treasures of energy hidden in the earth's darkness. The quest is well paid, if you're successful, but that is never what captures your soul. It's the hunt, the careful gathering and then analysis of data—retaining some, discarding lots—and at last a judgement. Stick your neck way out, and then put up your money or your job or your reputation; you are always alone with a new idea. Finally, drill. No prospect is ever certain. In the end, you are always shooting dice. Do the best you can, then "Let's roll!"

Preparation is vital. Intelligence is demanded. Determination is essential. But all of this fails without confidence. And confidence can only be absorbed from the positive elements of your life.

As long as I'm here, what I know how to do and want to do is keep current with new exploration data, assemble the puzzle pieces that form the Big Picture, pursue the Big Idea, and climb the next Big Mountain that life puts in front of me. Doing that, I intend to play a part in solving America's energy problem. Because, for all I've been given, I bear a continuing sense of responsibility that will not end until I do.

Alan would understand. My other kids know—and so does Lenora.